African Studies and Research Forum Series

The African Studies and Research Forum Series invites monographs and contributed volumes on Africa and related topics written by authors from across the academic disciplines. The contributors will encompass the more than 400 active members of the African Studies and Research Forum (ASRF) across the globe and other non-members interested in the organization's broader and global conceptualization of Africa and, thus, topics dealing with Africa and its diaspora. Members of the AFSR hail from political science, economics, international relations, the humanities, social sciences, natural sciences, formal sciences, and applied sciences.

All titles in this series are peer-reviewed.

Janeen Guest

China's Infrastructure Aid and Investment

Impact on Development in Africa, with a Focus on Nigeria, Ethiopia, and Kenya

Springer

Janeen Guest
Woodbridge, VA, USA

ISSN 2948-2399 ISSN 2948-2402 (electronic)
African Studies and Research Forum Series
ISBN 978-3-032-11963-6 ISBN 978-3-032-11964-3 (eBook)
https://doi.org/10.1007/978-3-032-11964-3

This Springer imprint is published by the registered company Springer Nature Switzerland AG
The registered company address is: Gewerbestrasse 11, 6330 Cham, Switzerland

This book is dedicated to those who are diligently working to alleviate poverty, ensure that aid and foreign direct investment is mutually beneficial to all parties, and promote equitable economic development throughout Africa.

Preface

This book explores the landscape of China's infrastructure aid in three pivotal African nations: (1) Nigeria, (2) Ethiopia, and (3) Kenya. The book comprehensively analyzes the developmental impacts of China's infrastructure aid initiatives over the past two decades from 2000 to 2022.

The book begins by understanding the history of the Sino-African relationship and Chinese aid initiative by examining China's foreign aid policies, tracing their historical evolution, and examining the motivations for China's engagement in Africa. The diverse forms of hard infrastructure projects are dissected to establish a foundational understanding of their impacts on the gross domestic products (GDPs) of Nigeria, Kenya, and Ethiopia.

The book employs a combination of quantitative and qualitative methodologies by carefully selecting countries based on criteria that ensure a representative analysis. In terms of the theoretical framework, this work assesses the relevance of Dependency Theory and other developmental theories in determining the effectiveness of Chinese infrastructure development aid in Nigeria, Ethiopia, and Kenya. It adds to the body of knowledge pertaining to the Dependency Theory as it relates to economic development measured by GDP. This work also contributes to Dependency Theory and its current relevance in international relations, helping the reader to understand Dependency Theory as it relates to South-South relations.

The data collection process is outlined in the quantitative analysis of each chapter, and a statistical framework using basic regression models provides a solid analytical foundation. Ethical considerations and limitations are discussed, thereby maintaining the integrity of the research. This book studies Nigeria, Ethiopia, and Kenya, with each country receiving a thorough examination, thereby providing readers with a historical context of China's relations with these nations. The analyses of infrastructure projects go beyond surface-level assessments, delving into the economic and social impacts while addressing challenges and criticisms. The statistical insights enrich the qualitative findings, thereby offering a holistic perspective. The heart of this book lies in its comparative analysis. By identifying patterns, trends, and variances in development impacts, the book offers a nuanced understanding of how China's infrastructure aid and investment strategies unfold in the three African countries investigated. The lessons from each case study contribute to a broader comprehension of China's infrastructure aid and investment effectiveness. Thus, this exploration extends beyond the retrospective, providing insights into the sustainability of projects and offering actionable recommendations for the future. Emphasis is placed on strengthening partnerships, fostering collaboration, and delivering policy recommendations tailored to the unique needs of each host country.

Woodbridge, USA Janeen Guest

Rationale for Country Selection

Nigeria, Kenya, and Ethiopia were selected to give a diverse sample size of African countries, each with unique characteristics and strategic importance. Nigeria, located in West Africa, is Africa's most populous country, providing a significant market and a wealth of natural resources. Its economic potential and regional influence make it a key player in African geopolitics and development. Nigeria's selection also highlights the challenges and opportunities in managing vast natural resources and a large population.

Kenya, chosen for its location in East Africa, is a port country with the bustling port of Mombasa serving as a crucial gateway for regional trade. As a major economic hub, Kenya's strategic location on the Indian Ocean makes it a vital point for trade routes and economic activities. The country's relatively stable political environment and its role as a financial and communication hub in East Africa provide an exciting contrast to Nigeria's resource-driven economy, offering a unique perspective for our research.

Lastly, Ethiopia was chosen for its unique position as one of the fastest-growing economies in Africa, despite being a landlocked country. This presents unique challenges in terms of logistics, transportation, and trade. Ethiopia's rapid economic growth, driven by significant investments in infrastructure and industrialization, provides a compelling case study for examining how infrastructure development can spur economic growth even in landlocked nations. Moreover, Ethiopia's ambitious development plans, including the Grand Ethiopian Renaissance Dam, underscore the transformative potential of large-scale infrastructure projects, thereby offering a unique perspective for this book.

By studying these three countries, a comprehensive is gained in understanding of the varying impacts and strategies of Chinese infrastructure aid across different geographical, economic, and logistical contexts within Africa. This diverse selection allows for a more nuanced analysis of the effectiveness and adaptability of infrastructure development programs in the continent. It also provides insights into how infrastructure investments can address different developmental needs and challenges ranging from resource management and market expansion in Nigeria, trade facilitation, and regional integration in Kenya to overcoming logistical constraints and fostering industrial growth in Ethiopia. This multifaceted approach enhances an understanding of the broader implications of infrastructure aid and investment on Africa's development trajectory.

Acknowledgments

I want to express my sincere gratitude to those who contributed to the realization of this work. I am thankful to three phenomenal women, Janelle Guest-Bakker, my late grandmother, Hattie M. Guest and my late mother, Kandis J. Guest. I am forever indebted to you for the sacrifice, love, and support that you have given me.

I would like to express my heartfelt gratitude to Abdul Karim Bangura. Your mentorship and support, from dissertation to publication, have been invaluable. Thank you for your guidance and support throughout this journey.

Organization of the Book

Introduction

This book is divided into nine chapters. Chapter 1 explores the historical evolution of the Sino-African relationship, focusing on Chinese infrastructure aid to Africa. It examines the origins, distribution, and impact of this aid through both quantitative and qualitative lenses. The chapter highlights the importance of theoretical perspectives, comparative analysis, and the detailed data collection process. It also addresses the integration of statistical frameworks with qualitative insights, specifically analyzing China's aid to Nigeria, Ethiopia, and Kenya. By combining these approaches, the chapter aims to offer a comprehensive understanding of the implications of China's infrastructure projects and foreign direct investment (FDI) on development in these countries. Additionally, it underscores the significance of this research for providing actionable recommendations and fostering partnerships for host countries. Topics covered include African colonialism, the Sino-African relationship, the history of Chinese aid, and the importance of addressing ethical considerations and study limitations.

Competing Perspectives

Chapter 2 examines the intricate link between infrastructure development and economic growth in Africa, highlighting both the opportunities and challenges involved. It discusses how quality infrastructure can reduce inequality and support sustainable development, referencing the MDGs and SDGs. The chapter presents diverse views on China's aid and FDI in Africa, with some seeing it as a development driver and others warning of potential risks and dependencies. It also explores the impact of infrastructure, especially in electricity and telecommunications, on GDP growth and contrasts modernization and dependency theories. Additionally, the chapter discusses the debate over whether China's aid fosters development or perpetuates neocolonialism, advocating for balanced, transparent cooperation to achieve sustainable development.

Methodological Framework and Analysis—Nigeria Case Study

Chapter 3 investigates whether Chinese infrastructure development aid impacts economic growth in Nigeria by exploring key statistical concepts essential for data analysis. It covers hypothesis testing, regression analysis, and terms like Null Hypothesis, R-Value, R-Square, and Statistical Significance to assess the strength and direction of relationships between variables. Through quantitative analysis, the chapter examines empirical data to uncover correlations between Chinese infrastructure aid and Nigeria's GDP growth. It also integrates qualitative findings to provide a comprehensive view of the aid's effects. The chapter is structured to include a historical overview of China-Nigerian relations, detailed analyses of infrastructure aid projects, and an evaluation of both economic and social impacts. It concludes with a summary of key findings and their implications, offering insights into the broader relationship between Chinese infrastructure aid and economic development in Nigeria.

Methodological Framework and Analysis—Kenya Case Study

Chapter 4 investigates whether Chinese infrastructure development aid impacts economic growth in Kenya by exploring key statistical concepts essential for data analysis. It covers hypothesis testing, regression analysis, and terms like Null Hypothesis, R-Value, R-Square, and Statistical Significance to assess the strength and direction of relationships between variables. Through quantitative analysis, the chapter examines empirical data to uncover correlations between Chinese infrastructure aid and Kenya's GDP growth. It also integrates qualitative findings to provide a comprehensive view of the aid's effects. The chapter is structured to include a historical overview of China-Kenya relations, detailed analyses of infrastructure aid projects, and an evaluation of both economic and social impacts. It concludes with a summary of key findings and their implications, offering insights into the broader relationship between Chinese infrastructure aid and economic development in Kenya.

Methodological Framework and Analysis—Ethiopia Case Study

Chapter 5 investigates whether Chinese infrastructure development aid impacts economic growth in Ethiopia by exploring key statistical concepts essential for data analysis. It covers hypothesis testing, regression analysis, and terms like Null Hypothesis, R-Value, R-Square, and Statistical Significance to assess the strength and direction of relationships between variables. Through quantitative analysis, the chapter examines empirical data to uncover correlations between Chinese infrastructure aid and Ethiopia's GDP growth. It also integrates qualitative findings to provide a comprehensive view of the aid's effects. The chapter is structured to include a historical overview of China-Ethiopian relations, detailed analyses of infrastructure aid projects, and an evaluation of both economic and social impacts. It concludes with a summary of key findings and their implications, offering insights into the broader relationship between Chinese infrastructure aid and economic development in Ethiopia.

Theoretical Framework

Chapter 6 examines essential concepts and theoretical frameworks relevant to global development and economic theory. It explores distinctions between the Global North and Global South and delves into theories such as Knowledge-Based Economy, Infrastructure-Based Economic Theory, and Social Infrastructure Development Theory, which offer insights into economic evolution. The chapter also considers alternative development models like the South-South Model and African Renaissance Theory, focusing on development strategies tailored to the Global South. It reviews Modernization Theory, Classical Dependency Theory, and Neoclassical perspectives to provide a comprehensive view of various development strategies. The discussion emphasizes the Dependency Theory, particularly in relation to Chinese infrastructure aid and foreign direct investment (FDI) in Nigeria, Kenya, and Ethiopia, highlighting how the theory interprets global economic imbalances and vulnerabilities. The chapter also addresses the theoretical and methodological approaches used to analyze these dynamics, noting that the study's theoretical framework is grounded in Dependency Theory and its impact on economic development in the Global South.

Comparative Analysis Nigeria, Kenya, and Ethiopia

Chapter 7 conducts a comparative analysis of Nigeria, Kenya, and Ethiopia to assess the impact of Chinese infrastructure aid and foreign direct investment (FDI) on their economies. It begins by summarizing the colonial histories of these countries and their influence on the effects of Chinese aid and investment. The chapter then examines geographical differences affecting the flow of goods and services and their economic implications. It compares the quantitative results of Chinese infrastructure aid and its relationship with GDP across the three countries. The analysis includes both quantitative and qualitative data to provide a comprehensive understanding of the impact. Additionally, the chapter reviews each country's policies on Chinese aid and FDI, evaluating their effectiveness in attracting investment and maximizing economic benefits, such as infrastructure development, job creation, and technology transfer. This comparison aims to identify best practices that could be adopted by other countries to enhance their investment environments.

Policy Recommendations and Conclusions

Chapter 8 provides the book conclusion as well as policy recommendations for Nigeria, Kenya, and Ethiopia. There is also discussion on plans for future research.

Postscript

Chapter 9 examines the sharp rise in Chinese infrastructure investment across Africa and its significance for countries such as Nigeria, Kenya, and Ethiopia within the context of the Belt and Road Initiative (BRI). The BRI argues that China's economic pivot toward Africa is driven by its strategic goal of reducing reliance on Western markets, especially considering escalating trade tensions with the United States. While these investments offer opportunities for growth and development, they also raise concerns about debt dependency, reduced policy autonomy, and imbalanced trade relationships. This chapter also highlights how US-China tariffs are reshaping global trade flows, pressuring China to seek alternative markets, and increasing Africa's strategic importance. However, without equitable and transparent agreements, Chinese infrastructure aid risks reinforcing historical patterns of dependency as emphasized by Samir Amin's theory of unequal exchange (Haselby, 2018).

About This Book

This book is about the combination of infrastructure development aid and foreign direct investment from China and its impact on economic growth in three African countries: (1) Nigeria, (2) Kenya, and (3) Ethiopia. The issue is important because over the last 22 years, 2000–2022, these countries and others in Africa South of the Sahara have seen significant growth in terms of gross domestic product (GDP) compared to the previous two decades, 1980–1989 and 1990–1999. Nonetheless, work must still be done to eliminate poverty and sustain economic development. This book is written to help understand the intricate relationship between China's infrastructure development aid, foreign direct investment (FDI), and the economic trajectories of Nigeria, Kenya, and Ethiopia. By analyzing the impact of Chinese infrastructure development aid and FDI in these countries, the book aims to provide insights for policymakers, development practitioners, and scholars on how to effectively leverage external investment for long-term, sustainable growth. It also seeks to shed light on the broader implications of China's growing influence in Africa, offering lessons that can inform future strategies to foster inclusive development and reduce poverty across the continent.

The book seeks to provide a comprehensive understanding of Chinese infrastructure development aid and foreign direct investment (FDI) and its impact on economic development in Africa, specifically Nigeria, Ethiopia, and Kenya. The book examines whether a positive correlation exists between Chinese infrastructure aid and investment in Nigeria, Ethiopia, and Kenya and its impact on per capita GDP in those countries. The primary postulate hinges upon the necessity of a thorough comparative analysis to unravel the complexities of China's infrastructure projects and their impacts on economic and social dimensions in diverse economic conditions. This book will be a crucial resource for scholars, policymakers, and practitioners seeking to navigate the intricate landscape of China's infrastructure aid and FDI in the three countries investigated. The book aims to foster a deeper comprehension of the dynamics at play, thereby contributing to informed decision-making and policy formulation by unraveling the development impact through a comparative lens.

This book is not just a textbook, but a tool for a reader's professional growth. It can be used as a supplementary reading for undergraduate and graduate students in academic disciplines such as development economics, security studies, international relations, African Studies, economic policy, economic development planning, political science, globalization and global studies, sustainable development, African economics, Africa's colonial history, public policy, geopolitical and geo-economics of Africa, international business, trade, and aid development studies. Its comprehensive insights and comparative analysis will equip the reader with a deeper understanding of China's infrastructure aid dynamics in Africa, enhancing the reader's ability to make informed decisions and formulate effective policies.

Contents

List of Figures

List of Tables

Introduction to China's Infrastructure Development Aid in Africa

1

It was John Haar who stated that "In the past, infrastructure investments have accounted for more than half the continent's economic growth, increases in productivity, improvement in human development, and reduction of poverty, according to the African Development Bank, proving that infrastructure investments are necessary for Africa to sustain its growth" (Haar, 2023). The quote by John Haar highlights the crucial role that infrastructure investments have played in driving economic growth, productivity, human development, and poverty reduction in Africa. The quote underscores the importance of infrastructure as a foundation for sustained economic growth. In the case of Nigeria, Kenya, and Ethiopia, Chinese infrastructure projects—such as roads, railways, and energy facilities—are not just short-term boosts but are expected to have long-lasting effects on their economies. Chinese infrastructure aid in these African countries is often tied to projects that improve access to essential services like transportation, electricity, and water, directly contributing to better living standards and poverty alleviation.

This chapter introduces key concepts essential for understanding the complex historical and contemporary dynamics that shape global development and international relations. The definitions were adapted from general definitions from multiple sources (Kegley, & Blanton, Sultan, Riddell, Encyclopedia Britannica). These concepts, such as **Colonialism, Decolonialization**, and **Neocolonialism**, provide a framework for analyzing the lasting impacts of European dominance on the political and economic structures of formerly colonized regions. It is important to note that the terms Global North and Global South help to delineate the economic and political disparities between wealthier, industrialized nations and less developed, often marginalized regions particularly in the context of development aid, foreign direct investment, and international diplomacy. While these terms are widely used in development and international relations literature, I acknowledge that they are contested and do not capture the full heterogeneity within regions

J. Guest, *China's Infrastructure Aid and Investment*, African Studies and Research Forum Series, https://doi.org/10.1007/978-3-032-11964-3_1

or countries. These terms are used as heuristic tools rather than fixed categories, recognizing their limitations while retaining their value in framing global systemic disparities. South-South Cooperation emerges as a critical response to these imbalances, emphasizing collaboration among developing countries. The chapter also examines the influence of **Neoliberal Experiments**, particularly through the **Washington Consensus** and **Structural Adjustment Programs**, which have shaped the economic policies of Global South nations. By defining and exploring these key concepts, this chapter aims to equip readers with the analytical tools necessary to critically engage with the ongoing processes of global inequality and development.

1. Colonialism: Colonization refers to the practice by which a powerful country establishes control over a less powerful region or country, exploiting it economically, politically, and culturally. The colonizing country exerts dominance over the local population, often leading to significant socioeconomic changes and resource exploitation. In the case of Nigeria and Kenya, they were colonized by the British, who established control over the territory, exploiting its resources, particularly oil, and imposing Western educational and political systems in Nigeria. The British exploited Kenya's agricultural resources in Kenya, mainly through settler farming of cash crops like tea and coffee. Ethiopia successfully resisted colonization during the Scramble for Africa but was occupied by Italy from 1936 to 1941 during the Second Italo-Ethiopian War.
2. Global North: The Global North includes many of the world's most developed and influential countries, known for their high standards of living, advanced infrastructure, and significant global impact.
3. Neoliberal Experiments: It refers to policies primarily established by the Washington Consensus or market-oriented reforms and policy prescriptions advocated by international financial institutions, including the International Monetary Fund (IMF), the World Bank, and the US Treasury.
4. Decolonialization: It is the process by which colonies achieve independence from their colonial rulers, establishing sovereign governance and control over their own resources and political systems. Nigeria gained independence from British colonial rule on October 1, 1960. Kenya attained independence on December 12, 1963, and Ethiopia was liberated from Italian occupation in 1941 with the help of Allied forces during World War II. Decolonization in these countries involved complex negotiation, resistance, and rebuilding processes, with lasting legacies that continue to influence their economic development trajectories, such as infrastructure challenges highlighted in the textbook.
5. Global South: Nigeria, Kenya, and Ethiopia are emblematic of the Global South, marked by developing economies, infrastructural challenges, and sociopolitical issues. These nations persist in their efforts toward economic growth and development.
6. Washington Consensus: Market-oriented reforms and policy prescriptions advocated by international financial institutions, including the International Monetary Fund (IMF), the World Bank, and the US Treasury.

7. Neocolonialism: Indirect control and influence exerted by former colonial powers and other developed nations over formerly colonized countries is often maintained through economic, political, cultural, and military means, rather than direct governance (Rahaman et al., (2011). For purposes of this book, in the cases of Nigeria, Kenya, and Ethiopia, this influence manifests through economic dependencies and reliance on foreign aid and investment.
8. South-South Cooperation: Collaboration among developing countries, primarily in the Global South, is needed to share knowledge, skills, resources, and technologies to address common development challenges and promote sustainable development. In the context of Chinese aid and foreign direct investment (FDI) to Nigeria, Kenya, and Ethiopia, this cooperation aims to foster mutual development and economic growth. This includes investments in infrastructure, such as roads, railways, and ports, as well as energy, manufacturing, and telecommunications initiatives.
9. Structural Adjustment Programs: Structural adjustment programs (SAPs) were economic policies and reforms that countries implement, often as prerequisites for obtaining loans from international financial institutions like the International Monetary Fund (IMF) and the World Bank. These programs were designed to stabilize economies, enhance international competitiveness, and correct balance-of-payments issues. SAPs typically include measures such as currency devaluation, reducing government intervention, eliminating subsidies, and liberalizing trade (Riddell, J.B, 1992).

In line with what is stated in the Preface of this book, this chapter offers a comprehensive overview of the historical evolution of the Sino-African relationship, explicitly focusing on Chinese infrastructure aid to Africa. It delineates this aid's initiation, distribution, and beneficiaries, seamlessly incorporating both quantitative and qualitative dimensions. The quantitative aspect investigates the exploration of data regarding the significance of Chinese infrastructure aid, while the qualitative aspect augments the narrative of the benefits to African countries. The chapter also emphasizes the importance of understanding various theoretical perspectives concerning Chinese infrastructure aid to Africa. The book strategically selects representative countries, meticulously detailing the data collection process, and introduces a statistical framework utilizing regression models. Ethical considerations and limitations are also discussed to ensure the integrity of the research.

The qualitative analysis delves into the historical, economic, and social context of China's relations with Nigeria, Ethiopia, and Kenya, dissecting infrastructure projects for deeper insights. The statistical analysis enriches the qualitative findings, thereby fostering a holistic understanding. The book distinguishes itself through a comparative analysis, identifying patterns, trends, and variances in the development impacts across the selected African countries. The lessons drawn contribute to a comprehensive view of China's infrastructure aid effectiveness, extending beyond retrospection, exploring projects into the future, and offering insights into project sustainability and actionable recommendations. Emphasizing partnerships, collaboration, and tailored policy recommendations for host countries, the book contributes to unraveling the complexities of China's infrastructure aid in Africa.

Concomitantly, eight aspects are covered in this chapter. They are as follows: (1) Brief Overview of African Colonialism, (2) Brief Historical Overview of Sino-African Relationship, (3) History of China's Aid to Africa, (4) Importance of Exploring the Quantitative Data on China's Aid to Africa, (5) Importance of Exploring the Qualitative Data on China's Aid to Africa, (6) Importance of Understanding Various Theoretical Perspectives, (7) Why Conduct a Comparative Analysis? (8) Ethical Considerations and Limitations of the Book, and (9) Chapter Summary.

1.1 Brief Historical Overview of African Colonialism

To comprehend why China provides infrastructure development aid to African countries, it is crucial to first delve into the historical relationship between Africa and colonialism. The exploration in this section therefore aims to shed light on the paradox of Africa, which harbors some of the world's poorest nations despite its abundant wealth in natural resources.

The Berlin Conference of 1884–1885 marked a significant time in African history. First, the purpose of that conference was to prevent conflict over the division of the continent of Africa among the Western countries. In 1884, the Berlin Conference brought together leaders from 14 European countries and the United States to discuss the partitioning of Africa and establish rules for dividing its resources among Western nations. Notably, no African representatives were present at the conference. France, Germany, Great Britain, and Portugal were major players. The conference aimed to bring "civilization" to Africa through Christianity and trade, with European countries claiming possession of African territories (Heath, 2010).

King Leopold II of Belgium, a significant participant, formally claimed the Congo as his possession. The Congo was rich in natural resources, including ivory, palm oil, timber, and rubber. Leopold exploited these resources to increase his wealth, causing vast environmental damage. Nonetheless, the larger story involves corruption and inhumanity. Leopold subjected the Congolese people to slave labor, extracting resources under severe conditions. Failure to meet production targets led to punishments ranging from the severing of hands to death. The exploitation of the Congo exemplified the ruthless pursuit of wealth at the expense of both the environment and the African people (Heath, 2010).

This historical background is crucial for understanding concerns related to the foreign aid received by Africa today, as it underscores the exploitation of African countries by Western powers during colonialism, whereby the primary objective was extracting resources. The information about the Berlin Conference of 1884–1885 is therefore crucial in understanding the historical context of Western exploitation in Africa. The conference, which aimed to prevent conflict among

Western nations over the division of Africa, resulted in the partitioning of the continent and establishing rules for resource distribution. This colonial history, marked by the absence of African representation, involved major European players like France, Germany, Great Britain, and Portugal.

The claim of King Leopold II over the Congo highlighted the rich natural resources, including ivory, palm oil, timber, and rubber. The exploitation of these resources for personal gain led to significant environmental damage. Moreover, Leopold's brutal treatment of the Congolese people, subjected to slave labor and harsh punishments for failing to meet production targets, exemplifies the darker aspects of colonial exploitation. Understanding this historical backdrop is thus imperative for assessing the dynamics of Chinese infrastructure development aid to Africa. It underscores the historical precedent of external powers exploiting Africa for its resources and inhumane practices of the Western powers on the African people, shaping perceptions and raising concerns about foreign interventions and aid (Johnson, 2014).

In terms of the environmental damage caused by colonialism, colonial powers exploited Africa's rich natural resources, leading to extensive deforestation, mining, and overexploitation of wildlife. This legacy of resource extraction has left lasting scars on the landscape, contributing to issues like soil degradation and loss of biodiversity.

In the late nineteenth century, French colonizers in North and West Africa prohibited traditional farming practices, leading to severe environmental degradation. Forests were cleared for cash crops like cotton, causing soil moisture loss and vegetation decline. The term "desertification" was coined, and colonizers blamed the indigenous people for the degradation caused by their own interventions. This history reflects a recurring theme of environmental exploitation and dispossession driven by colonial powers (Varanasi, 2022).

The examination of historical exploitation underscores the significance of understanding the motives and dynamics of the China-Africa relationship. In this context, evaluating the impact of Chinese infrastructure development aid on Africa becomes pivotal. By tracing the historical context, we can better grasp the nuances of the evolving partnerships and discern whether they align with mutual benefit or reflect potential neocolonial tendencies. This holistic understanding aids in assessing the true nature and implications of contemporary collaborations in infrastructure development between China and Africa.

While approximately 71 colonies exist today, the Western Sahara is the only known colony in Africa (United Nations, 2023). Although decolonization is complete in Africa, except for the Western Sahara region, much of the conflict taking place is rooted in colonialism due to the artificial borders established by the colonial powers. Nevertheless, Europeans no longer directly manage or control the former colonies. According to nationalist leaders in the Global South, the economic disparity between the affluent Global North and the impoverished Global South is attributed to neocolonialism. Unequal trade practices characterize this neocolonial relationship. The economically advantaged Global North exploits the Global South by entering the latter's markets and establishing economic systems that perpetuate this exploitation (Kegley & Blanton, 2010). Although China is considered a Global South country, the question remains about whether a neocolonial relationship exists between China and Africa.

According to the United Nations, China is praised for raising 800 million people from poverty, establishing influence surpassing many Western nations, and emerging as a major global economic power (United Nations Secretary-General, 2019). China's economic and poverty alleviation achievements position it as a significant global player. Understanding these accomplishments is important for comprehending China's approach to infrastructure development aid in Africa. China's experience in economic growth and poverty reduction questions its strategies and motivations when engaging with African nations, influencing the dynamics of its infrastructure projects in the continent.

1.2 Brief Historical Overview of Sino-African Relationship

It is important to provide a brief history of the Sino-African relationship from the 1950s to now. This timeframe is significant for understanding how the Sino-African relationship evolved over the years and how this relationship led to China providing infrastructure development aid to African countries. While the relationship between China and the African countries began before the 1950s, the 1950s were when China started to support the African liberation movement. During this time, many African countries gained independence from the colonizers. The Bandung Conference brought together leaders from 29 Asian and African countries. The conference aimed at promoting a neutral stance in the Cold War, advocating for non-alignment with either the Western or Eastern bloc (Ministry of Foreign Affairs of the People's Republic of China, 2024). The Bandung conference was therefore instrumental in shaping the relationship between China and the African countries. This relationship established the groundwork for diverse forms of collaboration, including educational and cultural exchanges, which would later become integral aspects of China's engagement with Africa. China positioned itself as a champion of the Global South's struggle against Western dominance. This shared history continues to influence China's relationship with Africa, forming a basis for today's diplomatic, economic, and cultural cooperation.

In the post-Cold War era (which is noted to have ended in late 1991 when the Soviet Union dissolved into its component republics), the pursuit of mutually beneficial economic cooperation became the focal point of Chinese policy toward Africa. Deng Xiaoping introduced the opening of the Chinese economy and reform in 1978. China aspired to become a prominent industrial power by adopting globalization and global integration as its development strategy. China's status as a leading contributor to foreign direct investment (FDI) from emerging economies is tied to its "Going Global" strategy and its vision for an alternative international system (Oqubay & Lin, 2019).

China became Africa's most valuable partner post-1990 amid skepticism about neoliberal prescriptions and structural adjustment reforms. Structural adjustment programs (SAPs) were economic policies and reforms that countries implement, often as prerequisites for obtaining loans from international financial institutions like the International Monetary Fund (IMF) and the World Bank (Archibong et al., 2021). It is important to point out that neoliberals'prescriptions refer to policies primarily established by the Washington Consensus or market-oriented reforms and policy prescriptions advocated by international financial institutions, including the International Monetary Fund (IMF), the World Bank, and the United States Treasury. The criticism of structural adjustment programs during the 1980s and 1990s in Africa revolves around their perceived failure to foster genuine economic development. Scholars argue that these programs, often influenced by neoliberal Washington Consensus policies, did not yield the anticipated positive outcomes but instead exacerbated existing challenges and left many African nations burdened with substantial debt, leading to economic stagnation and underdevelopment (Archibong et al., 2021).

The effects of structural adjustment programs (SAPs) in Africa generally worsened conditions, leading to increased poverty and a decline in quality of life. Prices rose, infrastructures crumbled, services deteriorated, and employment opportunities diminished. While almost everyone suffered, the negative impacts were most severe for the most vulnerable populations compounded by drought and conflict (Riddell, 1992).

The preceding situation coincided with a period of African introspection on why the continent's development trajectory had faltered despite long-standing ties with Europe and North America. The disillusionment with neoliberal experiments prompted African leaders to explore China's development experience for alternative models. China's historical background as a former semi-colony and its remarkable growth under a strong developmental state intrigued African policymakers, inspiring a quest for alternative development strategies beyond conventional neoliberal approaches. The interest is in learning from China's domestic policies and the role of the state in implementing measures for rapid economic growth, becoming a manufacturing powerhouse, reducing poverty, and expanding markets (Oqubay & Lin, 2019). This point is important in that China's own history of overcoming colonial challenges resonated with African nations, fostering a sense of shared historical struggle and a belief that similar development paths were viable for them. In addition, the interest appears not only in overarching principles but also in the practical application of policies, especially those involving a proactive role of the state in guiding economic development.

Understanding the historical context of China's relationship with Africa, especially the influence of events like the Bandung Conference from the 1950s, neoliberal policies, and shared histories, is crucial for comprehending Chinese infrastructure development aid to Africa from 2000 to 2020. Historical background information is also essential in understanding the history of China's aid to Africa and why China has historically provided aid to Africa.

1.3 History of China's Aid to Africa

The questions probed in this section are the following: What type of aid has China traditionally provided to Africa? Why does China give aid to Africa? When did China begin providing aid to Africa? How has the nature and composition of China's aid to Africa evolved? Are there specific African regions or countries that have been primary recipients of Chinese aid, and why? Have challenges or controversies been associated with China's aid projects in Africa?

Within the past 15 years, China has become Africa's largest trading partner, a top-five investor, and a significant source of development finance. Chinese demand for African resources, particularly oil, has profoundly influenced African economies. Since 1956, China has provided African countries eight types of foreign aid: "complete projects, goods and materials, technical cooperation, human resource development cooperation, medical assistance, emergency humanitarian aid, volunteer programs, and debt relief…This aid covers agriculture, education, transportation, energy, communications and health" (Sun, 2014). Additionally, China's increased investments in African infrastructure, such as roads, power generation, ports, and airports, have generated opportunities for local producers to enhance production and swiftly transport goods to various markets. This has led to an increased income for Africans (Oqubay, Arkebe & Lin 2019).

The type of aid that China provides to Africa usually takes on four different forms that include (1) grants, (2) concessional loans, (3) non-concessional loans, and (4) interest-free loans. China also provides support for programs that include medical teams and scholarships (China Africa Research Initiative, 2024). China's foreign aid also includes supporting small- and medium-sized projects in social welfare, collaborating on human resource development, providing technical assistance, offering material support, contributing to South-South cooperation assistance funds, and delivering emergency humanitarian aid. Interest-free loans primarily focus on enhancing public facilities and people's well-being, while concessional loans are designated for economically and socially beneficial projects, involving large- and medium-sized infrastructure initiatives (China Africa Research Initiative, 2024). The exploration of quantitative data on Chinese aid to Africa is crucial for understanding the scale, impact, and effectiveness of these diverse forms of assistance, aiding in informed decision-making and policy formulation. The next section of this chapter discusses the importance of exploring quantitative data to get a better understanding of China's aid to Africa.

1.4 Importance of Exploring the Quantitative Data on China's Aid to Africa

For several compelling reasons, exploring quantitative data is indispensable in the context of Chinese aid to Africa. First, it furnishes a comprehensive understanding of the scale and magnitude of the aid directed to Africa. This not only empowers policymakers in Africa but also provides a global audience, researchers, and stakeholders with the tools to assess the overall impact of Chinese aid on recipient countries. Given the ongoing debate about whether Chinese aid represents neocolonialism, quantitative data contributes objectivity by removing subjectivity, offering a clearer understanding of the impact of China's aid in Africa. Furthermore, this quantitative approach facilitates the identification of patterns, trends, and disparities in aid distribution, thereby aiding in the critical evaluation of its effectiveness.

Second, quantitative analysis facilitates comparisons over time and across different regions, helping to identify shifts in China's aid priorities and strategies. In this book, the comparisons among Nigeria, Kenya, and Ethiopia are being used because each country has received similar infrastructure development aid packages from China. In addition, there are geographical differences between the three countries, and these comparisons will be flushed out to determine what is working as it relates to Chinese aid to these select countries. This temporal and geographical perspective is essential for adapting policies, addressing emerging challenges, and maximizing the positive outcomes of aid initiatives.

Moreover, quantitative data are instrumental in promoting transparency and accountability. By quantifying aid flows, it becomes possible to track the allocation and utilization of resources, ensuring that aid serves its intended purpose of being mutually beneficial and benefits the targeted communities. This transparency is essential for fostering trust among stakeholders and ensuring aid resources' responsible and ethical use.

In summary, exploring quantitative data on Chinese aid to Africa is paramount for gaining insights into its scope, impact, and patterns. It will in turn contribute to evidence based decision-making, effective policy formulation, and increased accountability in the realm of international development. In the ensuing section, I discuss the importance of exploring qualitative data on Chinese aid to Africa.

1.5 Importance of Exploring the Qualitative Data on China's Aid to Africa

In research, it is essential to not only analyze the quantitative data but also the qualitative data pertaining to the topic under investigation. Indeed, examining qualitative data allows for a better understanding of quantitative data. Quantitative methods focus on explaining causation using statistics and modeling to assess the strength and generalizability of relationships (Ford & Goger, 2021). Qualitative research focuses on everyday human experiences and meaning making. Unlike quantitative techniques, qualitative methods aim to capture the depth and richness of a specific context, offering insights into diverse perspectives (Ford & Goger, 2021). In this book, qualitative data are used to assess the quantitative data, which involves the examination of case studies on infrastructure development aid projects in Nigeria, Kenya, and Ethiopia. The objective is to comprehend the impact of these projects on economic development in the selected countries.

Accordingly, the study employs a triangulative methodology by integrating both qualitative and quantitative research methods in order to investigate the impact of Chinese infrastructure development aid on economic development in Nigeria, Kenya, and Ethiopia. Triangulation, as defined by Todd D. Jick, involves "combining methodologies in the study of the same phenomenon. This approach dates to Campbell and Fiske, who emphasized the use of multiple methods for testing results to enhance data accuracy and ensure that differences in data operationalization reflect traits rather than methodological variations" (Jick, 1979). Case studies will be employed to investigate specific projects in Nigeria, Kenya, and Ethiopia, aiming to comprehend their purpose and impact on these countries. Furthermore, a qualitative thematic content analysis will be conducted by scrutinizing media coverage to understand the narratives surrounding these projects (Content Analysis, 2024). In the next section, the discussion turns to the importance of understanding various theoretical perspectives on foreign aid.

1.6 Importance of Understanding Various Theoretical Perspectives

In this book, the exploration of diverse theoretical frameworks serves a pivotal role by offering readers a comprehensive understanding of the varying lenses through which China's role in Africa, particularly in Nigeria, Kenya, and Ethiopia, can be interpreted. Including theoretical perspectives is instrumental in enriching the analytical depth of the study. Drawing on established theories, the book aims to provide a structured and nuanced examination of China's infrastructure development aid and foreign direct investment, facilitating a more informed and insightful discussion. The theoretical frameworks contribute to the study's intellectual rigor and empower readers to critically engage with the complexities inherent in the subject matter, thereby fostering a more profound appreciation for the multifaceted dynamics at play in international relations and development. I will now broach the essence of comparative analysis.

1.7 Why Conduct a Comparative Analysis?

A comparative analysis will be employed to comprehend the diverse Chinese infrastructure development aid projects and their impacts on economic development in Nigeria, Kenya, and Ethiopia. The analysis will encompass a comparative assessment of the GDPs of the three countries from 2000 to 2022. In conjunction with the GDP examination, a comparative analysis will be conducted on similar infrastructure development projects to evaluate their influence on GDP, citizens' quality of life, and job generation. Additionally, these infrastructure projects will be reviewed to understand both successes and failures in order to provide the reader with a multifaceted view of the various outcomes. The comparative analysis aims to elucidate each country's different policies regarding its relationship with China. The research will explore which policies are effective, whether one method of aid management is more efficient, and how each country is handling its aid for infrastructure projects. The exploration of these questions seeks to offer suggested recommendations and policy prescriptions. In the section that follows, I discuss the ethical considerations and limitations of the book.

1.8 Ethical Considerations and Limitations of the Book

In undertaking this research, ethical principles and standards have been paramount in shaping the methodology and analysis. While the study primarily involves the analysis of existing data and documents without direct interaction with human subjects, there are additional ethical considerations that are considered, such as informed consent and data usage. Thus, due diligence has been exercised in ensuring that the data used adhere to relevant data usage agreements, copyright regulations, and respect for the terms under which they were made available. Regarding cultural sensitivity, the information analysis considers the cultural context in which the data were generated. Efforts have been made to interpret findings with cultural sensitivity by acknowledging the potential implications and nuances of the content. In addition, throughout the research process, transparency was maintained. The methodology, data sources, and possible limitations are communicated to foster trust and understanding of the research process. Lastly, this research adheres to all relevant ethical guidelines and legal regulations governing data and intellectual property use.

To overcome the challenge of limited transparency in China's aid statistics, this study employed various data sources encompassing media-based, academic, and data from financial institutions. Given the inherent constraints in accessing comprehensive and accurate data on China's foreign aid, the collection of these sources involved meticulous extrapolation from official sources. It is important to note that using multiple datasets was imperative in order to construct a holistic and nuanced understanding of China's infrastructure aid to Nigeria, Kenya, and Ethiopia. Despite these efforts, it is essential to also acknowledge potential limitations arising from data gaps in the sources.

To address these limitations and strengthen the overall dataset, this study also incorporated statistical techniques to estimate missing values where data gaps remained despite extensive sourcing efforts. Specifically, in this study, the Expectation-Maximization (EM) algorithm was applied to estimate missing values in the dataset on Chinese infrastructure development aid to Nigeria, Kenya, and Ethiopia from 2000 to 2022. The EM technique was implemented using Microsoft Excel, beginning with preliminary imputations based on available means, and iteratively refining these estimates until statistical convergence was reached. To enhance the reliability of these estimates, public news sources, to include newspaper archives, government press releases and infrastructure project announcements were reviewed to supplement data gaps for specific years. This dual strategy of statistical estimation and qualitative verification provided a more complete dataset, enabling evaluation of the relationship between Chinese infrastructure aid and economic development in these three countries. It is important to note that the COVID-19 pandemic significantly altered the distribution and timing of Chinese infrastructure aid during the affected years of 2020–2022, which may have influenced quantity, volume, and sector focus of aid commitments.

While the enhanced dataset with the use of the Expectation-Maximization (EM) algorithm provides a more comprehensive foundation for analysis, it is essential to acknowledge a methodological limitation in the use of a simple linear regression model to assess the relationship between Chinese infrastructure aid and economic development, measured by GDP per capita in Nigeria, Kenya, and Ethiopia. The simplicity of this model makes it a practical and accessible starting point for inducing readers to econometric techniques. However, this model does not account for the complex interplay of multiple factors that can simultaneously affect economic outcomes, such as political stability, domestic policy, foreign aid from various countries, labor market conditions, or fluctuations in commodity prices. It is essential to note that this approach assesses whether a linear and direct relationship exists between Chinese infrastructure development aid and GDP in the selected countries. To account for other external factors that may influence GDP in these countries, in the theoretical framework discussion of the book, a multivariate analysis was conducted that incorporated aid and FDI from other major donors in addition to China. This broader model allowed for the isolation of China's specific effects thereby enabling an assessment of whether a dependency relationship exists even after controlling for Chinese aid.

Despite some limitations, the simple linear regression model offers key benefits, such as its ease of implementation and interpretation, as well as a clear visual and statistical understanding of the general relationship between infrastructure aid and GDP. Additionally, this model provides a solid foundation for more complex analyses. This foundation is adequate for new students and early-stage researchers in building critical analytical skills, econometric basics, and interpretive confidence.

1.9 Chapter Summary

This introduction chapter underscores the book's focus on the historical evolution of the Sino-African relationship, a topic of immense significance and relevance. Specifically, it delves into the dynamics of Chinese infrastructure aid to Africa and the importance of exploring its initiation, distribution, and beneficiaries by using a robust mix of quantitative and qualitative data. The chapter also places a strong emphasis on understanding various theoretical perspectives and the importance of comparative analysis, the selection of representative countries, and the detailed data collection process. It in addition discusses the essence of utilizing a statistical framework while addressing ethical considerations and limitations. The qualitative analysis will provide a rich exploration of the historical, economic, and social contexts of China's relations with Nigeria, Ethiopia, and Kenya, thereby offering deeper insights into infrastructure projects. The chapter further discusses the importance of combining statistical analysis with qualitative findings to fully understand China's infrastructure aid and FDI impact on development in the selected countries. This chapter then discusses why this research is important in making this holistic approach to offer actionable recommendations and policy suggestions for host countries, emphasizing partnerships and collaboration. In sum, the topics covered include African colonialism, the Sino-African relationship, the history of Chinese aid to Africa, the importance of quantitative and qualitative data exploration, and the importance of understanding theoretical perspectives, comparative analysis, ethical considerations, and study limitations.

References

Archibong, B., Coulibaly, B. S., & Okonjo-Iweala, N. (2021, February 19). How have the Washington consensus reforms affected economic performance in sub-Saharan Africa? *Brookings*. Retrieved from https://www.brookings.edu/articles/how-have-the-washington-consensus-reforms-affected-economic-performance-in-sub-saharan-africa/

China Africa Research Initiative. (2024, July 1). Data: Chinese Global Foreign Aid. http://www.sais-cari.org/data-chinese-global-foreign-aid.

Content Analysis. *Population Health Methods*. Columbia University Mailman School of Public Health. Last modified August 16, 2024. https://www.publichealth.columbia.edu/research/population-health-methods/content-analysis

Encyclopedia Britannica. (2025). *Neocolonialism*. Britannica. Retrieved: May 15, 2025.https://www.britannica.com/topic/neocolonialism

Ford, T. N., & Goger, A. (2021, October 14). The value of qualitative data for advancing equity in policy. Brookings Institution. Retrieved 7/2/2024 https://www.brookings.edu/articles/value-of-qualitative-data-for-advancing-equity-in-policy/

Haar, J. (2023). Modernizing infrastructure vital to fulfilling Africa's promise. *Insight & Analysis*. https://www.wilsoncenter.org/article/modernizing-infrastructure-vital-fulfilling-africas-promise.

Heath, E. (2010). Berlin conference of 1884–1885. *Encyclopaedia of Africa.*. https://www.oxfordreference.com/view/10.1093/acref/9780195337709.001.0001/acref-9780195337709-e-0467

Jick, T. D. (1979). Mixing qualitative and quantitative methods: Triangulation in action. *Administrative Science Quarterly, 24*(4), 602–611.

Johnson, S. (2014). King Leopold II's Exploitation of the Congo From 1885 to 1908 and Its Consequences. 1642.B https://stars.library.ucf.edu/honorstheses1990-2015/1642. Date accessed: December 15, 2023.

Kegley, C & Shannon Blanton. World Politics Trend and Transformation. Twelfth Edition. 2009–2010 Update. Wadsworth, Cengage Learning. 2010.p.141.

Ministry of Foreign Affairs of the People's Republic of China. (2024, May 31). *The Asian–African Conference*. Retrieved June 16, 2025, from https://www.mfa.gov.cn/eng/zy/wjls/3604_665547/202405/t20240531_11367588.html.

Oqubay, A., & Lin, J. Y. (2019). Introduction to China-Africa and an Economic Transformation. In *China-Africa and an Economic Transformation*, 3. Oxford University Press, 2019. Oxford University Press. © Oxford University Press. DOI: https://doi.org/10.1093/oso/9780198830504.003.0001.

Rahaman, Md., Shahinoor, Md., Rajib Yeazdani, & Raihan Mahmud. The Untold History of Neocolonialism in Africa (1960–2011). *History Research* 5, no. 1 (2017): 9–16. doi:https://doi.org/10.11648/j.history.20170501.12.

Riddell, J. B. (1992). Things Fall Apart Again: Structural Adjustment Programmes in Sub-Saharan Africa. *The Journal of Modern African Studies, 30*(1), 53–68. http://www.jstor.org/stable/161046.

Sultan, N. (2025). What is colonialism? The dual claims of a twentieth-century political category. *American Political Science Review, 119*(1), 435–448. https://doi.org/10.1017/S0003055424000388

Sun, Y. (2014) Africa in China's New Foreign Aid White Paper. Accessed July 6, 2024. https://www.brookings.edu/articles/africa-in-chinas-new-foreign-aid-white-paper/.

United Nations (2023). "Non-Self-Governing Territories." Date accessed January 5, 2024. Accessed from https://www.un.org/dppa/decolonization/nsgt.

United Nations Secretary-General. (2019, September 26). *Helping 800 million people escape poverty was greatest such effort in history, says Secretary-General, on seventieth anniversary of China's founding* [Press release SG/SM/19779]. United Nations.

Varanasi, A. (2022, September 21). How Colonialism Spawned and Continues to Exacerbate the Climate Crisis. Columbia Climate School. Accessed April 3, 2024. https://news.climate.columbia.edu/2022/09/21/how-colonialism-spawned-and-continues-to-exacerbate-the-climate-crisis/.

Competing Perspectives

2

This chapter is dedicated to unpacking key concepts that are central to understanding the economic development and integration of Africa South of the Sahara in the contemporary global economy. The concepts of Foreign Direct Investment and Infrastructure Development are explored to highlight their critical roles in driving economic growth, particularly through theories such as the Solow Growth Model and Infrastructure-Led Growth Theory. The Millennium Development Goals (MDGs) provide a backdrop for evaluating progress in social and economic outcomes across the region, while the African Continental Free Trade Area (ACFTA) represents a significant step toward regional economic integration. Additionally, New Economic Geography Theory offers insights into how spatial dynamics influence economic development, while the concept of Neocolonialism serves as a critical lens for understanding ongoing external influences on Africa's economic policies. By defining and examining these key concepts, the chapter aims to provide a comprehensive framework for analyzing the complex interplay of factors shaping Africa's economic landscape in the twenty-first century. These definitions have been developed from the combination of sources (World Bank, Brittanica, Investopedia, Oxford Reference, *Journal of the Practice of Cardiovascular Sciences,* Pierre-Richard Agénor, and Bernstein and Hayes). The definitions are as follows:

1. Foreign Direct Investment: Foreign Direct Investment (FDI) occurs when an individual, company, or government from one country (in this case, China) invests in a business or project in another country (in this case, Nigeria, Kenya, and Ethiopia). This typically involves acquiring a significant share or the entirety of a foreign business to expand operations in a new market. FDI

J. Guest, *China's Infrastructure Aid and Investment*, African Studies and Research Forum Series, https://doi.org/10.1007/978-3-032-11964-3_2

is more than just purchasing stocks in a foreign company; it entails substantial investments that create strong and lasting connections between different economies (Bernstein, 2023; Hayes, 2024).

2. Infrastructure: Infrastructure includes the various activities, services, and facilities necessary to support a country's economic and social development. It comprises the backbone of an economy, supporting sectors like agriculture, industry, and services. Infrastructure is essential for both economic growth and social progress (Sureiman & Mangera, 2020). Infrastructure development is referring to the process of planning, developing, improving, constructing, and maintaining these critical facilities and systems, such as transportation networks, energy production, communication systems, and water supply, to enhance a country's capacity for sustainable economic growth and improve the quality of life for its citizens.
3. Solow Growth Model:- A neoclassical perspective on economic growth, challenging the Harrod-Domar model. Solow focuses on the interplay between capital accumulation, labor force growth, and technological change in driving long-term economic growth.
4. Infrastructure-Led Growth Theory: Infrastructure-led growth is an economic development strategy that emphasizes significant investments in infrastructure projects, including transportation networks (roads, railways, airports), utilities (electricity, water supply, telecommunications), and social infrastructure (schools, hospitals). The goal is to stimulate economic growth and development by enhancing the foundational facilities and systems that support economic activities. In countries like Nigeria, Kenya, and Ethiopia, this involves targeted investments in key areas such as transportation, energy, and urban development. These projects aim to boost economic growth, improve connectivity, and support industrial and urban development within each nation.
5. Millennium Development Goals (MDGs): The Millennium Development Goals (MDGs) were eight international development objectives established at the United Nations Millennium Summit 2000. Adopted by the 191 UN member states and at least 22 international organizations, the MDGs aimed to tackle a wide range of global development challenges by 2015. These goals were designed to enhance social and economic conditions in the world's poorest countries, marking a significant milestone in international development policy (United Nations, 2015).
6. Neocolonialism (see definition in Chap. 1).

Accordingly, the chapter examines competing perspectives on the relationship between infrastructure development and economic growth. The discussion on the importance of infrastructure development in Nigeria is enriched by contrasting viewpoints, with some asserting that substantial infrastructure investment is pivotal for the nation's growth and others questioning the benefit of China's aid to Africa.

The debates surrounding China's foreign aid to African nations and its impact on economic growth are multifaceted, with a rich diversity of scholars presenting divergent views on the benefits and potential drawbacks of this aid. Similarly, the examination of China's FDI and its influence on economic growth reveals contrasting perspectives, as some experts laud FDI as a driver of development, while others caution against its potential pitfalls.

This chapter therefore encompasses a spectrum of viewpoints in the context of development theories, from modernization theories that emphasize economic growth to dependency theories that underline the potential risks and imbalances in global economic relations.

Also, the chapter delves into the debated question of whether China's aid is ultimately beneficial or detrimental to Africa. Different perspectives weigh in, with some highlighting the advantages of Chinese aid, such as infrastructural improvements, while others draw attention to potential risks and dependencies. These competing perspectives contribute to a comprehensive and balanced exploration of the multifaceted issues addressed in the book. The following topics covered in this chapter: (a) the relationship between infrastructure development and economic growth, (b) the importance of infrastructure development in Africa, (c) China's foreign aid to Africa and its impact on economic growth, (d) China's foreign direct investment and its impact on economic growth, (e) theories of development, (f) whether China's aid is good or bad for Africa, and (g) if a neocolonial relationship exists.

2.1 Relationship between Infrastructure Development and Economic Growth

The African continent confronts significant challenges related to infrastructure capacity, with the African Development Bank (AfDB) identifying an infrastructure deficit as a hindrance to growth. Challenges include providing a growing population with affordable electricity, housing, and transportation. Specific issues involve a low percentage of paved roads (53%), limited access to all-season roads for less than half the population, and significant road safety concerns leading to approximately 225,000 deaths annually. Outdated and insufficient maintenance negatively impacts railway systems in Africa South of the Sahara. Water and sanitation costs account for 5% of the GDP, with nearly half of those lacking access to these services living on less than two dollars a day. The contribution of the Internet to overall GDP is currently low, but it is anticipated to increase to 5–6% by 2025. Household electrification is at a rate of only 43%, leaving nearly 600 million people without electricity, and there is a projected 93% growth in power demand between the present and 2035 (AfDB 2023).

The challenges outlined in the preceding paragraph highlight the critical issues the African continent faces regarding infrastructure capacity. The AfDB has specifically identified the infrastructure deficit as a significant obstacle to growth in the continent. The deficiencies in essential services like affordable electricity, housing, and transportation for the growing population directly impact economic development. As aforementioned, the inadequate infrastructure, characterized by a low percentage of paved roads, limited access to all-season roads, and significant road safety concerns, not only hampers mobility and accessibility but also contributes to a staggering number of annual deaths (AfDB 2023).

The outdated and insufficient maintenance of railway systems further underscores the infrastructure challenges, affecting the efficiency of transportation networks. Additionally, the high water and sanitation costs, coupled with the lack of access for a significant portion of the population, especially those living on less than two dollars a day, intensify the economic struggles faced by the region (AfDB 2023).

Furthermore, the low contribution of the Internet to overall GDP, although anticipated to increase in the future, signifies a digital infrastructure gap that can hinder economic growth. The household electrification rate at 43% leaves a substantial part of the population, nearly 600 million people, without electricity, posing a direct constraint on productivity and quality of life. The projected 93% growth in power demand between the present and 2035 emphasizes the urgency to address these infrastructure challenges to meet the increasing energy needs of Africa (AfDB 2023).

In total, infrastructure deficits and challenges, ranging from transportation and water to energy and digital connectivity, directly impact economic growth in the African continent. Addressing these infrastructure gaps is essential for improving the quality of life for the population and is also pivotal for unlocking economic opportunities and fostering sustainable development in the long term.

The preceding verity underscores the critical importance of comprehensively understanding the existing perspectives on the symbiotic relationship between infrastructure development and economic growth in Africa. The perspectives provide valuable insights for formulating effective strategies to address the continent's infrastructure challenges and propel sustainable development.

A significant number of perspectives have been proffered on the impact of infrastructure development and economic growth. While infrastructure development is generally considered crucial for economic growth in Africa, several factors can influence the effectiveness of such investments. Some observers suggest a positive correlation between infrastructure development and economic growth, emphasizing the importance of quality infrastructure in reducing inequality and fostering development. The imperative for infrastructure development is highly significance for developing nations, particularly in Africa. In these places, the absence of modern infrastructure is seen as a hindrance to economic progress that poses substantial obstacles not only to poverty reduction but also to the achievement of the Millennium Development Goals (MDGs) in Africa South of the Saharan countries (United Nations, 2015). The MDGs were eight international development objectives established at the United Nations Millennium Summit 2000. Adopted by the 191 United Nations member states and at least 22 international organizations, the MDGs are aimed at tackling a wide range of global development challenges by 2015. These goals were designed to enhance social and economic conditions in the world's poorest countries, marking a significant milestone in international development policy (United Nations, 2015).

MDG 8 ("Develop a Global Partnership for Development") underscores the importance of global partnerships in achieving development goals. For Nigeria, Kenya, and Ethiopia, these partnerships are critical in securing financial resources, technological expertise, and policy support needed to build and maintain vital infrastructure. This, in turn, fosters economic growth, reduces poverty, and improves the overall quality of life in these countries. Securing aid from international partners helps Nigeria, Kenya, and Ethiopia to fund critical infrastructure projects that might otherwise be unaffordable. These include transportation, energy, and water supply projects, which are essential for economic growth and poverty reduction (United Nations, 2015).

Understanding the MDGs in the context of infrastructure development is essential for grasping the broader development challenges and opportunities in Nigeria, Kenya, and Ethiopia. Infrastructure development is critical in achieving economic growth, reducing poverty, improving access to education and healthcare, promoting gender equality, ensuring environmental sustainability, and fostering global partnerships. These countries have made significant strides in their development agendas by aligning their infrastructure projects with the MDGs, thereby establishing a foundation for continued progress under the SDGs.

Nonetheless, poor infrastructure, inadequate quantity and types of infrastructure needed, and limited access hinder the desired outcomes. Corruption is also identified as a factor that negatively affects the impact of infrastructure on productivity and growth. Additionally, the effect of infrastructure on reducing inequality in Africa South of the Sahara is noted to be relatively modest compared to other regions due to poor infrastructure quality. The observers that support infrastructure development and economic growth in Africa include Owusu-Manu, Jehuri, Edwards, and Asumadu who reveal a statistically significant relationship between infrastructure development and economic growth in Ghana. Specifically, the electricity-generating capacity is highlighted as the infrastructure component with the most substantial positive impact on the country's economic growth. Nevertheless, it is also noted that electricity-distribution loss has a significant negative effect over both long and short terms, indicating potential challenges in this aspect of infrastructure development (Owusu-Manu et al., 2019). This example underscores the importance of addressing issues such as electricity-distribution loss to ensure the effectiveness of infrastructure investments. Overall, these observers imply that strategic and targeted infrastructure development, particularly in the energy sector, can play a crucial role in fostering economic growth in African nations.

According to Timilsina et al. (2023), the impact of infrastructure, specifically transport, electricity, and telecommunications, on economic growth is evident. Using data from 87 countries spanning 1992 to 2017, these scholars employ the Pooled Mean Group (PMG) estimator to assess the weak exogeneity of infrastructure variables. The main finding suggests that an increase in infrastructure, particularly in electricity generation capacity and telecommunications, has substantial positive long-term effects on GDP. Nonetheless, the short-term effects are smaller and more negative for roads and railways. Additionally, the scholars highlight that the influence of electricity and communication infrastructure is more pronounced in developing economies compared to the industrialized ones (Timilsina et al., 2023).

Abdullahi and Sieng (2023) investigated the impact of infrastructure development on economic growth in ten African countries in South of the Sahara from 2010 to 2020. These investigators used balanced panel data and the African Infrastructure Development Index (AIDI) to analyze the effects of water supply and sanitation, electricity, transport, and information and communications technology (ICT) on GDP per capita. Their findings reveal that 74% of the variation in economic growth can be explained by the four independent variables. They further explain that a positive relationship exists between water supply, sanitation, and electricity indexes with economic growth, which aligns with the World Bank's report on improvements in water and sanitation and electricity infrastructures in Africa South of the Sahara. Nevertheless, the negative relationship observed for the ICT and transport indices may be attributed to the continent's infrastructure deficits in these areas. The scholars emphasize the importance of infrastructure development in promoting economic growth and recommend the need for increased investment in poor infrastructure to drive productivity and economic growth in Africa South of the Sahara (Abdullahi & Sieng, 2023).

A dissertation titled "Chinese Infrastructure Development Aid and its Effect on Economic Growth and Productivity: The Nigerian Case, 2000-2015," this study examined the impact of Chinese infrastructure development aid on Nigeria's economic growth and productivity from 2000 to 2015, utilizing GDP per capita and GDP per hour worked as key indicators. Grounded in Dependency Theory, the research examined whether Nigeria's reliance on Chinese aid impacted its development trajectory and whether such aid is correlated with significant economic outcomes. Quantitative analysis through regression modeling revealed that while Chinese infrastructure aid is positively associated with GDP growth, it is not the strongest predictor when compared to other variables, such as consumption, exports, and expenditures. Notably, Chinese aid has a limited impact on worker productivity, whereas Development Assistance Committee (DAC) aid and combined aid from multiple donors exhibit a more substantial influence. The findings challenge the assumption of a dependency dynamic, as the data suggest that Chinese aid alone does not create a statistically significant dependency relationship (Guest, 2017).

In terms of the qualitative analysis used in this study, insights were gathered from expert interviews conducted across Nigeria, the United States, and Canada. Most respondents acknowledge improvements in Nigeria's infrastructure and economic performance, with over half attributing these changes in part to Chinese aid. However, opinions differ on whether the China-Nigeria relationship fosters dependency, especially given concerns that many Chinese-funded projects rely heavily on Chinese labor. While GDP growth has been observed, several experts point to broader factors—like oil revenue, political stability, and middle-class expansion—as more significant contributors. The study concluded that although Chinese infrastructure development aid plays a significant role in Nigeria's economic landscape, it operates as part of a broader ecosystem of domestic and international influences rather than as a singular or dominant force (Guest, 2017).

2.2 Importance of Infrastructure Development in Africa

According to the World Bank (2023), Africa South of the Sahara is a diverse region with various income levels characterized by rich natural resources and the world's largest free trade area. Despite this potential, the region faces many challenges with projected economic growth slowing to 2.5% in 2023. Rising conflict, climate shocks, and a complex poly-crisis which encompasses climate issues, the Coronavirus Disease (COVID)-2019 and on-going geo-political conflicts have exacerbated debt issues and left 462 million people in extreme poverty. Uneven growth persists, with East Africa at 1.8% and West Africa at 3.3% in 2023. Energy and transportation bottlenecks hinder South Africa, while Nigeria faces challenges in its oil sector. Conflicts in Sudan, Niger, and Gabon affect Central Africa and Sahel nations (World Bank 2025).

Understanding the significance of infrastructure involves considering its impact on our daily lives. The roads we use for commuting to work, traveling between states, and reaching the supermarket, as well as the means through which we communicate via telephone and the Internet, send and receive mail, and access to clean water for consumption and bathing, all highlight the crucial role of infrastructure. These aspects are integral to our daily functioning and paramount for the sustained survival and prosperity of any nation's economy. A well-developed infrastructure enhances the quality of life for individuals and serves as a foundation for economic activities, thereby facilitating trade, communication, and the overall functioning of society.

Let us explore the importance of transportation infrastructure. Adequate transportation infrastructure, encompassing well-maintained roads, ports, and airports, is crucial in facilitating the smooth movement of goods and people. A strong transportation network not only minimizes logistics costs and time, but also enhances business competitiveness. Consequently, it promotes economic growth by stimulating trade and commerce on both domestic and international scales.

According to the World Bank (2025), the potential for regional trade in Africa remains largely untapped, accounting for only 12% of the region's total economic activity, compared to 60% in Europe and 40% in Asia. The African Continental Free Trade Area (ACFTA) presents a unique opportunity to elevate regional trade, fostering economic growth and job generation continent-wide. Given the current challenges, a key priority is improving cross-border transport efficiency by addressing insufficient road and rail networks, limited use of regional maritime transport, and lengthy border crossing times. The World Bank's research on West Africa's Road corridors emphasizes the importance of combining investments in road infrastructure with trade facilitation reforms. Ongoing projects, such as the $228-million initiative to modernize the Abidjan-Lagos Corridor, have already reduced border crossing times and improved road quality. A newly launched $470-million project aims to further enhance regional integration and economic opportunities in Burkina Faso, Niger, and Togo (Lebrand, 2022).

Well-developed transportation infrastructure is essential for facilitating the movement of goods within and between African countries. Efficient road, rail, and port networks contribute to seamless trade, fostering regional integration and economic cooperation. This is especially important for the landlocked countries. Adequate transportation infrastructure reduces the costs and time associated with logistics, making businesses more competitive. Improved connectivity enables more accessible access to markets, promotes entrepreneurship, and attracts FDI, contributing to overall economic development. In addition, constructing, maintaining, and operating roads, ports, airports, and railways generate employment opportunities. This stimulates economic activity in the short term and contributes to long-term employment stability related to road maintenance and construction repairs.

Reliable transportation is crucial for agricultural productivity which is a major contributor to many African economies. It facilitates the transportation of agricultural products from farms to markets, reducing post-harvest losses and ensuring food security. This, in turn, supports rural development and poverty reduction.

In terms of quality of life and access to essential services such as healthcare and education, well-connected regions can more easily access medical facilities, educational institutions, and other critical services, thus contributing to improved quality of life for the population. Insufficient healthcare or medical facilities in a specific region of a country can be addressed through efficient transportation, enabling citizens to travel to areas with adequate healthcare facilities.

Infrastructure development also influences other aspects of development. Well-planned and connected transport networks can spur the development of urban centers, industrial zones, and trade corridors. When strategically managed, this spatial development can lead to balanced regional growth that ripples throughout a country.

Transportation infrastructure is crucial for responding to and recovering from shocks such as natural disasters or health crises. It enables the efficient movement of relief goods to badly hit areas, medical supplies, and personnel during emergencies, contributing to the overall resilience of an economy that will translate to a better quality of life and the resilience of the people of a nation. As the African continent continues to grow and integrate, strategic investments in roads, railways, ports, and airports are imperative to unlock the full potential of trade, agriculture, and transportation. Healthcare, daily lives, foreign direct investments, longer lifespan, stimulation of other economic activities, and improvement of the population's overall well-being will be positively impacted.

In terms of telecommunication infrastructure, effective communication networks, including telephone and internet systems, are essential for any economy. These networks connect businesses, individuals, and government entities to enable seamless communication. In a globalized world, instant communication is vital for conducting business transactions, sharing information, and participating in the global marketplace.

To better understand the relationship between infrastructure development and economic growth in Africa, it is important to examine various theoretical perspectives on infrastructure investment and economic growth. Understanding these theoretical perspectives will assist in formulating and implementing policies that align with specific economic conditions. Different theories may suggest different policy approaches, and policymakers can choose the most suitable strategies based on theoretical insights. The following infrastructure economic development theories are examined here: (a) Infrastructure-Led Growth Theory, (b) Solow Growth Model, and (c) New Economic Geography Theory.

In terms of Infrastructure-led Growth Theory, Agénor (2010) presents a theory of long-term development centered on public infrastructure as a catalyst for economic growth. In this framework, the government not only invests in physical infrastructure but also allocates funds to health services. The provision of health services is posited to enhance labor productivity and reduce the rate of time preference. The impact of infrastructure is not only on the production of goods but also on health services (Agénor, 2010). It is important to analyze the premise behind the Infrastructure-led Growth Model. The theory argues that investment in infrastructure will help to promote economic growth in a country. The theory posits that investing heavily in infrastructure, such as transportation, energy, and communication systems, can stimulate economic development and promote long-term growth. The idea is that improved infrastructure establishes suitable environment for businesses to thrive, attracts investments, and enhances productivity. The theory suggests that by addressing infrastructure deficiencies, a country can overcome key obstacles to economic growth. Some critics, however, argue that this theory does not take into consideration the debt that the African countries take on as a result of infrastructure projects. This is reflected in the article by David NDII titled "Africa's Infrastructure-led Economic Growth Experiment is Faltering: It's Time to Focus on Agriculture (2022)" in which he questions the paradigm and suggests that Africa's massive infrastructure investments over the past two decades have led to debt distress rather than accelerated growth. He advocates for a pragmatic approach, urging African policymakers to consider successful agriculture-led transformations in Latin America as a viable alternative. The author concludes by encouraging a more flexible and pragmatic stance in setting economic agendas, akin to Deng Xiaoping's famous dictum: "Black cat or white cat, if it can catch mice, it's a good cat" (NDII, 2022). In considering the aid extended by China to Africa, it predominantly manifests as loans allocated for various infrastructure projects across the continent. Although these loans are characterized by low-interest rates, they remain financial obligations that recipient countries are obligated to repay. The crucial point of evaluation revolves around determining whether the advantages derived from the implemented infrastructure projects surpass the financial burden posed by the repayment of these loans. In essence, the key inquiry involves assessing the overall impact and long-term benefits of the infrastructure developments facilitated by Chinese loans against the economic cost incurred through the repayment process. This analysis often delves into the socioeconomic returns, improved connectivity, enhanced productivity, and other tangible benefits that the infrastructure projects bring to the recipient nations by seeking to ascertain whether the accrued value justifies the financial commitments associated with the loans.

The second theory examined is the Solow Growth Model. Robert M. Solow's, 1956 paper, "A Contribution to the Theory of Economic Growth," offers a neoclassical perspective on economic growth, challenging the Harrod-Domar model (the Harrod-Domar model is an economic theory that posits that higher savings rates lead to greater investment and economic growth, but warns that imbalances between savings and investment can result in economic instability, such as inflation or unemployment) (Solow, 1956) (Harrod, 1939); (Domar, 1946). Solow focuses on the interplays among capital accumulation, labor force growth, and technological change in driving long-term economic growth. He introduces the production concept under variable proportions and constant returns to scale, questioning the assumption of fixed proportions in the Harrod-Domar model. Solow's analysis explores the impact of variable savings ratios, technological change, taxation, and population growth on the equilibrium capital-labor ratio and long-term growth. While acknowledging the neoclassical model's limitations, such as neglecting factors like rigid wages and liquidity preference, Solow's work enriches the understanding of economic growth by scrutinizing assumptions, introducing new variables, and recognizing the framework's constraints in explaining real-world economic dynamics (Solow, 1956).

According to Oxford Reference (, 2024), the Solow Growth Model is a theoretical framework that explains economic growth based on capital accumulation. This model assumes that output is generated through capital and labor with constant returns to scale. The produced output is then either saved or consumed. The capital stock represents the accumulated savings from previous periods, adjusted for depreciation (Oxford Reference 2024). While looking at this definition, many may wonder how this relates to infrastructure investment and economic growth and development. To fully explicate the meaning, I will examine each element of the model to determine its relationship to infrastructure development.

In the Solow Growth Model, the major element in the equation is the accumulation of capital (k). Hard infrastructure, such as roads, bridges, and technology, can be considered as a form of capital. The crucial role of increased investment in infrastructure projects in contributing to the accumulation of capital, leading to higher productivity and economic growth, cannot be overstated.

Productivity improvement is another critical element of the Solow Growth Model; infrastructure development, especially in technology and efficient transportation networks, can enhance productivity. The model emphasizes the importance of technological progress for sustained growth, investments in infrastructure that improve efficiency, and innovation that aligns with the model's principles by generating more efficiencies that increase productivity. The model suggests that savings contribute to capital accumulation. Infrastructure projects often require significant investment, and the financing of these projects involves savings. Governments or private entities funding infrastructure development are, in a way, contributing to the savings that drive capital accumulation in the model (Solow, 1956).

The preceding aspect of the Solow Growth Model introduces a potential conflict compared to the Infrastructure-led Growth Model. In the context of infrastructure development projects in African countries, a significant portion of the funding often comes from loans. A concern arises when these countries are burdened with substantial debt, raising questions about their ability to accumulate savings. The issue becomes more complex as the need to repay loans may limit the capacity for savings, potentially affecting the overall economic growth trajectory. The interplays among infrastructure investment, debt accumulation, and the ability to save become critical in evaluating the effectiveness and sustainability of development initiatives in these countries.

The Solow Growth Model also implies that economies reach a steady state whereby growth becomes flat unless external factors like technological improvements exist. Infrastructure development can be seen as one such external factor. For example, the adoption of advanced technologies in infrastructure could lead to sustained growth by continuously raising productivity levels. This situation suggests that policies supporting infrastructure development, innovation, and technological progress can be essential for promoting long-term economic growth.

The third theory examined here is the New Economic Geography Theory, which argues that the new economic geography (NEG) offers a comprehensive and micro-founded approach to the uneven distribution of economic activities across geographic space. It focuses on the interplay between agglomeration (centripetal) and dispersion (centrifugal) forces, shaping observed spatial configurations. While some refer to the term "new economic geographies" to encompass diverse outputs inspired by an institutional-cultural shift in economic geography, others propose "geographical economics" as an alternative to NEG (Chen & Peng, 2020). It appears that this theory encourages a comprehensive examination of how the spatial distribution of infrastructure projects and economic activities can impact regional growth and development. It underscores the need for nuanced approaches to policy interventions and spatial planning, considering the complex interactions between economic agents and geography. Overall, the NEG Theory provides a valuable framework for analyzing the geographical aspects of economic development, including the role of infrastructure in shaping regional economic patterns.

The NED Theory highlights the importance of agglomeration effects, whereby industries and economic activities cluster in specific regions. Infrastructure facilitates agglomeration, including transportation networks, communication systems, and other public services. A well-developed infrastructure can enhance regional connectivity, reduce trade costs, and attract businesses to cluster in specific areas. It underscores the importance of understanding geographic factors and interactions between economic agents when planning and implementing infrastructure projects to foster balanced regional development and economic growth across the continent. Accordingly, the questions probed in the next sections are imperative (Chen & Peng, 2020).

2.2.1 Is China's Aid Good or Bad for Africa? Does a Neocolonial Relationship Exist?

This book is one of the many pieces of literature on Chinese aid to Africa. Some scholars note that the aid China provides to Africa is beneficial in helping the African economies to grow. Other scholars argue that the aid China provides is neocolonial. It is first important to define neocolonialism, a term coined by Kwame Nkrumah, which is considered "the final stage of imperialism." It is characterized by the indirect control of less developed countries by developed nations (Shafiqur Rahaman et al., 2017). In Encyclopedia Britannica, Sandra Halperin defines neocolonialism as the domination of underdeveloped or developing countries by developed nations through colonial exploitation rules, particularly in economic, political, and cultural aspects. The concept emerged after World War II when colonies gained political independence but remained economically dependent on their former colonial masters. Neocolonialism involves exploiting newly independent countries through hidden economic means while politically and culturally cloaking the exploitation (Encyclopedia Britannica 2025) (Shafiqur Rahaman et al., 2017). Charles Kegley Jr. and Shannon Blanton in *World Politics Trend & Transformation* define neocolonialism as "The economic rather than military domination of foreign countries" (Kegley & Blanton, 2010). Based on the preceding definitions, does China's relationship with African countries represent neocolonialism?

The argument that China's aid to African countries is neocolonial stems from the definitions of neocolonialism, particularly its economic, political, and cultural aspects. As aforementioned, neocolonialism, as coined by Kwame Nkrumah, involves the control of less developed countries by developed nations through indirect means, exploiting them economically while covering up the exploitation politically and culturally under the guise that they are helping to improve the lives of people in one developing country to another developing country. The concept emerged post-World War II, highlighting the economic dependence of politically independent colonies on their former colonial powers.

Kegley and Blanton (2010) further define neocolonialism as the economic domination of foreign countries. Considering this and the preceding definitions, the scholars question whether China's relationship with African countries, characterized by economic influence through aid, aligns with the definition of neocolonialism. This question underscores the concern that China's economic assistance may come with hidden agendas, potentially leading to economic dependence and exploitation, echoing patterns reminiscent of historical colonial practices. The analysis raises a critical perspective on China's role in Africa, framing it within the discourse of neocolonialism (Kegley & Blanton, 2010).

Assessing the impact of China's aid on Africa is a crucial task for researchers, students, and scholars. By critically evaluating the information provided in this book alongside the findings of other scholars, individuals can make informed decisions grounded in factual evidence. Understanding the nuances of China's aid is essential for comprehensively evaluating its implications for the African continent. The article titled "Is China Good or Bad for Africa?" (2012) by Peter Eigen explores the contrasting views on China's impact on Africa. According to him, critics argue that China exploits Africa for its resources and supports oppressive governments, while supporters contend that China aims for neutral economic growth rather than fostering dependency. Eigen also suggests that Africa can improve its relationship with China by diversifying its economies, encouraging labor-intensive Chinese investments, negotiating better terms, and enhancing working conditions. The evolving dynamics, marked by increased Chinese businesses in Africa, make it challenging to definitively categorize the China-Africa relationship as either positive or negative (Eigen, 2012).

The article, "Chinese Development Aid in Africa: What, Where, Why, and How Much?" (2011), by Deborah Brautigam explores the definition of aid according to the Organisation for Economic Co-operation and Development's Development Assistance Committee (OECD DAC) and categorizes China's financial instruments. The analysis distinguishes between official development assistance and other forms of finance, including grants, loans, and debt relief. China's aid, including scholarships, medical teams, and infrastructure development, is linked to diplomatic ties rather than resource patterns. Brautigam also examines aid projects in Ghana and the Democratic Republic of Congo, illustrating how resource-backed loans are linked to infrastructure projects with repayment mechanisms tied to revenue generation. She further delves into the complexities of distinguishing aid from investment in Chinese economic financing abroad (Brautigam, 2011).

The paper by Wang and Ozanne titled "Two Approaches to Aid in Africa: China and the West" (2010) challenges the Western aid paradigm, noting that the economic context endogenously determines governance. The West faces the following dilemma: conditionality aims to prevent aid misuse, but aid is needed for development, which can address corruption and governance issues. In contrast, the Chinese approach targets development constraints directly through infrastructure provision, thereby minimizing government involvement and corruption opportunities. While providing limited direct employment, this approach enhances trade opportunities and is argued to be more effective in fostering economic dynamics and long-term growth. Also discussed is aid effectiveness, the Chinese approach, and its potential to resolve the aid dilemma (Wang & Ozanne, 2010).

In the article titled "Rogue Aid? The Determinants of China's Aid Allocation" (2011), Axel Dreher and Andreas Fuchs investigate China's aid allocation, suggesting that it is driven more by self-interest than the interests of recipient countries. Using data from 1956 to 2006, the authors analyzed China's food, project aid, total aid, and medical support allocations. Their findings indicate that China's aid distribution is not primarily motivated by access to natural resources. While political considerations play a role in China's aid distribution, they are deemed less crucial compared to other traditional and emerging aid donors (Dreher & Fuchs, 2011).

A Brookings Institution article titled "Africa in China's New Foreign Aid White Paper" (2014) written by Yun Sun discusses China's new foreign aid white paper released in 2014. The paper is said to emphasize a shift in focus from general aid policies to specific priorities and implementation of current foreign assistance. China is shown to have increased its foreign aid efforts since 2009, with a notable rise in aid to Africa, reaching 51.8% from 2010 to 2012. Concessional loans now dominate China's aid financing, accounting for 55.7%, while zero-interest loans and grants have declined. Sun highlights China's engagement in poverty alleviation, capacity building, and development projects in Africa, downplaying natural resource-centric relations. Scrutiny has influenced China's changing perspective on Africa, and African countries are urged to align China's interests and aid with their needs (Sun, 2014).

The article "Africa-China Cooperation: Forging a Path to a Shared Future" (2024), by Olalekan A. Babatunde, discusses the evolving relationship between Africa and China, emphasizing the need for cooperation and shared benefits. The author acknowledges the historical ties between the two regions and highlights China's growing influence in Africa through investments, infrastructure projects, and trade partnerships. Babatunde argues that while there have been criticisms of China's engagement in Africa, including concerns about debt sustainability and environmental impact, the partnership presents opportunities for economic growth, development, and technological advancement. He also advocates for a balanced approach to Africa-China cooperation, emphasizing the importance of transparency, accountability, and mutual respect. He further calls for African countries to leverage their resources and negotiate favorable terms in their engagements with China, while also urging China to uphold ethical standards and contribute to sustainable development initiatives in the continent. Overall, Babatunde advocates for a constructive and mutually beneficial partnership between Africa and China as they navigate the complexities of globalization and seek to build a shared future (Babatunde, 2024).

Indeed, assessing the impact of China's aid on Africa is a complex, yet vital, task. The divergent perspectives presented by various scholars highlight the nuanced nature of China-Africa relations. Eigen suggests avenues for improving this relationship, emphasizing the evolving dynamics marked by increased Chinese businesses in Africa. Brautigam delves into the intricacies of distinguishing aid from investment in Chinese economic financing abroad, highlighting the role of diplomatic ties. Wang and Ozanne challenge the Western aid paradigm, proposing that China's direct targeting of development constraints may offer a more effective solution. Dreher and Fuchs argue that China's aid allocation is driven more by self-interest than by the interests of recipient countries. The Brookings Institution article underscores China's evolving aid focus, emphasizing poverty alleviation, capacity building, and sustainable development in Africa. Despite the complexities and ongoing scrutiny, this evolving relationship allows African countries to shape China's new interests and aid according to their needs.

2.3 Chapter Summary

This chapter has examined the intricate relationship between infrastructure development and African economic growth, highlighting the critical challenges and opportunities. It delved into the potential of quality infrastructure to reduce inequality and foster sustainable development, thereby referencing the MDGs and the SDGs. The chapter presented diverse perspectives on China's aid and FDI in Africa, with some scholars praising these as development drivers. In contrast, others caution about potential risks and dependencies. Empirical studies underscore the significant long-term positive impact of infrastructure, particularly in electricity and telecommunications, on GDP growth. The chapter also contrasted modernization and dependency theories to provide a balanced exploration of the multifaceted issues surrounding infrastructure development and economic growth in Africa.

The importance of infrastructure development in Africa is multifaceted, significantly impacting daily life and economic activities. Despite its potential, Africa South of the Sahara faces challenges like slow economic growth, conflicts, climate shocks, and extreme poverty. Infrastructure, including transportation and telecommunications, is crucial for enhancing quality of life, facilitating trade, and promoting economic growth. Effective transportation networks reduce logistics costs, boost business competitiveness, and support agricultural productivity. Telecommunication infrastructure connects businesses and individuals, enabling participation in the global marketplace. The chapter also examined various theoretical perspectives on infrastructure investment and economic growth, including the Infrastructure-led Growth Model, the Solow Growth Model, and the New Economic Geography Theory. These theories provide insights into how infrastructure development can drive productivity, attract investment, and foster development despite challenges like debt from infrastructure loans.

China's aid to Africa is a topic of intense debate, sparking discussions over whether it fosters development or perpetuates neocolonialism. Neocolonialism, as defined by Kwame Nkrumah, raises concerns about hidden agendas behind China's aid. Scholars like Charles Kegley Jr. and Shannon Blanton argue that China's economic influence aligns with neocolonialism's definition of economic domination. Critics fear economic dependence and exploitation akin to historical colonialism, while others argue that China promotes growth and independence. Deborah Brautigam distinguishes China's aid from Western aid, noting its ties to diplomacy and infrastructure projects. Wang and Ozanne contrast China's direct aid approach with Western conditionalities, suggesting effectiveness in development. Axel Dreher and Andreas Fuchs find China's aid driven by self-interest rather than recipient needs. Despite criticism, Olalekan A. Babatunde advocates for balanced, mutually beneficial Africa-China cooperation, urging transparency and negotiation for sustainable development. The diversity of these perspectives makes the debate on China's aid to Africa a compelling and engaging one.

References

Abdullahi, A., & Sieng, L. W. (2023). The effect of infrastructure development on economic growth: The case of sub-Saharan Africa. *Journal of Infrastructure, Policy and Development, 7*(2), 1994. https://doi.org/10.24294/jipd.v7i2.1994

Agénor, P.-R. (2010). A theory of infrastructure-led development. *Journal of Economic Dynamics and Control, 34*(5), 932–950. https://doi.org/10.1016/j.jedc.2010.01.009

Babatunde, Olalekan A. Premium Times. Africa-China Cooperation: Forging a Path to a Shared Future. Retrieved April 16, 2024. https://www.premiumtimesng.com/opinion/688847-africa-china-cooperation-forging-a-path-to-a-shared-future-by-olalekan-a-babatunde.html

Bernstein, Larry. EBSCO (2023). Foreign direct investment (FDI). In Business and management: Research starters. EBSCO. Retrieved June 17, 2025, from https://www.ebsco.com/research-starters/business-and-management/foreign-direct-investment-fdi.

Brautigam, Deborah, Chinese Development Aid in Africa: What, Where, Why, and How Much? (June 2011). Available at SSRN: https://ssrn.com/abstract=2013609 or doi:https://doi.org/10.2139/ssrn.2013609. Date Retrieved July 15, 2024.

Chen, Chung, & Shiyuan Peng. New economic geography. Oxford Research Encyclopedia of Economics and Finance, October 27, 2020. Retrieved May 24, 2024. https://oxfordre.com/economics/view/10.1093/acrefore/9780190625979.001.0001/acrefore-9780190625979-e-338.

Domar, E. D. (1946). Capital expansion, rate of growth, and employment. *Econometrica, 14*(2), 137–147. https://doi.org/10.2307/1905364

Dreher, Axel, & Andreas Fuchs. Rogue Aid? The Determinants of China's Aid Allocation. Working Paper No. 164, Princeton University, 2011.

Eigen, Peter. Is China Good or Bad for Africa? October 29, 2012 Special to CNN - Global Public Square.

Guest, Janeen (2017). *Chinese infrastructure development aid and its effect on economic growth and productivity: The Nigerian case, 2000–2015.* (Unpublished doctoral dissertation). Howard University.

Harrod, R. F. (1939). An essay in dynamic theory. *The Economic Journal, 49*(193), 14–33. http://www.jstor.org/stable/2225181

Hayes, Adam. Foreign Direct Investment (FDI). *Investopedia.* Retrieved July 6, 2024. https://www.investopedia.com/terms/f/fdi.asp.

Kegley, Charles & Shannon Blanton. World Politics Trend and Transformation. Twelfth Edition. 2009–2010 Update. Wadsworth, Cengage Learning. 2010.p.141.

Lebrand, Mathilde (2022). World Bank. Better transport can bring African countries closer together and support their economies. World Bank Blogs. Retrieved May 12, 2024. https://blogs.worldbank.org/en/transport/better-transport-can-bring-african-countries-closer-together-and-support-their-economies.

NDII, David. Carnegie Endowment for International Peace. "Africa's Infrastructure-led Growth Experiment Is Faltering. It Is Time to Focus on Agriculture." Last modified December 20, 2022. Accessed July 6, 2024. https://carnegieendowment.org/2022/12/20/africa-s-infrastructure-led-growth-experiment-is-faltering.-it-is-time-to-focus-on-agriculture-pub-88662.

Owusu-Manu, D.-G., Jehuri, A. B., Edwards, D. J., Boateng, F., & Asumadu, G. (2019). The impact of infrastructure development on economic growth in sub-Saharan Africa with special focus on Ghana. *Journal of Financial Management of Property and Construction, 24*(3), 253–273. https://doi.org/10.1108/JFMPC-09-2018-0050

Shafiqur Rahaman, M., Rawshan Yeazdani, M., & Mahmud, R. (2017). The untold history of neocolonialism in Africa (1960-2011). *History Research, 5*(1), 9–16. https://doi.org/10.11648/j.history.20170501.12

Solow growth model. *Oxford Reference*; Retrieved 17 Aug. 2024. https://www.oxfordreference.com/view/10.1093/oi/authority.20110803100517469.

Solow, R. M. (1956). A contribution to the theory of economic growth. *The Quarterly Journal of Economics, 70*(1), 65–94. https://doi.org/10.2307/1884513

Sun, Yun. (2014) Africa in China's New Foreign Aid White Paper. Retrieved July 6, 2024. https://www.brookings.edu/articles/africa-in-chinas-new-foreign-aid-white-paper/.

Sureiman, O., & Mangera, C. M. (2020). F-test of overall significance in regression analysis simplified. *Journal of the Practice of Cardiovascular Sciences, 6*, 116. https://doi.org/10.4103/jpcs.jpcs_18_20

Timilsina, G. R., Stern, D. I., & Das, D. K. (2023). Physical infrastructure and economic growth. *Applied Economics*. https://doi.org/10.1080/00036846.2023.2184461

United Nations. *The Millennium Development Goals Report 2015*. United Nations, 2015. Retrieved January 15, 2024. https://www.un.org/millenniumgoals/2015_MDG_Report/pdf/MDG%202015%20rev%20(July%201).pdf.

Wang, X., & Ozanne, A. (2010, September). *Two approaches to aid in Africa: China and the West* (Paper presented at Ten Years of 'War Against Poverty': What Have We Learned Since 2000 and What Should We Do 2010–2020?, Brooks World Poverty Institute, University of Manchester). Retrieved from ResearchGate.

Methodological Framework and Analysis: Nigeria Case Study

3

This chapter introduces a range of key concepts essential for analyzing the economic and developmental impacts of Chinese involvement in Nigeria, Kenya, and Ethiopia. Concepts like **Quantitative Data** and **Qualitative Data** are foundational for understanding the methods used to assess the effects of **Chinese Foreign Direct Investment** and **Chinese Infrastructure Aid** on economic indicators such as Per **Capita** Gross Domestic Product in these countries. The relationship between **Independent** and **Dependent Variables** is examined to understand how various factors interact, while concepts like **Correlation** help clarify the connections between Chinese investments, including those under the **Belt and Road Initiative**, and economic outcomes in these target nations. By defining and exploring these terms, the chapter aims to equip readers with the tools necessary to critically assess the broader implications of China's economic strategies in these three African countries. The definitions have been formally defined within the textbook and have been adapted from multiple sources to include the Carnegie Endowment for International Peace, IMF, World Bank, Council on Foreign Relations, and OECD. The definitions are as follows:

1. Quantitative Data: Quantitative data refer to any information that can be quantified, counted, or measured and expressed numerically. In this case, a regression analysis is used to determine if a relationship exist between Chinese infrastructure aid and FDI and per capita GDP.
2. Qualitative Data: Qualitative data in the content analysis of newspapers in Nigeria, Kenya, and Ethiopia involve examining the textual and visual elements of news coverage to understand how these countries' media perceive and portray Chinese infrastructure aid and FDI. This approach provides a comprehensive and nuanced understanding of the attitudes, opinions, and narratives surrounding Chinese involvement in their infrastructure development.

J. Guest, *China's Infrastructure Aid and Investment*, African Studies and Research Forum Series, https://doi.org/10.1007/978-3-032-11964-3_3

3. Chinese Foreign Direct Investment: Foreign Direct Investment (FDI) is when an individual, company, or government from one country (in this case China) invests in a business or project in another country (in this case, Nigeria). This usually means buying a significant share or the entire foreign business to grow their operations in a new area. FDI is not just about buying stocks in a foreign company; it involves more substantial investments that create strong and lasting connections between different economies.
4. Chinese Infrastructure Aid grants concessional loans, non-concessional loans and interest-free loans provided by China to Nigeria, Kenya, and Ethiopia. For purposes of this research, Chinese infrastructure aid is also the independent variable provided in the regression equation.
5. Per Capita Gross Domestic Product (GDP) is the total value of all goods and services produced within a country's borders during a specific time, like a year or a quarter. It's a common measure used to understand how well a country's economy is performing and how big it is. GDP considers the value of everything people buy and sell, plus government spending, investments, and exports minus imports.
6. Dependency Theory: A condition which theorists argue is a result of exploitation of the Global South by the Global North, which results in subordination of the Global South to the Global North. In addition, resulting in vulnerabilities of the Global South to the Global North business cycles.
7. Concessional Loans: Concessional loans are designated for economically and socially beneficial projects, involving large- and medium-sized infrastructure initiatives. These are loans provided at interest rates lower than the market rate or with extended grace periods, offering more favorable terms for borrowers (Foster et al., 2009; Usman, 2021).
8. Non-Concessional Loan: Non-concessional Chinese loans have played a crucial role in financing infrastructure development in Africa, driving economic growth and modernization. However, the higher interest rates, shorter repayment periods, and less transparent terms pose Significance Financial and economic challenges for borrower nations. Kenya has secured significant non-concessional loans for projects such as the constructions of roads in Nairobi. While these projects have stimulated economic activity, they have also increased the country's debt burden (Foster et al., 2009).
9. Independent Variable: For this book, the independent variable is Chinese infrastructure aid and FDI.
10. Dependent Variable: Dependent variable (GDP per capita in this case) is the variable in an experiment or study that is affected by changes in the independent variable (Chinese infrastructure aid and FDI to Nigeria, Kenya, and Ethiopia).
11. Correlation: Correlation refers to the statistical relationship between two variables, indicating the strength and direction of their linear relationship. In the case of this research, it is the relationship between Chinese infrastructure development aid and FDI relationship to GDP from 2000 to 2022.

12. Belt & Road Initiative: China's Belt and Road Initiative (BRI), launched in 2013 by President Xi Jinping, is a large-scale infrastructure project designed to connect East Asia with Europe through an extensive network of railways, highways, pipelines, and maritime routes. Initially focused on East Asia and Europe, the initiative has expanded to include Africa, Oceania, and Latin America, significantly increasing China's global economic and political influence. The BRI consists of the Silk Road Economic Belt, which covers the land routes, and the 21st Century Maritime Silk Road, which includes the sea routes (McBride et al., 2023).

Appropriately, this chapter explores the following question: Does Chinese infrastructure development aid affect economic growth? It is hypothesized that Chinese infrastructure development aid and FDI to Nigeria, Kenya, and Ethiopia does not represent a neocolonial relationship but instead promotes economic development in Nigeria, Kenya, and Ethiopia. The chapter unfolds through a systematic exploration of several essential areas. The chapter begins by presenting quantitative analysis, drawing on empirical data to uncover the effects of Chinese infrastructure development aid and its impact on economic growth in Nigeria. Through statistical examinations, this chapter examines measurable correlations while providing insight into the relationship between Chinese infrastructure development aid and economic growth measured by GDP. In addition to quantitative findings, the chapter examines the non-quantifiable facets of Chinese infrastructure development aid and economic growth in Nigeria.

Thereafter, building on the quantitative and qualitative findings, the chapter comprehensively analyzes the results. This analytical exploration aims to draw meaningful conclusions and identify potential patterns or variations. The chapter also provides a concise and insightful summary, highlighting the key takeaways and implications of the study's findings, thereby setting the stage for a deeper understanding of the relationship between Chinese infrastructure development aid and economic growth in Nigeria. The chapter therefore covers the following topics: (a) a brief historical context of China-Nigeria relations, (b) an in-depth analysis of infrastructure aid projects, (c) quantitative analysis (economic impact) and qualitative analysis (social impact), (d) an analysis of the findings, and (e) the chapter summary.

3.1 Brief Historical Context of China-Nigeria Relations

China's involvement in building the Tanzam/TAZARA Railway was a monumental project linking Zambia and Tanzania. This project marked a significant chapter in Chinese foreign aid endeavors during the 1960s and 1970s. Motivated by geopolitical considerations rather than immediate economic gains, China extended an interest-free credit of $400 million. This gesture surpassed contributions by the Soviet Union and other international actors at that time. The completion of the Tanzam Railway in 1975 provided Zambia with an alternative sea route and served as a strategic move to reduce vulnerability to economic retaliation for supporting liberation movements. This ambitious project showcased China's determination to outspend its global counterparts in Africa, reinforcing its anti-imperialist stance and challenging Western aid norms. The Tanzam Railway was one of China's most significant overseas aid projects. This project involved extensive collaboration with Chinese experts overseeing exploration, surveying, and design. The challenging construction, featuring mountainous terrain and inhospitable conditions, required immense effort. Despite facing economic constraints, China shouldered the project's entire cost, deploying over 50,000 engineers and technicians to East Africa. The completion of the railway in 1976 contributed to regional economic development, breaking South Africa's economic blockade and providing Zambia with a secure trade route. Despite subsequent challenges, the Tanzam Railway remains a symbol of China's impactful aid efforts in Africa, earning praise from leaders like Julius Nyerere and Kenneth Kaunda and being hailed as a model for South-South cooperation (Globalsecurity.org, 2024).

China's decision to invest in large-scale infrastructure projects like the Tanzam Railway was driven by strategic geopolitical considerations. Its aim was to enhance its global stature by outspending other international players, including the Soviet Union, in Africa. This approach reflected China's broader foreign policy goals during that era (Globalsecurity.org, 2024).

The Tanzam Railway remains one of China's most significant and impactful aid projects abroad. Understanding this project's scale, challenges, and outcomes provides insights into China's capabilities, motivations, and methods in providing foreign assistance. This historical context informs the perception of China's aid initiatives in subsequent years, including its engagements with Nigeria.

Sino-Nigerian relations began in 1971. Nigeria's pro-Western stance and China's support for the Biafran secession bid initially strained diplomatic ties. Nonetheless, in 1971, Nigeria supported China's bid for recognition in the United Nations, establishing formal diplomatic relations between the two countries. The relationship was politically driven, aligning with China's support for African national liberation movements. Nigeria's President General Yakubu Gowon's visit to China in 1971 marked an early diplomatic engagement, but subsequent political changes in Nigeria limited the impact. During the Olusegun Obasanjo Administration (1999–2007), efforts were made to address trade imbalances, resulting in China providing limited aid to Nigeria. In the 1980s and 1990s, while China underwent significant economic transformation, Nigeria experienced a series of military coups. Notably, during General Sani Abacha's rule from 1993 to 1998, contact was initiated with the Chinese government, leading to the establishment of the Nigerian Chinese Chamber of Commerce in 1994 (Egbula & Zheng, 2011). Economic relations gained momentum in the 1990s, notably during General Sanni Abacha's regime. The return to democratic rule in 1999 saw increased economic relations attributed to China's changing orientation toward Africa. President Obasanjo's administration (1999–2007) witnessed significant Chinese investment, including contracts for infrastructure projects. Nevertheless, policy inconsistencies and changes in leadership affected the continuity of certain foreign policy objectives. Despite challenges, economic relations between Nigeria and China intensified during Obasanjo's second term (2003–2007), marked by the founding of the Nigeria-China Investment Forum in 2006 (Odeh, 2011).

A concise overview of the history of Sino-Nigerian relationships helps one to comprehend the foundational aspects of their connection, thereby facilitating an understanding of why China extends infrastructure aid to Nigeria. This chapter will delve into an in-depth analysis of infrastructure aid projects in Nigeria and the GDP in current dollars from 2000 to 2022 (see Fig. 3.1). Analyzing GDP in current dollars is crucial for grasping the immediate market value of goods and services produced in Nigeria during this timeframe. Current dollars offer a snapshot of economic conditions without adjusting for inflation, providing a real-time view of Nigeria's monetary output. This perspective proves valuable for assessing the immediate economic health, enabling informed decision-making based on current market conditions and the evolving economic landscape in Nigeria throughout this period.

As shown in Fig. 3.1, Nigeria's GDP exhibited a dynamic trend from 2000 to 2022, reflecting growth and challenges. From 2000 to 2008, one can notice a steady increase in GDP, primarily driven by the booming oil sector, a cornerstone of the Nigerian economy. Nonetheless, the global financial crisis in 2009 led to a significant drop in GDP, highlighting the vulnerability of Nigeria's economy to external shocks. Subsequently, there was a gradual recovery and growth until 2014, buoyed by increased oil prices and government efforts to diversify the economy. The sharp decline in GDP from 2015 to 2017 can be attributed to the oil price slump during this period, exposing the country's over-reliance on oil revenue. The subsequent increase in 2018–2019 can be linked to moderate oil price recovery and ongoing diversification initiatives. The drop in 2020, a year marked by the COVID-2019 pandemic, reflects the broader economic challenges faced globally,

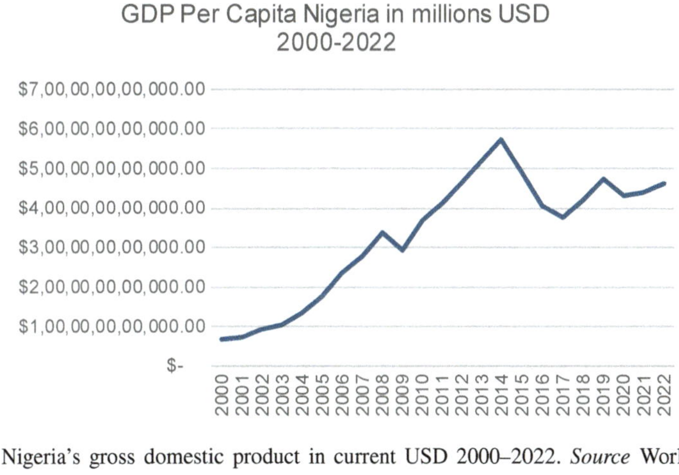

Fig. 3.1 Nigeria's gross domestic product in current USD 2000–2022. *Source* Worldbank.org, 2024

affecting various sectors, including oil. Overall, this analysis underscores the need for Nigeria to address its economic vulnerabilities, diversify revenue sources, and build resilience to external shocks for sustained and inclusive economic growth.

The fluctuations in Nigeria's GDP from 2000 to 2022 provide a crucial backdrop for analyzing the impact of infrastructure projects across key sectors. During the period of steady GDP growth from 2000 to 2008, there was an increased investment in infrastructure, particularly in energy, transport, ICT, and water and sanitation. The subsequent drop in GDP in 2009 affected the funding and implementation of infrastructure projects, leading to a slower growth trajectory. The gradual recovery until 2014 suggests a resurgence in infrastructure development, aligning with economic diversification efforts. Nonetheless, the sharp decline from 2015 to 2017 hampered infrastructure investments, especially given the susceptibility of Nigeria's economy to oil-related shocks. The subsequent GDP increase in 2018–2019 indicates a renewed focus on infrastructure; but the drop in 2020, influenced by the global pandemic, posed challenges for ongoing and planned projects. Analyzing infrastructure development in energy, transport, ICT, and water and sanitation against, these economic shifts provide valuable insights into the efficacy and resilience of these projects amid various economic conditions. In 2021, there was an ease in some of the restrictions that were put in place due to the pandemic, and economic activities resumed, leading to an increase in GDP. This recovery continued into 2022, contributing to higher GDP per capita. In 2021 and 2022, global oil prices increased compared to 2020, positively impacting Nigeria's oil export revenue.

In researching the Chinese infrastructure development projects, approximately 24 infrastructure loan projects were assessed from 2000 to 2022. When evaluating the loans and the impact on Nigeria's GDP, based on this information, regression testing and analysis were conducted on the 24 infrastructure loans to Nigeria. Regression analysis helps identify patterns and trends in the relationship between GDP and Chinese aid/loans over the specified period. Examining these patterns reveals the impact of Chinese financial assistance on Nigeria's economic performance. In addition, regression analysis provides quantitative measures of the relationships among variables. It helps quantify how changes in Chinese aid/loans are associated with fluctuations in GDP, giving valuable insights into the magnitude of the impact. It is important to remember that various economic, political, and global factors can influence the relationship between GDP and Chinese aid/loans over a two-decade period. Regression analysis helps one to understand this relationship's dynamic nature and how it evolves over time. It is essential to define the variables before conducting the analysis. See definitions below:

1. GDP: Gross Domestic Product (GDP) is the total value of all goods and services produced within a country's borders during a specific time, like a year or a quarter. It's a common measure used to understand how well a country's economy is performing and how big it is. GDP considers the value of everything people buy and sell, plus government spending, investments, and exports minus imports (Fernando, 2024).

2. Chinese Infrastructure Development Aid to Nigeria: Chinese infrastructure development aid to Nigeria differs from traditional aid models as it primarily revolves around financing rather than grants. The emphasis is on funding infrastructure projects rather than providing direct assistance (Debt Management Office Nigeria, 2024).
3. Chinese Foreign Direct Investment to Nigeria: Foreign Direct Investment (FDI) is when an individual, company, or government from one country (in this case, China) invests in a business or project in another country (in this case, Nigeria). This usually means buying a significant share or the entire foreign business to grow their operations in a new area. FDI is not just about buying stocks in a foreign company; it involves more substantial investments that create strong and lasting connections between different economies (Hayes, 2024).

3.2 Quantitative Analysis

To establish a foundational understanding of the relationship between Chinese infrastructure development aid and economic development, this study begins with a simple linear regression model: $\text{GDP per capita} = \beta_0 + \beta_1 \times \text{Chinese Infrastructure Aid} + \epsilon$. This model was selected as an entry point to explore whether there is a measurable association between the volume of infrastructure aid provided by China and economic performance measured by GDP per capita to Nigeria, Kenya, and Ethiopia. By isolating Chinese infrastructure aid as the primary independent variable and GDP per capita as the dependent variable, this approach allows for a clear and interpretable estimate of the potential influence Chinese infrastructure aid has on economic development. While the model does not account for all possible determinants of economic development measured by GDP, it is effective in introducing readers to economic analysis by focusing on a direct testable hypothesis. The simplicity of this framework is useful for students, new researchers, providing a foundation for understanding linear relationships before progressing to more complex multivariate models.

The following is the equation for the suggested relationship:

$$\text{GDP} = \beta_0 + \beta_1 \times \text{Chinese Infrastructure Aid} + \epsilon$$

where GDP is the GDP of Nigeria; β_0 is the intercept term, representing the value of GDP when Chinese aid is zero; β_1 is the coefficient for Chinese aid, indicating the change in GDP for a one-unit change in Chinese aid; ChineseInfrastructureAid is the amount of infrastructure development aid received from China; and ϵ is the error term, representing the difference between the observed GDP and the GDP predicted by the regression equation. After assessing the 24 infrastructure loans from China, the results of the regression testing are presented in Fig. 3.2.

For the regression analysis of the hypothesized relationship between GDP (dependent variable) and Chinese infrastructure aid to Nigeria from 2000 to 2022

SUMMARY OUTPUT

Regression Statistics	
Multiple R	0.212842357
R Square	0.045301869
Adjusted R Square	-0.000159947
Standard Error	1.57005E+11
Observations	23

ANOVA

	df	*SS*	*MS*	*F*	*Significance F*
Regression	1	2.45637E+22	2.45637E+22	0.99648173	0.329527594
Residual	21	5.17659E+23	2.46504E+22		
Total	22	5.42223E+23			

	Coefficients	*Standard Error*	*t Stat*	*P-value*	*Lower 95%*	*Upper 95%*	*Lower 95.0%*	*Upper 95.0%*
Intercept	3.17151E+11	36399560686	8.713045614	2.04033E-08	2.41454E+11	3.92848E+11	2.41454E+11	3.92848E+11
X Variable 1	24.88938925	24.93328891	0.998239315	0.329527594	-26.96222357	76.74100207	-26.96222357	76.74100207

Fig. 3.2 Regression output Chinese infrastructure aid to Nigeria 2000–2022. *Source* self-generated by the Author from Data Obtained from the World bank (2024), OECD.org (2024), aiddata.org (2023), & China Africa Research Initiative (2024), Boston University Global Development Policy Center, 2024), and Debt Management Office Nigeria (2024)

(independent variable), a Multiple R value of 0.212842357 represents the correlation coefficient. The Multiple R measures the strength and direction of the linear relationship between the two variables.

In this case, the value of 0.212842357 suggests a positive correlation between Chinese infrastructure aid and Nigerias GDP. Nevertheless, the magnitude of the correlation is relatively low, indicating a weak positive linear relationship. The closer the Multiple R is to 1, the stronger the positive correlation, and the closer it is to −1, the stronger the negative correlation.

The value of 0.212842357 also implies a positive association between the amount of Chinese infrastructure aid received by Nigeria and the country's GDP, but the relationship could be stronger because the correlation coefficient is relatively low, indicating that while there is a positive association between Chinese infrastructure aid and Nigeria's GDP, the impact of this aid may be diluted by other factors affecting economic growth. Additionally, the presence of other influential variables, such as domestic economic policies, political stability, or global economic conditions, might also contribute to the overall strength of the relationship, and the strength of the relationship is only approximately 21%. Factors beyond Chinese infrastructure aid are likely influencing Nigeria's GDP, and the aid alone may not be a highly reliable predictor of GDP changes.

An R-Square value of 0.0453018, which can be expressed as a percentage (4.53%), represents the proportion of the variance in the dependent variable (in this case, Nigerias GDP) that can be explained by the independent variable (Chinese infrastructure aid to Nigeria from 2000 to 2022) in the regression analysis. The R-Square indicates how well the independent variable(s) account for the variability observed in the dependent variable. In this case, the R-Square of 0.0453018 suggests that variations in Chinese infrastructure aid can explain approximately 4.53% of the variability in Nigerias GDP.

In terms of the Significance F of 0.33, a low P-Value (typically less than 0.05) suggests enough evidence to reject the null hypothesis (the null hypothesis typically tests whether the coefficients of the independent variables in the model are equal to zero, indicating no significant relationship between those variables and the dependent variable), indicating that at least one independent variable in the model contributes significantly to explaining the variability in the dependent variable. The independent variables, which include Chinese infrastructure aid, may not collectively provide a significant explanation for the variations in Nigerias GDP.

The regression analysis of the hypothesized relationship between Nigeria's GDP and Chinese infrastructure aid from 2000 to 2022 yielded a significance F of 0.33. This P-Value, which assesses the overall statistical significance of the regression model, indicates that the model might not be statistically significant at the conventional significance level of 0.05. In practical terms, this suggests that the set of independent variables, including Chinese infrastructure aid, may not collectively provide a significant explanation for the variations observed in Nigeria's GDP during the specified period. It emphasizes the need for further examination, potential refinement of the model, and consideration of additional factors that might influence the relationship between Chinese aid and Nigeria's economic performance.

Examining the economic relationship between China and Nigeria from 2000 to 2022 involves delving into Chinese foreign aid, particularly loans extended to Nigeria and Chinese FDI. This dual perspective provides a more comprehensive understanding of China's contributions to Nigeria's economic landscape. While Chinese foreign aid in the form of loans has played a role in supporting various projects and initiatives, Chinese FDI has been instrumental in fostering long-term economic development. Assessing the benefits of these two financial mechanisms involves considering the scale of investment and the impact on infrastructure, technology transfer, job generation, and overall economic growth. This holistic approach allows for a nuanced analysis of how China's financial engagement has influenced Nigeria's trajectory over the past two decades, providing valuable insights for policymakers and analysts alike.

Thus, the following question emerges: What is FDI? According to the Organization for Economic Co-Operation and Development (OECD), foreign direct investment (FDI) is a form of cross-border investment whereby an investor residing in one economy establishes a lasting interest and exerts a degree of influence over an enterprise in another economy. The ownership of ten percent or more of the voting power in an enterprise demonstrates this substantial relationship. FDI plays a pivotal role in fostering stable and enduring connections among economies, serving as a key element in international economic integration. It facilitates the transfer of technology between countries, boosts international trade by providing access to foreign markets, and acts as a significant driver for economic development. This category of indicators encompasses both inward and outward values for stocks, flows, and income, categorized by partner country and industry, along with indicators related to FDI restrictiveness (OECD, 2024).

SUMMARY OUTPUT								
Regression Statistics								
Multiple R	0.86359564							
R Square	0.74579743							
Adjusted R Sq	0.72990977							
Standard Err	6.9366E+10							
Observations	18							
ANOVA								
	df	*SS*	*MS*	*F*	*Significance F*			
Regression	1	2.2587E+23	2.2587E+23	46.9419277	3.8933E-06			
Residual	16	7.6986E+22	4.8117E+21					
Total	17	3.0285E+23						
	Coefficients	*Standard Erro*	*t Stat*	*P-value*	*Lower 95%*	*Upper 95%*	*Lower 95.0%*	*Upper 95.0%*
Intercept	1.8808E+11	3.0144E+10	6.23928268	1.183E-05	1.2417E+11	2.5198E+11	1.2417E+11	2.5198E+11
X Variable 1	116.928185	17.0662754	6.85141793	3.8933E-06	80.7492978	153.107073	80.7492978	153.107073

Fig. 3.3 Chinese Foreign Direct Investment & Nigeria's GDP, 2000–2022. Self-generated by the Author Using Data from https://data.worldbank.org (2024) and China Africa Research Initiative (2024)

The OECD also defines FDI stocks as a comprehensive measure of the total direct investment in a specific period, typically at the end of a quarter or year. Outward FDI stock represents the value of equity and net loans from resident investors to enterprises in foreign economies. Conversely, inward FDI stock reflects the value of equity and net loans from foreign investors to enterprises within the reporting economy. These FDI stocks are measured in United States dollars and as a share of GDP. FDI plays a crucial role in establishing enduring and stable connections among economies, thereby fostering economic integration and development (OECD, 2024).

When examining the impact of Chinese FDI to Nigeria during the period covered in this chapter, the regression analysis revealed the results summarized in Fig. 3.3.

Based on the information in Fig. 3.3, a multiple R of 0.86359564 means that the value suggests a strong and positive correlation; this signifies that as Chinese FDI increases, there is a substantial tendency for the GDP of Nigeria to increase as well. The closer the multiple R value is to 1, the stronger the correlation. In other words, the multiple R is 86%; and the closer the correlation is to 100%, the stronger the correlation. In this case, there is a strong correlation between Chinese FDI in Nigeria and Nigeria's GDP. As Chinese FDI to Nigeria increases, Nigeria's GDP also has a substantial tendency to increase. This correlation also suggests that the economic activities associated with Chinese FDI, such as investments, projects, or collaborations, positively impact Nigeria's overall economic output. It is important to note, however, that correlation does not imply causation; thus, further analysis would be needed to understand the specific mechanisms and factors influencing this relationship.

In terms of the R-Square, approximately 74.6% of the variability in Nigeria's GDP can be attributed to the changes in Chinese FDI. A higher R-Square suggests the stronger the ability of an independent variable (in this case, Chinese FDI) to explain the changes in the dependent variable (here, Nigeria's GDP). An R-Square value of 0.745797427 indicates that about 74.6% of the changes in Nigeria's GDP can be attributed to the variations in Chinese FDI during the specified time. This suggests a strong relationship between the amount of Chinese FDI entering Nigeria and the fluctuations observed in Nigeria's economic output. It is important, however, to remember that other factors not considered in the regression analysis may influence Nigeria's GDP.

In terms of Significance, an F-Value of 3.89335E-06 (in scientific notation, this is equivalent to 0.00000389335) indicates that the overall regression model, which examines the relationship between Chinese FDI and Nigeria's GDP, is statistically significant. In practical terms, the model's findings are not likely due to random chance. The low P-Value associated with the F-statistic suggests that there is evidence to reject the null hypothesis, indicating that at least one independent variable (such as Chinese FDI) significantly influences Nigeria's GDP.

When I state that I reject the null hypothesis, it means the following: H_0: $\beta 1 = \beta 2 = \ldots = \beta k = 0$. H_0: represents the null hypothesis. $\beta 1 = \beta 2 = \ldots = \beta k = 0$ are the coefficients of the independent variables in the regression model. The dependent variable is GDP, and the independent variable is Chinese FDI. The null hypothesis typically tests whether the coefficients of the independent variables in the model are equal to zero, indicating no significant relationship between those variables and the dependent variable. As mentioned earlier, the Significance F is statistically significant, so one must reject the null hypothesis because there is a significant relationship between the variables in the study; in this case, Chinese FDI and Nigeria's GDP.

H_1 is the alternative hypothesis, which hypothesizes that a significant relationship exists between at least one independent variable and the dependent variable. In this case, as noted previously, Chinese FDI to Nigeria during this period is statistically significant. As a result, one can reject the null hypothesis in favor of H_1, i.e., the alternative hypothesis based on the observed data and statistical analysis.

On account of the preceding information, it is shown in Fig. 3.3 that the null hypothesis pertaining to Chinese infrastructure aid to Nigeria cannot be rejected because there was no statistical significant relationship between Chinese infrastructure development aid and Nigeria's GDP. When Chinese infrastructure development aid to Nigeria is found not to be statistically significant in a regression analysis, while Chinese FDI to Nigeria and GDP show statistical significance, it implies that within the examined data and model there is insufficient evidence to conclude a significant relationship between Chinese infrastructure aid and Nigeria's GDP. Contrastively, a statistically significant relationship is observed between Chinese FDI to Nigeria and the country's GDP. All this suggests that, based on the available data and analysis, on the one hand, the impact of Chinese infrastructure development aid (in the form of loans) may not have a distinct and measurable influence on Nigeria's GDP. On the other hand, the statistical significance observed with Chinese FDI indicates that changes in Chinese FDI to Nigeria are associated with statistically measurable variations in Nigeria's GDP.

Transitioning from the quantitative analysis, exploring qualitative data adds depth to our understanding of the dynamics among Chinese foreign aid, foreign direct investment (FDI), and Nigeria's economic landscape. While statistical significance provides valuable insights, qualitative data can unveil nuanced aspects such as diplomatic considerations, geopolitical influences, and the specific nature of aid and investment projects. Delving into qualitative dimensions complements the statistical findings, offering a more comprehensive perspective on the multifaceted relationship between China and Nigeria and their economic interactions. This dual approach enhances the overall comprehension of the intricate factors shaping the economic ties between these two nations.

3.3 Qualitative Analysis

This qualitative analysis focuses on selected Chinese infrastructure aid and investment projects to understand their impact on Nigeria's GDP. Data for the analysis were gathered from official documents, reports, news articles, and academic publications. The projects analyzed include the Abuja-Kaduna Railway Line, the Abuja Light Rail Project, and the Abuja-Keffi-Makurdi Road Rehabilitation and Upgrade.

The Abuja-Kaduna Railway Line, a standard gauge railway modernization project in Nigeria, connects the federal capital city Abuja with its commercial capital Kaduna. Constructed with China's support, it was started in February of 2011 and completed in December of 2014. Nigerian President Muhammadu Buhari inaugurated the line for commercial services in July of 2016. The project, executed by the China Civil and Engineering Construction Company (CCECC), employed around 4000 people during construction and is anticipated to generate over 5000 additional jobs during operation (Railway Technology, 2020).

The railway modernization initiative in Nigeria aimed to upgrade the existing narrow-gauge system to a standard gauge system, allowing for high-speed train operations. The $8.3 billion Lagos-Kano standard gauge modernization project was awarded to CCECC in 2006, marking this initiative's beginning. Still, funding issues led to a re-scoping of the project. The Abuja-Kaduna segment, a 186-kiliometer line with standard gauge railway tracks, was the first to be implemented under this project. The next segment is the Lagos-Ibadan rail line, a double-track standard gauge line that was scheduled for completion in 2020. Other standard gauge line projects in the pipeline include the Lagos-Benin City, Benin-Abakiliki, and Lagos-Abuja high-speed lines. The Abuja-Kaduna Railway Line, constructed with China's support, saw the addition of new locomotives and coaches to accommodate increasing passenger traffic. CCECC broke ground for Nigeria's first rolling stock assembly unit in November of 2019, which aimed to support the railway modernization project (Railway Technology, 2020).

During the post-COVID-2019 era, the Chinese government withdrew capital financing for rail projects in Nigeria. Nigerian officials' concerns about alternative funding sources for the federal government emerged, given the significant capital requirements of these projects. Previously, many rail projects were financed through loans from the Chinese government. As of March 31, 2020, Nigeria's borrowing from China totaled US$3.121 billion, with rail projects such as the Nigerian Railway Modernization Project (Idu-Kaduna section) and the Abuja Light Rail Project being major recipients. Some attribute the Chinese retreat to concerns over the Nigerian government's accountability and the perceived lack of good use of the funds. Additionally, there are suggestions that the withdrawal may be linked to a shift in Chinese investment priorities toward digital infrastructure and telecommunications, away from heavy infrastructure projects like railways. Others attribute the Chinese government's withdrawal from financing infrastructural projects in Nigeria to include the economic impact of the COVID-2019 pandemic on China's economy, the dire debt position and revenue strain of Nigeria, uncertainties regarding loan repayment, and concerns about the Nigerian government's accountability. Due to the uncertainty with finance from the Chinese government, the Nigerian government is now seeking private financing from Standard Chartered Bank (SCB) for the remaining projects, although the funding structure remains uncertain (BusinessDay, 2024).

Regarding examining the economic benefits of this project, railway development is integral to China's Belt and Road Initiative (BRI), launched in 2013 by President Xi Jinping, which is a large-scale infrastructure project designed to connect East Asia with Europe through an extensive network of railways, highways, pipelines, and maritime routes. Initially focused on East Asia and Europe, the initiative has expanded to include Africa, Oceania, and Latin America, significantly increasing China's global economic and political influence. The BRI consists of the Silk Road Economic Belt, which covers the land routes, and the 21st Century Maritime Silk Road, which includes the sea routes (McBride et al., 2023). BRI emphasizes its potential for economic and social benefits in Nigeria. Railways offer advantages over road networks, including lower maintenance needs and higher efficiency for freight traffic. Connecting Nigeria's inland regions with coastal markets would reduce transport costs, boost competitiveness, and promote trade. Additionally, railway development stimulates employment and supports industries like steel and construction materials. Socially, railways facilitate mobility, cultural integration, and rural-urban migration. Improved infrastructure could foster peacebuilding and attract investment in regions like the oil-producing Delta. Despite concerns about Chinese labor, railway projects have generated local jobs, but continued Chinese involvement is needed for technology and skills transfer (Chen, 2018).

Examining the economic benefits of the Abuja-Kaduna Railway Line project is essential for understanding the benefits it has provided to promote economic development measured by GDP in Nigeria. Based on the reports, this railway project is necessary to connect different regions of the country and aid in transporting goods and services. This allows people to obtain work in other areas of the country when they may not be able to receive work in their local areas. In addition, the railway is essential in the transporting of goods from one part to another part of the country. This is particularly important in the case of local farmers or manufacturers who are looking to increase their business reach. With the increase in railway transportation, local farmers and producers now have access to new markets. In addition, with railway transportation, jobs were generated because of this project, including workers for railcar trains, railway station workers, maintenance workers, and those in railway-related industries. While it was noted in some of the research that Chinese transfer of knowledge is essential in the continual transition of this project, this will be important in employing more local labor in Nigeria. A social benefit of the Abuja-Kaduna Railway Line project is that the train allows for the connection of goods and services and people in different parts of the country. The railway promotes cultural integration and social cohesion by bringing together people from various regions and backgrounds. It enables more accessible access to employment opportunities, educational institutions, healthcare facilities, and other essential services, thereby fostering greater social mobility and inclusivity. The Abuja-Kaduna Railway Line project contributes to the overall quality of life for residents in both urban and rural areas along the route. It helps alleviate traffic congestion, reduce travel time, and lower transportation costs, improving access to economic opportunities and overall well-being. Overall, the project serves as a catalyst for economic growth by enhancing connectivity, promoting trade, and generating employment opportunities, all of which ultimately contribute to increasing GDP in Nigeria.

In terms of assessing the Abuja Light Rail Project, according to Chima Okereke (2012), it was initiated in 2009 and aims to establish an intra-city rail network connecting key areas within the Federal Capital Territory, including routes from the city center to Kubwa and the Nnamdi Azikiwe International Airport, as well as to Masaka in Nasarawa State. Currently, at 25% completion, the project includes multiple lots, with the first lot focusing on the city center, Kubwa, and the Abuja Airport. Additionally, plans for two light rails from Abuja to Masaka are in place, one designed for wagons and locomotives and the other for a smaller corridor, to be activated once the power supply improves. Furthermore, a portion of a loan amounting to $500 million was allocated for constructing four new terminals at various airports across Nigeria to increase passenger capacity and generate jobs. Another $100 million will fund the National Security Development System by Galaxy Backbone Plc to enhance security efforts and technology connectivity in underserved rural areas. Additionally, Nigeria secured a $1 billion facility loan from the Exim Bank in China to partially finance a double-carriage railway between Lagos and Ibadan, with Nigeria providing $500 million in additional funding (Okereke, 2012). It is important to note that as of the time this book was written, the Abuja light rail services were suspended in 2020 after the COVID-2019 pandemic and have remained suspended since then. It is projected that services will resume sometime in 2024. This is an important fact to point out since repayment of the loan began in 2020. The suspension of the Abuja light rail services in 2020 due to the COVID-2019 pandemic and the subsequent continuation of this suspension until at least 2024 are significant in the context of Nigeria taking out a $500 million loan from China for the project and its impact on Nigeria's GDP. The interruption in services means that the revenue-generating potential of the rail system, which would normally contribute to economic growth and potentially assist in loan repayment, has been severely hindered. With services being halted, the ability of the project to stimulate economic activity, generate jobs, and facilitate transportation of goods and people, all of which would contribute to GDP growth, has been delayed. Additionally, the resumption of service in 2024, if it occurs, may require additional investments or resources to regain momentum, restore previous work completed, and fully realize the economic benefits initially anticipated from the project. Therefore, the suspension of the Abuja light rail services underscores the challenges and uncertainties surrounding the loan repayment and the overall economic impact of the project on Nigeria's GDP. This point is important when looking at not only the quantitative data but also the qualitative data. If one reflects on the quantitative data results, and it was determined that the value is 0.252487559, it implies that there is a positive association between the Chinese infrastructure aid received by Nigeria and the country's GDP, albeit the relationship is not very strong. The strength of the relationship is approximately 25%. Other factors beyond Chinese infrastructure aid are likely influencing Nigeria's GDP, and the aid alone may not be a highly reliable predictor of GDP changes. The Abuja Light Rail Project may help to explain the low correlation between Chinese infrastructure aid in the form of concessional and non-concessional loans and Nigeria's GDP growth. It highlights the intricate interplay between external investments, such as Chinese infrastructure aid, and domestic factors affecting economic performance.

The article titled "Lagos Light Rail: 17 Years After, Failed Promises, Rot, Neglect Trail Project" (2020) by Oladeinde Olawoyin Premium Times investigates the state of the Lagos Light Rail Project by highlighting its prolonged delays, mismanagement, and neglect. The article traces the project's history initiated 17 years ago with promises of transforming transportation in Lagos, Nigerias largest city. Nonetheless, despite significant investments and announcements by successive administrations, the project has faced numerous setbacks, including funding challenges, contractual disputes, and bureaucratic hurdles. As a result, the Lagos Light Rail Project still needs to be completed and is non-operational, with abandoned construction sites, decaying infrastructure, and overgrown vegetation along its routes. The article exposes the extent of the project's decay and neglect, raising questions about accountability, transparency, and the government's commitment to infrastructure development. It underscores the disappointment and frustration of Lagos residents who had hoped for improved transportation options but continue to face congestion, gridlock, and inadequate public transportation services. Overall, the article sheds light on the challenges and failures of the Lagos Light Rail Project and calling for urgent action to revitalize and complete the long-delayed initiative for the benefit of the city's residents and commuters (Olawoyin, 2020). While projects like the Abuja Light Rail have the potential to boost economic activity and contribute to GDP growth significantly, external disruptions like the COVID-2019 pandemic can lead to unforeseen challenges, delaying the realization of these benefits. This underscores the need for comprehensive risk assessment and mitigation strategies in infrastructure development projects to ensure long-term sustainability and positive economic impact. As Nigeria navigates its economic growth and development path, it must carefully balance the opportunities and risks associated with external financing while addressing domestic factors that influence its economic performance. Ultimately, the successful implementation of infrastructure projects like the Abuja Light Rail will not only depend on financial investments but also on effective governance, strategic planning, and adaptability to external shocks, all of which are essential for achieving sustained economic growth and prosperity.

The third project examined is the Abuja-Keffi-Makurdi Road Rehabilitation and Upgrade. Understanding the impact of road projects is essential in the same way that railway transportation is discussed. Having proper road access is essential for not only the transportation of goods but also the movement of people from one part of the country to the next. In November of 2018, the Nigerian government led by former President Muhammadu Buhari initiated a groundbreaking ceremony for the expansion and dualization project of the Abuja-Keffi Road, aiming to alleviate the difficulties faced by commuters and motorists on the Keffi-Akwanga-Lafia-Makurdi route. The project encompasses two main components: first, the extension of the Abuja-Keffi expressway by 5.4 km, connecting Abuja to Nasarawa; and second, the reconstruction and dualization of the 221.8-km Keffi-Akwanga-Lafia-Makurdi expressway, linking Nasarawa to Benue. China Harbour Engineering Company (CHEC) has been awarded the contract to complete the execution of the project, which includes expanding the Abuja-Keffi expressway by constructing a two-lane auxiliary road alongside the existing six-lane section. Furthermore, the Keffi-Akwanga-Lafia-Makurdi expressway will undergo widening from two lanes to a two-way, four-lane road (Yusuf, 2023).

Residents of Lafia and Keffi in Nasarawa State praised the completion of a phase of the road network, attributing it to China Harbour's efforts to enhance infrastructure development in Nigeria under the BRI. The residents commended China Harbour and the Nigerian government for their continuous efforts in building and rehabilitating roads nationwide. They expressed satisfaction with the quality of the road and emphasized the need for more funding to complete remaining projects, which would further enhance the economy and provide benefits to the citizens of Nigeria. Mohammed Agwai Mohammed, a major stakeholder in Keffi, praised the collaboration between the federal government and China Harbour, highlighting the positive impact on the skill, capacity, and technical expertise of the local community through knowledge sharing and technology transfer (Odoh, 2024). An article by Odoh (2024) highlighted quotes from Nigeria stakeholders some of whom have highlighted not only the construction of good roads but also the positive impact on the skill, capacity, and technical expertise of the local community. Some added that China Harbour has contributed to community development by engaging young men in skill acquisition and technical expertise and supporting them to expand their vocation and further their studies. Many young people have acquired technical competencies in road construction and related fields such as welding which they now use to add value to their lives and employ others, thereby showcasing a multiplier effect. One motorist added that the roads have resulted in a smoother and safer travel experience along that route. It was also highlighted that a positive transformation has taken place in the region, particularly in terms of increased business opportunities, as the availability of goods and services has expanded in these areas. It is important to note that the project was completed and handed over to the Nigeria government in April of 2023 (Odoh, 2024).

The completion of the project in April of 2023 further corroborates the quantitative data, indicating a low correlation of 0.252487559. This suggests a positive association between the amount of Chinese infrastructure aid received by Nigeria and the country's GDP, albeit relatively weak. Notably, there was no apparent or quantifiable financial impact on Nigeria's GDP from 2000 to 2022 due to the road project needing to be completed and handed over to the Nigerian government in April of 2023.

In terms of Chinese FDI, its massive influx has led to the closure of local firms due to competition with cheaper Chinese imports and services. This has adversely affected local employment and industrial growth, as Chinese firms often import their own labor and materials, thereby limiting local economic participation (Oyeranti et al., 2018). In addition, Chinese firms have established dominance in critical sectors such as manufacturing and construction, which has stifled local businesses and contributed to a trade imbalance. In 2006, the trade imbalance heavily favored China, with a significant surplus at the expense of Nigerian imports (Nabine, 2009). In addition, some scholars argue that the dependency on Chinese FDI and loans undermines Nigeria's economic sovereignty, limiting its ability to enforce regulations and negotiate favorable terms. This dependency is exacerbated by the lack of transparency in financial dealings, particularly in the oil sector, which has been subject to investigations related to corruption and bribery (International Monetary Fund, 2023; Xiang, 2023).

3.4 Analysis of Nigerian Newspapers

A comprehensive review of various Nigerian newspapers was conducted to gain deeper insights into how the people of Nigeria perceive Chinese infrastructure development aid and FDI in the country. This review encompassed well-known publications such as *The Premium Times*, *Punch*, *Vanguard*, *The Guardian Nigeria*, and *Daily Trust*. By analyzing the contents of these newspapers, the aim is to uncover diverse perspectives and opinions regarding Chinese investment and its impact on Nigeria's economic development.

As described by Columbia University Mailman School of Public Health (2024), content analysis is a research method that evaluates specific words, themes, or concepts in qualitative data such as text. Researchers gain insights into their presence, meanings, and relationships by quantifying and analyzing these elements. For example, studying language in news articles enables researchers to identify biases or partiality, facilitating inferences about the text's messages, authors, audiences, and contextual factors. In understanding the impact of Chinese infrastructure development aid and its effect on the lives of Nigerians, diverse perspectives are analyzed to better comprehend its influence on economic development in Nigeria and FDI.

According to a *Premium Times* article titled "Nigeria must lead Africa against neocolonialism—NDA Commandant" (2023) by Suleiman Qosim, Major General John Ochai, Commandant of the Nigeria Defence Academy (NDA), emphasized that Nigeria must lead African countries in resisting neocolonialism from developed nations. Speaking at a leadership lecture series, Ochai argued that countries like the United States, China, Russia, France, and Saudi Arabia are engaging in a new scramble for Africa by exploiting the continent through multinational companies, big tech, and foreign investments. He highlighted that these actions, including China's infrastructure projects and United States foreign direct investments, constitute neocolonialism (Suleiman, 2023).

Ochai also stressed that for Nigeria to assume a leadership role, it must first resolve its internal issues such as corruption, infrastructure deficits, and political instability. He then pointed out that Nigeria is seen as a regional leader and must therefore foster strong diplomatic ties with other African nations to effectively counter external influences (Suleiman, 2023).

A *Premium Times* article titled "What a Shared Day Means for China-Nigeria Relations" (2023) by Olalekan A. Babatunde focused on the shared partnership between the two countries: i.e., China and Nigeria. The author emphasized the mutual benefits of Nigeria-China relations, noting that Nigeria gains manufactured goods, expertise, funding, and aid from China while offering a favorable business climate and natural resources. Nonetheless, it also acknowledged the disparity in development between the industrialized China, which has eradicated absolute poverty, and Nigeria, which still faces challenges like poverty, unemployment, and corruption (Babatunde, 2023).

Reflecting on their cooperation, both nations are encouraged to draw lessons from each other to address the preceding issues. China's experience in rapid development can guide Nigeria in its journey. Babatunde further suggested that continued collaboration, particularly during President Bola Ahmed Tinubu's upcoming visit to Beijing, can strengthen their relationship and attract investments. The National Day celebrations serve as a reminder of their enduring diplomatic ties and the potential for future cooperation aimed at sustainable development and global community building (Babatunde, 2023).

There are some articles in the *Premium Times* that focus on proceeding with caution as it relates to Chinese aid to not only Nigeria but African countries overall. For example, in the article titled "Can China Be a More Attractive Security Partner for Africa?" (2023) by Jana de Kluiver pointed out that China's engagement has garnered support from African nations disillusioned with the Western-dominated international order and its paternalistic security cooperation. China's non-interference policy appeals to these countries, although it raises concerns about potential harm to human rights and governance. By providing technology and training to autocratic regimes, China's policies may undermine democracy and good governance, conflicting with the African Union's Agenda 2063. It is also noted that while China has some Western approaches, such as capacity building through training, it represents a more coordinated effort to promote China's brand of security assistance. Nevertheless, critics warn that this could lead to increased political repression in authoritarian regimes, as seen with advanced surveillance tools in Zimbabwe (de Kluiver, 2023).

For China's security cooperation to be beneficial, it must deliver on its commitments and support "African solutions" while addressing governance challenges. This includes involving civil society in discussions and ensuring that security projects complement existing peace and security strategies. Kluiver suggested that a nuanced definition of sovereignty, which includes protecting human rights, is essential. Overall, while China's increased security cooperation in Africa presents opportunities, it also poses significant challenges regarding human rights and governance. African stakeholders must carefully evaluate these implications to ensure that security cooperation benefits both governments and citizens (de Kluiver, 2023).

According to *Punch* newspaper, China has played a significant role in Nigeria's railway sector, primarily through the CCECC which handles major projects funded by Chinese loans. Examples include the Lagos-Ibadan railway and the Abuja-Kaduna line (Tunji, 2022).

In addition, *Punch* article titled "Chinese Loan Rises by $800 m in One Year, Hits $4.73bn" (2023) discussed the Abuja-Kano and Port Harcourt-Maiduguri rail projects that have been significant but have faced funding delays. Recently, China committed to refinancing and completing these projects following a bilateral meeting between Nigerian and Chinese leaders (Punch, 2023). In addition to concerns over excessive debt, *Punch* articles highlighted skepticism within China about extending further loans due to Nigeria's financial instability and legislative probes into loan terms and repayment capabilities (Punch, 2023). Overall, *Punch* provided a comprehensive view, balancing the benefits of infrastructure development with the potential risks associated with heavy borrowing from China.

The newspaper discussed Chinese infrastructure aid and FDI in the context of significant bilateral economic cooperation. Articles highlighted how China's BRI has facilitated numerous infrastructural projects in Nigeria such as the Abuja-Kaduna rail line, new airport terminals, and the Lekki deep seaport. These projects have boosted transportation, trade, and investment environments. The newspaper also reported about increasing trade volumes and the broader impact of Chinese enterprises contributing to Nigeria's economy (Vanguard, 2020).

The Guardian newspaper in Nigeria covered Chinese infrastructure aid and FDI in the country with a mixture of optimism and scrutiny. It acknowledged the significant contributions of Chinese investments to Nigeria's infrastructure and economy while highlighting some of the complexities and conditions associated with these investments. For example, in the article, "China gives stringent for 20bn loan to Nigeria" (2016), Chuka Odittah reported about the substantial financial support from China for key infrastructure projects such as railways and power generation, emphasizing the potential benefits for Nigeria's economic development. There are conditions for receiving the funding that include the Chinese supervising the funds (Odittah, 2016). This careful monitoring by the Chinese is part of broader efforts to safeguard their investments and maintain financial sustainability. Chinese investments have played a crucial role in various sectors, with around 160 Chinese firms operating in Nigeria and employing over 200,000 Nigerians (Odutola, 2019).

The Guardian covered the challenges and controversies arising from Nigeria-China relations. This includes issues of discrimination against Africans in China during the COVID-2019 pandemic which strained diplomatic ties and led to calls for better treatment of Nigerians and other Africans in China (Adekoya, 2020).

Reviewing *This Day* online newspaper article titled "China Debt Trap: Chinese Loan Terms Caution Africa: Project Implementation on Slow Mode" (2019) discussed the strategic cooperation between Nigeria and China, focusing on infrastructure renewal as a critical component of Nigeria's Economic Recovery and Growth Plan. Under President Buhari's administration, the Ministry of Works and Housing led by Mr. Babatunde Fashola prioritized infrastructure development in order to drive economic revival. The ministry collaborated with the CHEC, a firm with a 26-year presence in Nigeria, to build essential transport networks. The article added that the partnership between Nigeria and the CHEC aims to drive sustainable and inclusive economic growth by generating jobs, encouraging economic activities, and ensuring social stability. The CHEC has also played a crucial role in addressing Nigeria's infrastructure deficit, utilizing its extensive experience and global expertise to deliver high-quality projects efficiently. Nonetheless, the article also highlighted a growing caution among African countries regarding Chinese investments, especially loans that often lead to significant debts and potential mortgaging of assets. This caution is based on the experiences of neighboring countries and the broader implications of Beijing's debt diplomacy under the BRI (This Day, 2019).

In essence, various newspapers have discussed Chinese infrastructure aid and FDI in Nigeria with a mixture of optimism and scrutiny. While Chinese investments have contributed significantly to Nigeria's infrastructure and economy, concerns persist regarding loan terms, conditions, and potential debt traps. This is particularly important as Nigeria conducts a cost-benefit analysis of the aid versus the debt that it takes on in relation to the benefits it provides.

According to the journal article titled "China in Foreign Media: Assessing China's Image in Online Editions of Nigeria's Leading Newspapers in 2017" (Anunne & Yan, 2018), Nigerian newspapers largely depict Chinese activities in a positive light, with approximately 76% of news materials portraying China positively compared to 17% being neutral and 7% being negative (Anunne & Yan, 2018). This favorable coverage extends across various forms of media, including news stories, articles, opinions, and editorials, indicating a significant positive bias in the portrayal of China (Anunne & Yan, 2018). Such positive portrayal can influence public opinion favorably toward Chinese projects and play a role in shaping policy decisions, particularly in areas of economic partnerships and infrastructure development.

In assessing the newspapers in Nigeria, the coverage of China's role in Nigerian infrastructure varies significantly among leading Nigerian newspapers. *Vanguard*, known for its independent stance, facilitated public discourse on governmental policies including those concerning Chinese aid. *Punch*, a prominent newspaper, offered detailed reports on Chinese infrastructure projects across a wide range of topics (Thiombiano & Tulga, 2022).

3.5 Chapter Summary

In reviewing the quantitative and qualitative data, it was important to understand the relationship between Chinese infrastructure development aid and investment and its impact on economic development in Nigeria. The quantitative data revealed a weak positive relationship between Nigeria's infrastructure development aid and economic development as measured by GDP. The qualitative data supported the weak positive relationship in the quantitative result. Many projects still need to be completed, and we have yet to realize the true benefits of their ability to improve Nigeria's GDP. The analysis also revealed that Chinese loans to Nigeria are tied to specific projects, including the Nigerian Railway Modernization Project (Idu-Kaduna section), the Abuja Light Rail Project, and the expansion of four airport terminals in Abuja, Kano, Lagos, and Port Harcourt, among others. These loans positively and also negatively impact Nigeria's external borrowing practices. Some scholars argue that Nigeria's partnership with China has been more beneficial than its relationship with Western donor countries, as Chinese aid and trade come with fewer strings attached and focus more on practical support such as infrastructure development. Nevertheless, there are also complex challenges in Sino-Nigeria bilateral relations, and the increasing external borrowings pose socioeconomic challenges for Nigeria, especially as its democracy matures (Okeke, 2021).

In examining FDI in Nigeria, there was evidence of a strong and positive relationship between Chinese FDI and Nigeria's GDP. Based on the information, a multiple R of 0.86359564 means that the value suggests a strong and positive correlation, signifying that as Chinese FDI increases, Nigeria's GDP also has a substantial tendency to increase. In the provided comparison, two different forms of Chinese funding in Nigeria are examined: (1) FDI and (2) infrastructure aid in the form of loans. The analysis focuses on the correlation between these investments and Nigeria's GDP.

On the one hand, the multiple R value of 0.86359564 for Chinese FDI in Nigeria indicates a strong and positive correlation. This suggests that as Chinese FDI increases, Nigeria's GDP also has a substantial tendency to increase. This implies that Chinese FDI significantly drives economic growth in Nigeria through job creation, infrastructure development, and increased productivity. On the other hand, the multiple R value of 0.252487559 for Chinese infrastructure aid to Nigeria in the form of loans suggests a weaker correlation compared to FDI. While still positive, the correlation between Chinese infrastructure aid and Nigeria's GDP is less strong than that of FDI. This could indicate that while infrastructure projects financed by Chinese loans may contribute to economic development to some extent, other factors may significantly influence Nigeria's GDP growth.

To sum up, the comparative analysis underscores the contrasting effects of Chinese FDI and infrastructure aid on Nigeria's GDP. FDI exhibits a robust positive correlation with GDP, underscoring its pivotal role in propelling economic growth. In contrast, infrastructure aid in the form of loans manifests a weaker correlation, hinting at a more indirect influence on GDP growth compared to FDI. Since Chinese FDI shows a strong and positive correlation with Nigeria's GDP, Nigerian policymakers should focus on establishing an attractive investment climate to encourage more FDI inflows. This may involve streamlining regulations, reducing bureaucratic hurdles, and incentivizing foreign investors.

While Chinese infrastructure aid in the form of loans contributes to economic development, the weaker correlation with GDP suggests that more than relying on Chinese loans may be required. Policymakers should continue to explore diversifying sources of infrastructure funding, such as seeking investment from other countries, multilateral development banks, or private investors.

In addition, policymakers should prioritize transparency and accountability in negotiating and implementing infrastructure projects financed by Chinese loans. This may involve conducting thorough cost-benefit analyses, ensuring fair and competitive procurement processes, and promoting public disclosure of project details and financial terms.

Furthermore, the impact of Chinese FDI on Nigeria's economy is multifaceted. On the one hand, it has provided a critical boost to infrastructure and economic development. Significance funds have been funneled into major projects like railways, with China backing extensive rail developments such as the Lagos to Kano and Lagos to Calabar lines (Sow, 2018). On the other hand, concerns about economic dependency on China have surfaced. The influx of Chinese FDI is accompanied by the importation of Chinese labor and materials, which limits local employment opportunities and the development of domestic industries (Oyeranti et al., 2018). Moreover, the engagement of Chinese firms in sectors like construction and manufacturing has led to a competitive disadvantage for some Nigerian firms, potentially threatening local industries with closure (Oyeranti et al., 2018).

Thus, policymakers should invest in domestic capacity-building initiatives to maximize the benefits of Chinese FDI and infrastructure aid. This may include improving education and training programs to enhance local skills and expertise in sectors relevant to infrastructure development and attracting foreign investment. Investing in research and development to support innovation and technology transfer can stimulate economic growth and reduce dependency on external funding. In addition, focusing on jumpstarting stagnant infrastructure projects to generate income to repay the loans and generate revenue and jobs for Nigerian citizens could lead to economic growth and development in Nigeria.

Accordingly, establishing robust monitoring and evaluation mechanisms is essential to accurately assess the impact of Chinese aid and investments on Nigerias economy. Policymakers should regularly evaluate the effectiveness and outcomes of infrastructure projects funded by Chinese loans and FDI to ensure that they align with national development priorities and contribute to sustainable economic growth and development. By following these suggestions, Nigeria can better leverage Chinese investments to drive economic growth, enhance infrastructure development, and ultimately improve the well-being of its citizens.

References

Adekoya, F. (2020). *Nigeria Issues with Bilateral Ties with China Post Pandemic*. https://guardian.ng/business-services/issues-with-nigerias-bilateral-ties-with-china-post-pandemic/

Anunne, U. K., & Yan, L. (2018, December). China in Foreign Media: Assessing China's Image in Online Editions of Nigeria's Leading Newspapers in 2017. *European Scientific Journal*. https://eujournal.org/index.php/esj/article/view/11560/11027. Accessed July 6, 2024.

Babatunde, O. A. (2023, October 2). What a Shared National Day Means for Nigeria-China Relations. *Premium Times*. https://www.premiumtimesng.com/opinion/629981-what-a-shared-national-day-means-for-nigeria-china-relations-by-olalekan-a-babatunde.html. Accessed January 15, 2024.

BusinessDay. (2024). *Reflections on Nigeria's Rail Projects*. https://businessday.ng/editorial/article/reflections-on-nigerias-rail-projects/. Accessed February 6, 2024.

Chen, Y. (2018, April). *China's Role in Nigerian Railway Development and Implications for Security and Development*. United States Institute of Peace. https://www.usip.org/sites/default/files/2018-04/sr_423_chen_final.pdf. Accessed July 6, 2024.

China Africa Research Initiative. (2024). *Data: Chinese Global Foreign Aid*. http://www.sais-cari.org/data-chinese-global-foreign-aid. Accessed July 1, 2024.

Columbia University Mailman School of Public Health. (2024, August 16). *Content Analysis*. Population Health Methods. Columbia University Mailman School of Public Health. https://www.publichealth.columbia.edu/research/population-health-methods/content-analysis. Last modified August 16, 2024.

Debt Management Office Nigeria. (2024). *Facts About Chinese Loans to Nigeria*. https://www.dmo.gov.ng/facts-about-chinese-loans-to-nigeria. Accessed February 12, 2024.

de Kluiver, J. (2023, September 25). Can China be a More Attractive Security Partner for Africa? *Premium Times*. https://www.premiumtimesng.com/foreign/africa/628127-can-china-be-a-more-attractive-security-partner-for-africa.html. Accessed November 14, 2023.

Egbula, M., & Zheng, Q. (2011). *China in Focus: Lessons and Challenges*. OECD. https://www.oecd.org/china/49814032.pdf. Accessed July 6, 2024.

Fernando, J. (2024). *Gross Domestic Product (GDP)*. Investopedia. https://www.investopedia.com/terms/g/gdp.asp. Accessed June 5, 2024.

Foster, V., Butterfield, W. M., Chen, C., & Pushak, N. (2009). *Building bridges: China's growing role as infrastructure financier for Sub-Saharan Africa* (English). *Trends and policy options, 5*, World Bank Publications. http://documents.worldbank.org/curated/en/936991468023953753

GlobalSecurity.org. (2024). *Tanzania-Zambia Railway*. https://www.globalsecurity.org/military/world/tanzania/tanzam.htm. Accessed April 13, 2024.

Hayes, A. (2024). *Foreign Direct Investment (FDI)*. Investopedia. https://www.investopedia.com/terms/f/fdi.asp. Accessed July 6, 2024.

International Monetary Fund. (2023). *Nigeria 2022 Article IV Consultation—Press Release; Staff Report; Staff Statement; and Statement by the Executive Director for Nigeria*. International Monetary Fund.

McBride, J., Berman, N., & Chatzky, A. (2023, January 28). *China's Massive Belt and Road initiative*. Council on Foreign Relations. https://www.cfr.org/backgrounder/chinas-massive-belt-and-road-initiative. Accessed February 16, 2024.

Nabine, D.-W. (2009). *The Impact of Chinese Investment and Trade on Nigeria Economic Growth*. United Nations Economic Commission for Africa. https://repository.uneca.org/bitstream/handle/10855/4157/Bib-30980.pdf?sequence=1. Accessed March 1, 2024.

Odeh, L. E. (2011). Sino-Nigerian Economic Relations Under the Obasanjo administration. *Ilorin Journal of History and International Studies, 2*(1), 216–230. www.academia.edu/23146118/Sino-Nigerian_Economic_Relations_under_The_Obasanjo_Administration. Accessed March 15, 2016.

Odittah, C. A. (2016). China Gives Stringent Conditions for $20bn Loan to Nigeria. *The Guardian.* https://guardian.ng/news/china-gives-stringent-conditions-for-20bn-loan-to-nigeria/. Accessed March 1, 2024.

Odoh, I. (2024). Completion of Keffi-Akwanga-Lafia Road Project Spurs Sino-Nigeria Ties. *Leadership Newspaper*. https://leadership.ng/completion-of-keffi-akwanga-lafia-road-project-spurs-sino-nigeria-ties/. Accessed July 6, 2024.

Odutola, A. (2019, November 28). *How the Chinese Are Taking Over Nigeria's Economy.* Nairametrics. https://nairametrics.com/2019/11/28/how-the-chinese-are-taking-over-nigerias-economy/#:~:text=In%20a%20recent%20interview%2C%20the,have%20employed%20over%20200%2C000%20Nigerians. Accessed July 6, 2024.

OECD. (2024). *Foreign Direct Investment (FDI).* OECD-iLibrary. https://www.oecd-ilibrary.org/finance-and-investment/foreign-direct-investment-fdi/indicator-group/english_9a523b18-en. Accessed February 3, 2024.

Okeke, C. (2021). Contentious Issues in China-Nigeria Contemporary Economic Relations. *International Journal of Humanities and Social Science, 9*, 1–12.

Okereke, C. (2012, November). Long-term Project Management Analysis: Chinese Loan to Nigeria. *PM World Journal, 4*(11). https://pmworldlibrary.net/wp-content/uploads/2013/02/PMWJ4-Nov2012-OKEREKE-LongTermProjectManagementAnalysis-ChineseLoanToNigeria-FeaturedPaper.pdf. Accessed August 16, 2024.

Olawoyin, O. (2020). Lagos Light Rail: 17 Years After, Failed Promises, Rot, Neglect Trail Project. *Premium Times.* https://www.premiumtimesng.com/investigationspecial-reports/431862-lagos-light-rail-17-years-after-failed-promises-rot-neglect-trail-project.html#print. Accessed May 12, 2024.

Oyeranti, O. A. M., Adetunji Babatunde, E., Ogunkola, O., & Bankole, A. S. (2018). *The Impact of China-Africa Relations: The Case of Nigeria.* African Economic. https://aercafrica.org/old-website/wp-content/uploads/2018/07/NigeriaPB8.pdf. Date Accessed: March 1, 2024.

Punch. (2023). *Chinese Loan Rises by $800m in One Year, Hits $4.73bn.* https://punchng.com/chinese-loan-rises-by-800m-in-one-year-hits-4-73bn/. Accessed June 6, 2024.

Railway Technology. (2020). *Abuja-Kaduna Rail Line.* https://www.railway-technlogy.com/projects/abuja-kaduna-rail-line/?cf-view. Accessed March 1, 2024.

Sow, M. (2018, September 6). *Figures of the Week: Chinese Investment in Africa.* Brookings Institution. https://www.brookings.edu/articles/figures-of-the-week-chinese-investment-in-africa/.

Suleiman, Q. (2023, November 19). Nigeria Must Lead Africa Against Neocolonialism—NDA—Commandant. *Premium Times.* https://www.premiumtimesng.com/news/top-news/644519-nigeria-must-lead-africa-against-neocolonialism-nda-commandant.html. Accessed July 6, 2024.

This Day Live. (2019). *China Debt Trap: Chinese Loan Terms Caution Africa Project Implementation on Slow Mode.* https://www.thisdaylive.com/index.php/2019/05/15/china-debt-trap-chinese-loan-terms-caution-africa-project-implementation-on-slow-mode/. Accessed July 6, 2024.

Thiombiano, D., & Tulga, A. Y. (2022, January). A Sentiment Based Text Analysis of the Perception of Chinese Infrastructure Development in Africa: Cases from Nigeria and Ethiopia. *International Journal of Social Science Studies, 10*(1), 11.

Tunji, S. (2022, January 18). *Chinese Company Dominates Nigeria's N10.5tn Railway Projects, Says Fitch Report.* Punch Nigeria. https://punchng.com/chinese-company-dominates-nigerias-n10-5tn-railway-projects-says-fitch-report/. Accessed April 6, 2024.

Usman, Z. (2021, June). *What Do We Know About Chinese Lending in Africa?* Carnegie Endowment for International Peace. https://carnegieendowment.org/research/2021/06/what-do-we-know-about-chinese-lending-in-africa?lang=en&center=global. Accessed July 6, 2024.

Vanguard. (2020, January). *How China's Belt and Road Initiative Affects Nigeria, Africa.* https://www.vanguardngr.com/2020/01/how-chinas-belt-and-road-initiative-affects-nigeria-africa/. Accessed July 6, 2024.

World Bank. (n.d.). GDP (current US$) [Indicator 5.51.01.10]. *World Bank Databank Glossary.* Retrieved June 27, 2025, from https://databank.worldbank.org/metadataglossary/statistical-capacity-indicators/series/5.51.01.10.gdp

Xiang, W., & Oluduro, O. (2023). China's Investment in the Nigerian Energy Sector: A Prognosis of the Dispute Settlement Paradigm. *Laws, 12*(5), 81. https://doi.org/10.3390/laws12050081

Yusuf, K. (2023). Investigation: Real Reason Construction of Abuja-Keffi-Makurdi Highway Is Delayed. *Premium Times.* https://www.premiumtimesng.com/features-and-interviews/612608-investigation-real-reason-construction-of-abuja-keffi-makurdi-highway-is-delayed.html. Accessed July 6, 2024.

Methodological Framework and Analysis—Kenya Case Study

4

In this chapter, we delve into several key concepts that form the foundation of statistical analysis and data interpretation, particularly within the context of hypothesis testing and regression analysis. Understanding these concepts is crucial for accurately analyzing quantitative data and drawing valid conclusions. The *Null Hypothesis* serves as the baseline assumption that any observed effect is due to chance, and its rejection is pivotal in determining statistical significance. The terms *R-Value*, *R-Square*, and *Multiple R* are central to evaluating the strength and direction of relationships between variables, providing insights into *variability* and *variation* within data sets. The concept of *Statistical Significance* is essential for determining whether the results observed in the data are likely to reflect true effects rather than random variation. Each of these terms plays a critical role in interpreting data accurately, helping researchers make informed decisions based on empirical evidence. The definitions are adapted from multiple sources (Bahna (2009), Kenton (2025), and, Wooldridge (2006) as follows:

1. Null Hypothesis: The null hypothesis typically tests whether the coefficients of the independent variables in the model are equal to zero, indicating no significant relationship between those variables and the dependent variable.
2. R-Value: Also known as the multiple correlation coefficient, represents the overall correlation between the independent variable (Chinese infrastructure aid to Kenya) and the dependent variable (GDP), considering all the independent variables in the model.
3. R-Square: It measures the proportion of the variance in the dependent variable that is predictable from the independent variable(s). In this context, it reflects how much of the variability in infrastructural development outcomes can be explained by Chinese infrastructure aid in each country.

J. Guest, *China's Infrastructure Aid and Investment*, African Studies and Research Forum Series, https://doi.org/10.1007/978-3-032-11964-3_4

4. Multiple R: It measures the strength and direction of the linear relationship between the two variables.
5. Variability: It assesses how Chinese infrastructure aid and FDI vary in their amounts, types, and effectiveness across Nigeria, Kenya, and Ethiopia.
6. Variation: How changes in the independent variable(s) (X) relate to changes in the dependent variable (Y).
7. Statistical Significance: Statistical significance is a concept used to figure out if the results of a study are likely real or just happened by chance. This is usually done by looking at a p-value, which tells us how likely it is that the results could occur by random chance. In this study, if the p value is less than 0.05, it means there's less than a 5% chance that the results are random, making them statistically significant. This helps researchers decide whether to reject the idea that there's no effect (the null hypothesis) and instead believe that there is a real effect (the alternative hypothesis).

Concomitantly, this chapter explores this question: Does Chinese infrastructure development aid affect economic growth? The chapter unfolds through a systematic exploration of several essential areas. The chapter begins by presenting a quantitative analysis by drawing on empirical data to uncover the effects of Chinese infrastructure development aid and its effect on economic growth in Kenya. Through statistical examinations, the chapter examines measurable correlations while providing insight into the relationship between Chinese infrastructure development aid and economic growth measured by GDP. Besides quantitative findings, the chapter examines the non-quantifiable facets of Chinese infrastructure development aid and economic growth in Kenya. Building on quantitative and qualitative findings, the chapter comprehensively analyzes the results. This analytical exploration aims to draw meaningful conclusions and identify potential patterns or variations. This chapter also provides a concise and insightful summary, highlighting the key takeaways and implications of the findings, setting the stage for a deeper understanding of the relationship between Chinese infrastructure development aid and economic growth in Kenya. The chapter is structured as follows: (a) historical context of China-Kenya relations; (b) in-depth analysis of infrastructure aid projects—quantitative analysis (economic impact) and qualitative analysis (social impact); (c) analysis of the findings; (d) Kenya newspaper content analysis; and (e) chapter summary.

4.1 Brief Historical Context of China-Kenya Relations

After Kenya gained its independence from Britain in December of 1963, diplomatic relations were established with the People's Republic of China under the leadership of the ruling Kenya African National Union (KANU) party. Nonetheless, internal conflicts within KANU and external pressures from Western intelligence agencies led to the sidelining of the left wing by the late 1960s, putting China-Kenya relations on hold until the late 1970s. Despite this, economic ties between the two countries predated independence, with Kenya exporting raw materials to China and importing semi-processed and finished products in return. Trade volumes increased post-independence, laying the groundwork for further cooperation. In 1964, negotiations between the Chinese ambassador and the Kenyan Minister of Finance led to economic and technical cooperation agreements, including the construction of a textile factory and a sugar refinery. Nevertheless, these projects never materialized, despite initial commitments from both sides (Chege, 2008).

The Chinese-Kenyan relationship post-Kenya's independence underwent a transition marked by state visits, confidence-building measures at various government levels, and the establishment of friendship agreements common in China-Africa relations at the time. This period also saw the beginning of discussions on development projects, technical assistance, and limited state-managed trade. While the phase of increased trade and investment characteristic of the early twenty-first century had not yet begun, the confidence-building efforts, reduction in revolutionary rhetoric, and emphasis on trade and economic development in the 1980s laid the groundwork for a more mutually beneficial relationship in the following decades (Chege, 2008).

From 1978 to 2000, Kenyan delegations, including foreign ministers and KANU leaders, visited China, indicating the seriousness with which China regarded Kenya as a gateway to Eastern Africa. China reciprocated with numerous high-level visits to Kenya, resulting in various technical exchanges and commercial initiatives. China also sought to learn from Kenya's progress in sectors like agriculture and tourism (Chege, 2008). Kenya aimed to increase both concessional development aid and its capacity to absorb it, supplementing local and foreign direct investments (FDIs). The Kenya Joint-Assistance Strategy (KJAS) involves 17 mostly Western donors that aim to coordinate and harmonize aid efforts in line with the 2003 Paris Declaration on Aid Effectiveness. China, however, is not part of the KJAS, which has led to friction with Western donors due to China's increasing bilateral aid to Kenya. The traditional multilateral donors of Kenya include the European Union, the World Bank, and the African Development Bank, while its main bilateral partners are the United States and the United Kingdom. Traditionally, Kenya's prominent multilateral donors include the European Union, the World Bank, and the African Development Bank, while bilateral partners include the United States, the United Kingdom, Japan, Germany, France, and others. China's aid contribution to Kenya rose significantly from 0.08% in 2002 to 13% in 2005, making it the largest bilateral donor in 2005. The appeal of Chinese aid lies in its simplicity and efficiency, with projects completed more quickly than other donors, despite criticism for overlooking human rights and democracy issues in African states (Chege, 2008).

To understand the foundation of the relationship between China and Kenya and Kenya's interest in collaborating on infrastructure development projects, it is essential to delve into the historical context of their relationship. First, let us explore Kenya's GDP from 2000 to 2022 (see Fig. 4.1).

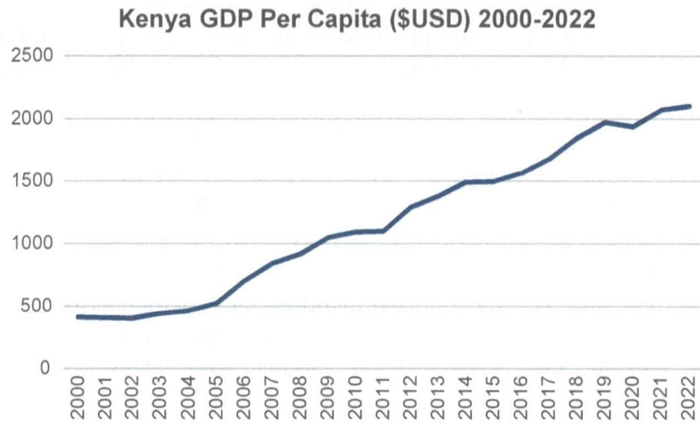

Fig. 4.1 Kenya's GDP per capita (USD), 2000–2022. *Source* Self-generated by Author Using Data from the World Bank (2024)

In assessing Kenya's GDP, one can observe an increasing trend in GDP over the years which indicates overall economic growth in Kenya. There are fluctuations in GDP figures from year to year, suggesting periods of economic expansion and contraction.

Kenya experienced a notable increase in GDP from 2006 to 2014, with a particularly significant jump between 2006 and 2007. There is a slight decline in GDP in some years, such as 2020, likely influenced by various factors such as economic downturns or external shocks like the COVID-2019 pandemic which is noticed also in Nigerian data. Overall, the upward trajectory of Kenya's GDP reflects the country's efforts toward economic development and growth during the analyzed period. I will explore Chinese infrastructure development aid to Kenya to determine if the Chinese support infrastructure projects contribute to economic growth and development in Kenya from 2000 to 2022 in the ensuing section.

4.2 Quantitative Analysis

In examining the data for Chinese infrastructure aid in the form of loans to Kenya, 97 projects were examined from 2000 to 2022. The infrastructure projects ranged from road construction, bridges, power distribution centers to solar power plants. Based on this information, the regression analysis was conducted, and the results are summarized in Fig. 4.2.

A Multiple R of 43% indicates that in the context of GDP being the dependent variable and Chinese infrastructure aid to Kenya being the independent variable, the direction of the linear relationship between these variables is strong. The Multiple R value, also known as the multiple correlation coefficient, represents the overall correlation between the independent variable (Chinese infrastructure aid to

SUMMARY OUTPUT

Regression Statistics	
Multiple R	0.42790301
R Square	0.183100986
Adjusted R Square	0.144201033
Standard Error	1659992379
Observations	23

ANOVA

	df	*SS*	*MS*	*F*	*Significance F*
Regression	1	1.29704E+19	1.29704E+19	4.706971892	0.041662853
Residual	21	5.78671E+19	2.75557E+18		
Total	22	7.08375E+19			

	Coefficients	*Standard Error*	*t Stat*	*P-value*	*Lower 95%*
Intercept	-398265037.8	788819497.8	-0.504887416	0.618895263	-2038704986
X Variable 1	1302371.352	600294.041	2.16955569	0.041662853	53991.5537

Fig. 4.2 Regression output China's infrastructure aid to Kenya & GDP. *Source* Self-generated by the Author Utilizing Data from aiddata.org (2023) and World Bank Data on Per Capita GDP (2024)

Kenya) and the dependent variable (GDP), considering all the independent variables in the model. In this case, it suggests that approximately 43% of the variation in GDP can be explained by the variation in Chinese infrastructure aid to Kenya.

This result means that changes in Chinese infrastructure aid to Kenya are associated with changes in GDP, and about 43% of the fluctuations or differences in GDP can be accounted for by fluctuations or differences in Chinese infrastructure aid to Kenya. In other words, when Chinese infrastructure aid to Kenya either increases or decreases, there tends to be a corresponding increase or decrease in GDP approximately 43% of the time. The remaining 57% of the variation in GDP is influenced by other factors not accounted for in the analysis, such as domestic economic policies, global economic conditions, government spending, and private investment.

An R-Square value of 18% means that approximately that portion of the variability of the dependent variable (GDP) can be explained by the independent variable (Chinese infrastructure aid to Kenya) and any other independent variables included in the model. This result suggests that Chinese infrastructure aid to Kenya accounts for about 18% of the variability observed in GDP. Put differently, when considering only Chinese infrastructure aid to Kenya, approximately 18% of the differences or fluctuations in GDP can be attributed to variations in Chinese infrastructure aid to Kenya. The remaining 82% of the variability in GDP is explained by factors other than Chinese infrastructure aid to Kenya that are not included in the model. These could include domestic economic policies, global economic conditions, government spending, private investment, and other factors influencing GDP.

In the case of Chinese infrastructure aid to Kenya, a Significance F-statistic of 0.041662853 suggests that the regression model, which includes Chinese infrastructure aid to Kenya as an independent variable, is statistically significant. This means that there is evidence to reject the null hypothesis, which posits that all the independent variables in the regression model are equal to zero, indicating no relationship between the independent variable (Chinese infrastructure aid to Kenya) and the dependent variable (GDP). Instead, the alternative hypothesis is favored, indicating that at least one of the coefficients is non-zero and the model has explanatory power. In this case, there is a statistically meaningful relationship between Chinese infrastructure aid to Kenya and the dependent variable (GDP). Specifically, a statistically significant coefficient for Chinese infrastructure aid to Kenya indicates that changes in the amount of aid provided by China to Kenya are associated with changes in the dependent variable (GDP). Stated differently, Chinese infrastructure aid to Kenya is a meaningful predictor of the variation in the dependent variable. As stated in the discussion of Nigeria, the closer the Multiple R is to 1, the stronger the positive correlation; and the closer it is to -1, the stronger the negative correlation.

This preceding significance result suggests that Chinese infrastructure aid to Kenya is not just random noise in the model but has a genuine impact on the outcome of interest. It also implies that policymakers, analysts, or researchers can rely on this relationship when making predictions or drawing conclusions about the effects of Chinese infrastructure aid on economic outcomes in Kenya.

In terms of analyzing the impact of Chinese FDI and its impact on economic development in Kenya, the regression analysis was conducted for 2000–2022. Based on this information, it is important to provide insights into the long-term trends and patterns of Chinese FDI flows and their effects on various economic indicators in Kenya over a substantial period. This extensive timeframe allows for a comprehensive examination of the relationship between Chinese investment activities and economic development outcomes, thereby offering a more robust understanding of the dynamics at play and enabling policymakers to formulate informed strategies and policies to maximize the benefits of Chinese FDI while mitigating potential risks or challenges. Additionally, by spanning multiple years, the analysis captures changes in investment patterns, economic conditions, and policy environments, and facilitating a comprehensive assessment of the evolving impact of Chinese FDI on Kenya's economic landscape. Based on the regression analysis conducted, the generated results are provided in Fig. 4.3.

Based on the regression results, the key measures used in this analysis are the Multiple R, R-Square, and the Significance F. These measures in the regression model are important in determining the overall strength and validity of the regression model and its ability to explain the variation in the dependent variable. The Multiple R value indicates the strength of the relationship between the independent and dependent variables and provides insight into how well the independent variables collectively predict the outcome. The R-Square value represents the proportion of variance in the dependent variable that is explained by the independent variables and offers a measure of the goodness-of-fit of the regression model. The

SUMMARY OUTPUT

Regression Statistics	
Multiple R	0.92691969
R Square	0.85918012
Adjusted R Square	0.85247441
Standard Error	226.445869
Observations	23

ANOVA

	df	SS	MS	F	Significance F
Regression	1	6570044.976	6570044.98	128.1266698	2.12102E-10
Residual	21	1076832.362	51277.7315		
Total	22	7646877.338			

	Coefficients	Standard Error	t Stat	P-value	Lower 95%
Intercept	684.203699	64.45245205	10.6156349	6.7378E-10	550.1674878
X Variable 1	7.0067E-07	6.19002E-08	11.3193052	2.12102E-10	5.71939E-07

Self-generated by author using data from UNCTAD 2010 & China Africa Research Initative

Fig. 4.3 Chinese Foreign Direct Investment to Kenya Regression Output 2000–2022. *Source* Self-generated by the Author Using Data from UNCTAD (2024a-b) and China Africa Research Initiative (2024)

Significance *F* value assesses whether the overall regression model is statistically significant and indicates whether the independent variables, as a group, have a significant impact on the dependent variable. These regression statistics help one to evaluate the reliability, explanatory power, and significance of the regression analysis results, thereby aiding to the interpretation and conclusions drawn from the results.

A Multiple R value of 0.926919694 in relation to the dependent variable being GDP and the independent variable being Chinese FDI to Kenya indicates a strong positive correlation between the two variables. Specifically, it suggests that approximately 92.69% of the variation in Kenya's GDP can be explained by the variation in Chinese FDI to the country. As Chinese FDI to Kenya increases, there tends to be a corresponding increase in Kenya's GDP and vice versa. The high Multiple R value indicates a significant relationship between Chinese FDI and economic output in Kenya. It also implies that Chinese FDI plays a substantial role in driving or influencing economic activity and growth within the country. Nevertheless, it is essential to consider other factors and conduct further analysis to comprehensively understand the mechanisms and impacts of Chinese FDI on Kenya's GDP.

An R-Square value of 0.859180118, also known as the coefficient of determination, indicates the proportion of variance in the dependent variable explained by the independent variable(s) in a regression analysis. In this case, the dependent variable is GDP in Kenya, and the independent variable is Chinese FDI to Kenya.

The preceding R-Square value means that approximately 85.92% of the variability in Kenya's GDP can be accounted for by variations in Chinese FDI to the country. In simpler terms, the R-Square value provides a measure of how well the independent variable (Chinese FDI to Kenya) can predict or explain changes in the dependent variable (GDP in Kenya). A higher R-Square value close to 1 indicates that the independent variable(s) are more effective at explaining the variability in the dependent variable, suggesting a stronger relationship between the variables. Conversely, a lower R-Square value closer to 0 indicates a weaker relationship or less explanatory power of the independent variable(s) on the dependent variable.

In summary, an R-Square value of 0.859180118 suggests a strong relationship between Chinese FDI to Kenya and Kenya's GDP, indicating that Chinese FDI significantly influences Kenya's economic output. Nonetheless, it is essential to consider other factors and conduct further analysis to fully understand the relationship between these variables.

A significance F value of 2.12102E-10, when GDP is the dependent variable and Chinese FDI to Kenya is the independent variable, indicates the statistical significance of the regression model. In regression analysis, the significance F value tests the overall significance of the regression equation, assessing whether the independent variable(s) significantly affect(s) the dependent variable(s). The minimal significance *F* value (2.12102E-10) suggests that the regression model is highly statistically significant because 2.12 -10 is smaller than.05. This means that the relationship between Chinese FDI to Kenya and the country's GDP is not likely due to random chance. Instead, it provides evidence that Chinese FDI to Kenya significantly impacts Kenya's GDP. In sum, a significance *F* value of 2.12102E-10 indicates strong evidence that Chinese FDI to Kenya is associated with changes in Kenya's GDP and that this relationship is unlikely to be an error.

The statistical significance of both Chinese infrastructure aid and FDI indicates that Chinese infrastructure aid has a substantial and meaningful impact on various aspects of the Kenyan economy. This aid contributes significantly to developing infrastructure projects such as roads, bridges, ports, and railways, which are crucial for economic growth and development. Chinese infrastructure aid and FDI are critical in bolstering Kenya's economic growth. The funds invested in infrastructure projects generate jobs, stimulate economic activity, and improve productivity, thereby contributing to economic expansion. Chinese infrastructure aid may help address some of Kenya's development challenges, such as inadequate transportation networks, limited market access, and disparities in regional development. By investing in infrastructure, China contributes to efforts to reduce poverty and inequality and promote inclusive growth. It is important to note that while Chinese infrastructure aid brings benefits, there may be concerns about debt sustainability. Kenya must therefore ensure that borrowing for infrastructure projects is managed responsibly to avoid over-indebtedness and potential financial risks in the future.

4.3 Qualitative Analysis

To determine the impact of Chinese infrastructure aid on the Kenyan economy, it is important to examine select projects to determine their social impact on Kenya's economy. The two projects examined in this study are the Kibwezi-Mutomo-Kitui Road Construction project and the Nairobi Western Bypass Road Construction (16.8 km). These projects are concrete examples of Chinese infrastructure aid in action within Kenya. These projects were selected because they represent infrastructure investments—road construction in rural areas (Kibwezi-Mutomo-Kitui Road) and urban transportation infrastructure (Nairobi Western Bypass). Examining rural and urban projects allows for a comprehensive understanding of the diverse impacts of Chinese aid on different regions and sectors of the Kenyan economy. These projects have significant social and economic implications for Kenya. The construction of roads improves connectivity, facilitates transportation of goods and people, enhances access to markets and services, and stimulates economic activity. Analyzing these projects' social and economic impacts provides insights into their contribution to Kenya's development goals. In addition, constructing roads also encourages more FDIs in countries that allow for easier access to goods and people.

According to *Yobesh Onwong'a* (2020), *Kenya* boosts socioeconomic development along this international highway. Kitui South constituency previously lacked any tarmac roads since independence but stands to benefit greatly from this project initiated by President Uhuru Kenyatta in December of 2016. The road project cuts across eight other constituencies and begins near Kibwezi Town and extends northward through various areas, offering access to natural resources like limestone and iron ore, tourism potential with proximity to the Tsavo East National Park, and agricultural opportunities such as beekeeping and drought-resistant crop cultivation (*Onwong'a*, 2020).

This road project aligns with Kenya's development agenda, particularly the Big Four Agenda, which aims to position the country as a regional transport and logistics hub. Increased government spending, foreign aid, and private sector involvement support Kenya's infrastructure plans. This road project is part of Vision 2030, Kenya's long-term development blueprint focusing on infrastructure development to drive economic growth and regional integration. This road is anticipated to serve as a crucial link between the Port of Mombasa, the Lower and Upper Eastern Regions, and Ethiopia in order to alleviate congestion on the Nairobi-Mombasa Highway and enhancing economic competitiveness. Overall, the road forms part of the larger Mombasa-Addis Ababa Transport Corridor by providing an alternative route to Addis Ababa, Ethiopia, and contributing to regional connectivity and trade facilitation (*Onwong'a*, 2020). Local newspapers were used to examine the Kibwezi-Mutomo-Kitui Road Construction project because newspapers serve as valuable sources of information for understanding the impact of Chinese aid on infrastructure projects like the Kibwezi-Kitui-Migwani road and provide important insights into the project's social, economic, and political implications for Kenya.

According to *Business Daily Africa*, the road development project named Kibwezi-Mutomo-Kitui Road Construction encompasses enhancements to several townships and involved the installation of storm-water drainage systems and the construction of tarmacked feeder roads. There are plans for a lorry park near Kibwezi Township that will serve as a resting area for transit trucks in order to foster business opportunities in the region. The road has gained popularity among various transportation vehicles, such as *matatus*, buses, and trucks traveling to destinations across multiple counties. One resident stated that the road has contributed to shorter routes and reduced fuel consumption, stimulating economic activities like the goat trade at Mutha market and attracting investors interested in minerals and real estate. Despite these benefits, increased competition among *matatu* operators has resulted in complaints among local operators, highlighting challenges associated with the road's development (Maundu, 2021).

While there appears that the road construction project has contributed to economic development in Kenya, it has also displaced some residents. According to James Mbaka, with *The Star* newspaper, since the initiation of the Sh21 billion project in 2017, approximately 5,000 title owners have yet to receive compensation for their relocation to make way for the multi-billion-dollar project. The delay in compensation has left affected families who were pushed out for the project and are now struggling with poverty (Mbaka, 2023).

While the road construction project undoubtedly contributes to Kenya's overall economic development, it is important to recognize and address the hardships faced by those displaced by the project and any other infrastructure development projects in the country. The delay in compensating approximately 5,000 title owners as reported by James Mbaka with *The Star* highlights the urgent need to prioritize the well-being of affected families. While infrastructure projects can bring numerous benefits to a country, including improved connectivity, trade, and economic growth, ensuring that the process is fair and equitable for all citizens is equally essential. Addressing the issue of delayed compensation is not only a matter of justice but also a critical step in fostering social cohesion and inclusive development. Therefore, the government must expedite the compensation process and support those adversely affected by the project's implementation.

The second project examined is the Nairobi Western Bypass which is valued at Sh17 billion and includes five interchanges at strategic points along its 14.7-km length, facilitates improved access to markets and boosts real estate development in Nairobi. Key features include noise control barriers, paved deviations, traffic bridges, pedestrian underpasses, and facilities like a bus park and separate footpaths for pedestrians and cyclists (Andeso, 2022).

According to Marystella Momanyi of the *Nation*, bypasses have positively impacted Nairobi's socioeconomic landscape. The writer highlights how the construction of bypasses like the Southern, Eastern, and Western Bypasses has eased traffic congestion, reduced travel time, and enhanced accessibility to various parts of the city. These improvements have not only benefited commuters but also stimulated economic activities, leading to increased investments, job generation, and real estate development along the bypass corridors. Additionally, the bypasses have helped decongest the city center, resulting in improved air quality and overall urban livability. The writer concludes by emphasizing the importance of continued investment in infrastructure projects like bypasses to support Nairobi's growth and development (Momanyi, 2023). The author also underscores the significance of the Western Bypass within the context of the broader infrastructure development in Nairobi. While the qualitative research primarily centered on the Western Bypass, it is crucial to recognize its pivotal role among the four key bypasses essential for alleviating traffic congestion in the city. The integration of the Western Bypass with the existing Southern, Eastern, and Northern Bypasses forms a comprehensive network that enhances transportation efficiency and connectivity across Nairobi. As part of this network, the Western Bypass not only contributes to easing congestion but also complements the functionality of the other bypasses, collectively driving Nairobi's socioeconomic progress and urban development forward.

During the timeframe of the research for this book, the Northern, Eastern, and Southern Bypasses were also completed. The Northern and Eastern Bypass Project in Nairobi was financed through a $108 million preferential buyer's credit agreement between China Eximbank and the government of Kenya, later revised to $104,400,000. The loan featured a 2% interest rate, a seven-year grace period, and a 20-year maturity, with semi-annual repayments between January 2015 and January 2029. It supported a 52-km road, comprising a 21-km northern bypass and a 31-km eastern bypass. The project was implemented by China Road and Bridge Corporation (CRBC), began on April 18, 2009, and was completed on March 30, 2012. The northern bypass starts in Ruaka, travels through Runda, Marurui, and Kahawa, ending at the Nairobi Eastern Bypass Highway in Ruiru. The eastern bypass begins at the Nairobi–Mombasa Road and Airport North Road junction, passes through Ruai, and ends at the Ruiru Kamiti Road in Ruiru (Aiddata.org, 2023). The Southern Bypass Highway was also constructed during the time of this research, began in 2011 and completed in 2016 to also ease congestion in Nairobi and promote socioeconomic development. The total amount for the project was $261,095,369.00 of which $183,600,000 was financed by China Exim Bank (Kenya National Highways Authority, 2020). The project's geographical area is depicted in Fig. 4.4.

Figure 4.4 illustrates how the Northern, Southern, Western and Eastern bypasses collectively alleviate congestion in Nairobi while fostering economic development across Kenya. These bypasses enhance connectivity and accessibility to different regions, making the country more appealing to investors. With improved transportation infrastructure, including bypasses, Kenya establishes a favorable business environment that attracts investment in key industries like logistics, manufacturing, and tourism, thereby driving economic growth.

Moreover, these bypasses play a crucial role in facilitating the movement of goods and services, reducing transportation costs, and boosting trade within Kenya and with its landlocked neighboring countries such as Ethiopia, South Sudan, and Uganda. By providing efficient routes, bypasses enhance market access and linking production centers to consumer markets more efficiently. This, in turn, stimulates economic development in previously underserved or remote areas by improving

Fig. 4.4 Map of Northern, Southern, Eastern, and Western Bypass in Nairobi, Kenya. *Source* Kenya National Highways Authority, 2020 (in public domain)

connectivity and accessibility. Additionally, bypasses offer improved access to tourist attractions, cultural sites, and natural landmarks.

Furthermore, bypasses often serve as catalysts for developing industrial clusters and special economic zones along their corridors, further driving economic activity and growth. Overall, the strategic implementation of bypasses contributes significantly to Kenya's economic development by improving transportation efficiency, enhancing trade links, and fostering regional development.

4.4 Analysis of Kenyan Newspapers

The analysis of Kenyan newspapers involved systematically reviewing and coding articles from major publications over a specific period. This method aimed to identify prevailing themes and sentiments regarding Chinese influence in Kenya and offer a comprehensive overview of the media landscape. The following Kenyan newspapers were examined: *The Daily Nation*, *The Standard*, *The Star*, *Business Daily Africa*, *Capital FM Kenya*, *Kenya Broadcasting Corporation*, and *The East African*. *The Daily Nation* is the most widely read newspaper in Kenya and reaches up to ten percent of adults (Řehák, 2016).

In reviewing *The Daily Nation*, it was found that it provided a nuanced view on Chinese infrastructure aid and FDI in Kenya. President William Ruto has been actively engaged with China with the aim of securing new infrastructure deals that build upon past successes such as the Mombasa-Nairobi railway and the oil terminal at the port of Mombasa. These projects have significantly enhanced connectivity and cross-border regional trade integration in Kenya. The article also described the relationship between Kenya and China as a comprehensive strategic cooperative partnership, with recent discussions focusing on future infrastructure projects and digital economy advancements. Ruto emphasizes the importance of making these infrastructure investments sustainable and beneficial for Kenya's development (Mutambo, 2023).

The article "After a Tricky Year, Kenya to Formalise China Policy" (2013) in *The Daily Nation* by Aggrey Mutambo discussed Kenya's plans to formalize its policy toward China after a challenging first year under Ruto. Prime Cabinet Secretary Musalia Mudavadi's recent trip to China aimed to establish a comprehensive strategic partnership for the next 60 years, focusing on infrastructure, green energy, and ICT. The policy will involve establishing focal points in the government to handle Chinese affairs. This move reflects Kenya's intent to correct past mistakes, enhance cooperation, and ensure sustainable development through clear guidelines and structured collaboration. While the newspaper provided articles highlighting the enthusiasm for the Sino-Kenyan partnership, there is also a cautious approach toward Chinese investments that reflects broader concerns about debt sustainability and the need for Kenya to balance infrastructure development with financial prudence. This balanced view acknowledges both the significant contributions of Chinese investments to Kenya's infrastructure and the complexities involved in managing such a partnership (Mutambo, 2024).

In *The Standard*, the article titled "Kenya Bets on Chinese Help in SGR expansion" (2023) by Brian Ngugi expressed optimism as it relates to Chinese infrastructure aid to Kenya. The article added that Kenya remains committed to securing Chinese support for completing the Standard Gauge Railway (SGR) to Malaba despite not reaching an agreement during recent talks between Ruto and Jinping. Transport Cabinet Secretary Kipchumba Murkomen emphasized ongoing engagement with China by focusing on extending the SGR from Naivasha to Malaba and eventually to Kampala. The BRI forum saw the signing of multiple cooperation agreements. Ruto praised the BRI projects for enhancing Kenya's regional connectivity and trade, marking a shift from his earlier stance on Chinese loans (Ngugi, 2023).

The Standard article titled "Can the Chinese Economic Model Work in Kenya?" (2011) explored the potential application of China's economic strategies in Kenya. The author, XN Iraki, highlighted China's success through FDI, discipline, focuses on economic growth over politics and market-oriented reforms since 1978. The article suggested that Kenya can learn from China by prioritizing economic policies, attracting investors, and leveraging national pride and discipline. It emphasized that Kenya should adapt Chinese economic principles to its context to stimulate growth and development. This article had a positive perspective on China's economic growth and suggested that Kenya can leverage Chinese expertise and investment to boost its economy (Iraki, 2011).

In terms of *The Star* article titled "Kenya-China Ties Have Unleashed Profound Benefits—Mudavadi" (2023), discussed is Chinese infrastructure aid to Kenya in a favorable light. Kenya's Prime Cabinet Secretary Musalia Mudavadi emphasized the deliberate steps taken by Ruto and his predecessors to strengthen Kenya's ties with China, resulting in significant benefits under the BRI. Key infrastructure projects funded by China include the Thika Superhighway, the Mombasa-Nairobi Standard Gauge Railway (SGR), and the Nairobi Expressway, all of which have greatly improved Kenya's transportation network and economic growth as discussed in the previous newspapers highlighted. Kenya also has seen an influx of Chinese investors and projects like the Nairobi Global Trade Center, SGR and Thika Superhighway, which indicates a robust partnership between the two countries. Mudavadi stressed the potential for further collaboration in other areas such as renewable energy, agriculture, and industrialization, aiming for 100% green energy access and enhanced food security with China (Xinhua, 2023).

Also, Stephen Ndegwa's article titled "Contrary to Critics, China-Kenya Relations Are Growing Stronger" (2013) talked about a high-level meeting during which Wang Yi, a top Chinese official, and Ruto marked a significant milestone in Kenya-China relations by showcasing strong support and mutual commitment to economic growth. China has pledged to consider Kenya's priority areas that include infrastructure, climate change, ICT, education, and security (Ndegwa, 2023).

It was added that Ruto highlighted Kenya's support for China's Global Development Initiative and praised the relationship's foundation of mutual respect. Both nations aim to strengthen political mutual trust, increase government and party exchanges, and support each other in international fora. China's approach to Kenya, characterized by strategic alignment and mutual benefit, has led to substantial economic and trade cooperation with over 100 major joint projects that include the transformative SGR and the Nairobi Expressway (Ndegwa, 2023).

Kenya's strategic position and favorable economic environment make it an attractive destination for Chinese investment. Future cooperation will focus on critical sectors like ICT, manufacturing, health, and housing which align with Kenya's sustainable development and climate resilience goals. The key to this article is that the no-strings-attached nature of China's support and patience has contributed to the enduring and mutually beneficial relationship. Observers therefore suggested that the best outcomes of this partnership are still to come (Ndegwa, 2023).

Indeed, Kenyan newspapers exhibited a nuanced approach when covering Chinese investments and aid by reflecting on both the benefits and challenges of the partnership. *The Daily Nation*, Kenya's most widely read newspaper, highlighted significant Chinese infrastructure projects like the Mombasa-Nairobi railway and the Nairobi Expressway by emphasizing the positive impact on connectivity and trade. Nonetheless, it also noted a cautious approach toward Chinese investments, especially concerning debt sustainability and the need for financial prudence (Mutambo, 2023, 2024).

The Standard expressed optimism about Chinese infrastructure aid and focused on the commitment to completing projects like the SGR, despite negotiation challenges. It also explored how Kenya might adapt China's economic strategies to stimulate local growth by underscoring the potential for learning from China's development model (Ngugi, 2023; Iraki, 2023).

The Star portrayed Chinese aid in a favorable light and highlighted significant infrastructure achievements under the BRI and the potential for future collaboration in renewable energy, agriculture, and industrialization. It also emphasized the Kenya-China relationship's strategic and mutually beneficial nature and suggested that the best outcomes of this partnership are yet to come (The Ndegwa, 2023; Star, 2023).

Kenyan newspapers recognized Chinese aid's significant benefits while also acknowledging the need for balanced and sustainable development strategies. They highlighted the optimism surrounding improved connectivity through projects like the SGR which have enhanced regional integration and boosted the economy by generating numerous jobs. Additionally, the newspapers discussed the complexities related to the extensive loans Kenya has taken from China by addressing concerns about the potential long-term impact on the nation's financial health. Overall, the coverage reflected a balanced view by appreciating the economic benefits while also being mindful of the financial risks involved.

4.5 Chapter Summary

Analyzing Kenya's infrastructure aid and investment data proved intriguing due to the significant number of Chinese projects undertaken between 2000 and 2022. During this period, Kenya received aid through loans for numerous infrastructure projects spanning various sectors. These projects encompassed initiatives such as underground electrical power distribution networks, road constructions, dam developments, expressway expansions, port enhancements, railway constructions, and pipeline water projects. In this chapter, the infrastructure projects were analyzed qualitatively and quantitatively to understand better the role of the Chinese infrastructure aid projects in impacting economic development in Kenya.

China and Kenya's post-independence relationship underwent several phases characterized by diplomatic ties, economic cooperation, and bilateral visits. Despite initial setbacks and delays in project implementation, both countries engaged in confidence-building measures and explored avenues for technical assistance and trade. China regarded Kenya as a crucial gateway to Eastern Africa, leading to numerous high-level visits and exchanges aimed at mutual learning and cooperation, particularly in sectors like agriculture and tourism.

Kenya, in its pursuit of development, has seen a significant shift in its aid sources. Once heavily reliant on Western donors, the country has now become a recipient of substantial Chinese aid. By 2005, China had emerged as Kenya's largest bilateral donor, a testament to the changing dynamics of global aid. Chinese aid, with its reputation for simplicity and efficiency, has expedited project completion, although it has not been without its share of criticism for its perceived disregard for human rights and democracy issues. Amid the changing aid landscape, Kenya's economic growth stands as a beacon of stability. This is evidenced by a consistent upward trend in GDP over the years, despite periodic fluctuations, a testament to the country's resilience and potential for further development.

The analysis of Chinese infrastructure aid and FDI in Kenya from 2000 to 2022 revealed Significance Findings regarding their impact on the country's economic development. Chinese infrastructure aid, comprising 97 projects from road construction to power distribution, demonstrates a moderate correlation with fluctuations in Kenya's GDP. The regression analysis indicated that approximately 43% of the variability in GDP can be attributed to changes in Chinese infrastructure aid, thereby highlighting its role in influencing economic output. Despite Chinese aid accounting for about 18% of the observed GDP variability, the remaining 82% was influenced by other factors not considered in the analysis which suggested the presence of additional determinants of economic performance.

In contrast, Chinese FDI exhibited a notably stronger correlation with Kenya's GDP, with approximately 92.69% of the variability in GDP explained by variations in Chinese FDI. The regression analysis underscored the substantial influence of Chinese FDI on Kenya's economic output, indicating a robust positive correlation between the two variables. Moreover, the statistical significance of the regression model confirmed the meaningful relationship between Chinese FDI and Kenya's GDP, thereby providing compelling evidence against the null hypothesis and affirming the pivotal role of Chinese investment in driving economic growth within the country.

Chinese infrastructure aid and FDI are crucial in bolstering Kenya's economic growth and development by funding vital infrastructure projects, stimulating economic activity, and improving productivity. Nevertheless, alongside their benefits, there are concerns regarding debt sustainability, necessitating responsible borrowing and financial management to mitigate potential risks in the future. Overall, the findings underscored the significance of Chinese investments in Kenya's economic landscape, highlighting the need for strategic planning and policy measures to maximize the benefits of these investments while addressing associated challenges.

Qualitatively, examining Chinese infrastructure aid in Kenya necessitated a focused analysis of specific projects to gauge their social and economic impacts on the country's development trajectory. Two critical projects under scrutiny are the Kibwezi-Mutomo-Kitui Road Construction and the Nairobi Western Bypass Road Construction. These projects symbolize diverse infrastructure investments, covering rural and urban areas, offering a comprehensive understanding of Chinese aid's effects across different regions and sectors. The construction of roads enhances connectivity and facilitates transportation of goods and people, promotes economic activities, and fosters access to markets and services, aligning with Kenya's development goals of becoming a regional transport and logistics hub.

For instance, the Kibwezi-Mutomo-Kitui Road Construction project demonstrated significant socioeconomic potential, particularly for previously underserved areas like the Kitui South constituency. Initiated by Uhuru Kenyatta in 2016, this project aims to unlock various economic opportunities, including access to natural resources, tourism potential, and agricultural ventures in order to contribute to regional development and the realization of Kenya's Big Four Agenda. Nonetheless, challenges such as delayed compensation for displaced residents highlight the importance of equitable development practices and fair treatment of affected communities.

Similarly, the Nairobi Western Bypass project, valued at Sh17 billion, is pivotal in enhancing market access and stimulating real estate development in Nairobi. Alongside other bypasses like the Southern, Eastern, and Northern Bypasses, it has significantly eased traffic congestion, reduced travel time, and improved urban livability in the city. Furthermore, integrating these bypasses into a comprehensive network has enhanced transportation efficiency, boosted trade links, and fostered economic growth within Nairobi and across Kenya and its neighboring countries.

Overall, the strategic implementation of infrastructure projects, including bypasses, underscores China's substantial contribution to Kenya's economic development by improving transportation infrastructure, facilitating trade, and fostering regional integration. Nevertheless, addressing challenges such as equitable compensation for affected communities is imperative to ensure that the benefits of such projects are inclusive and sustainable, aligning with Kenya's broader development aspirations and commitments to social justice.

References

AidData. (2023). *Global Chinese Development Finance Dataset, Version 3.0*. 2023. Retrieved July 6, 2024, from https://www.aiddata.org/data/aiddatas-global-chinese-development-finance-dataset-version-3-0

Andeso, A. (2022). Nairobi Western Bypass Construction Begins. *Construction Kenya*. Retrieved July 6, 2024, from https://www.constructionkenya.com/6895/nairobi-western-bypass/

Bahna, S. L. (Ed.). (2009). Statistics for clinicians (Suppl. 1). *Annals of Allergy, Asthma & Immunology, 103*(4 Suppl. 1). American College of Allergy, Asthma & Immunology. Retrieved June 17, 2024, from https://college.acaai.org/sites/default/files/Statistics%20for%20Clinicians%20-%20Annals%20Suppl%20Oct%2009%20-%20ALL.pdf#page=35

Chege, M. (2008). *Economic Relations Between Kenya and China*. https://www.csis.org/analysis/economic-relations-between-kenya-and-china-1963-2007

China Africa Research Initiative. (2024). *Data: Chinese Global Foreign Aid*. Retrieved July 1, 2024, from https://www.sais-cari.org/data

Iraki, X. N. (2011). Can the Chinese Economic Model Work in Kenya? *Standard Media*, October 20, 2011. https://www.standardmedia.co.ke/article/2000045500/can-the-chinese-economic-model-work-in-kenya

Kenton, W. (2025, March 28). *Statistical significance: What it is, how it works, and examples. Investopedia*. Retrieved June 18, 2025, from https://www.investopedia.com/terms/s/statistically_significant.asp

Kenya National Highway Authority. (2020). Kenya Nairobi Southern Bypass Project. *Parliament of Kenya*. Retrieved July 6, 2024, from http://www.parliament.go.ke/sites/default/files/2021-10/AG%20-%20KEnya%20Nairobi%20Southern%20Bypass%20Project%20-%20KNHA%2030th%20June%2C%202020.pdf

Maundu, P. (2021). Sh18bn Kibwezi-Kitui Road Project to Open Up Region for Trade. *Business Daily Africa*, May 18, 2021. Retrieved July 3, 2024, from https://www.businessdailyafrica.com/bd/corporate/shipping-logistics/sh18bn-kibwezi-kitui-region-for-trade-3405266

Mbaka, J. (2023). MP Seeks Answers on Delayed Kitui-Kibwezi Road Compensation. *The Star*, March 21, 2023. Retrieved June 1, 2024, from https://www.the-star.co.ke/news/2023-03-21-mp-seeks-answers-on-delayed-kitui-kibwezi-road-compensation/

Momanyi, M. (2023). Bypasses Have Improved Nairobi's Socio-Economy. *Daily Nation*. Retrieved July 6, 2024, from https://nation.africa/kenya/blogs-opinion/blogs/bypasses-have-improved-nairobi-s-socio-economy-4378636

Mutambo, A. (2023). Ruto Courts China with Eye on New Infrastructure Deals. *Daily Nation*. October 19, 2023. Retrieved July 6, 2024, from https://nation.africa/kenya/news/ruto-courts-china-with-eye-on-new-infrastructure-deals-4406014

Mutambo, A. (2024). After a Tricky Year, Kenya to Formalise China Policy. *Daily Nation*. January 29, 2024. Retrieved July 6, 2024. https://nation.africa/kenya/news/after-a-tricky-year-kenya-to-formalise-china-policy-4507314

Ndegwa, S. (2023). Contrary to Critics, China-Kenya Relations Are Growing Stronger. *The Star*. July 23, 2023. Retrieved July 6, 2024, from https://www.the-star.co.ke/opinion/2023-07-23-contrary-to-critics-china-kenya-relations-are-growing-stronger/

Ngugi, B. (2023). Kenya Bets on Chinese Help in SGR Expansion. *The Standard*. November 2023. Retrieved July 6, 2024, from https://www.standardmedia.co.ke/business/article/2001484069/kenya-bets-on-chinese-help-in-sgr-expansion

Onwong'a, Y. (2020). Sh 18.4 Billion Kibwezi-Kitui Road to Spur Socio-Economic Development. *Kenya News Agency*. Retrieved July 6, 2024, from https://www.kenyanews.go.ke/sh-18-4-billion-kibwezi-kitui-road-to-spur-socio-economic-development/

Řehák, V. (2016). China-Kenya Relations: Analysis of the Kenyan News Discourse. *Modern Africa: Politics, History and Society, 4*(2), 85–115. Retrieved from https://edu.uhk.cz/africa/index.php/ModAfr/article/view/35

The Star. (2023). MP Seeks Answers on Delayed Kitui-Kibwezi Road Compensation. *The Star*, March 21, 2023. https://www.the-star.co.ke/news/2023-03-21-mp-seeks-answers-on-delayed-kitui-kibwezi-road-compensation/

The Star. (2023). *Kenya-China ties have unleashed profound benefits—Mudavadi*. News.December 15, 2023. Retrieved July 6, 2024, from https://www.the-star.co.ke/news/2023-12-15-kenya-china-ties-have-unleashed-profound-benefits-mudavadi/

UNCTAD. (2024a). US FDI flows and stock. *UNCTADStat*. Retrieved from https://unctadstat.unctad.org/datacentre/dataviewer/US.FdiFlowsStock. Date Retrieved: August 14, 2024.

United Nations Conference on Trade and Development (UNCTAD). (2024b). *Statistics*. Retrieved August 19, 2024. https://unctad.org/statistics

Wooldridge, J. M. (2006). *Introductory econometrics: A modern approach* (3rd ed.). Cengage Learning.

World Bank. (2024). *GDP (current US$)—Kenya*. Retrieved May 12, 2024. https://data.worldbank.org/indicator/NY.GDP.MKTP.CD?end=2022&locations=KE&start=2000

Xinhua. (2023). Kenya-China Ties Have Unleashed Profound Benefits - Mudavadi. *The Star*. December 15, 2023. Retrieved July 6, 2024, from https://www.the-star.co.ke/news/2023-12-15-kenya-china-ties-have-unleashed-profound-benefits-mudavadi/

Methodological Framework and Analysis—Ethiopia Case Study

5

In this chapter, we will explore key concepts fundamental to understanding and conducting statistical analysis. These concepts provide the foundation for interpreting data, assessing relationships, and determining the validity of results. We will begin by defining **bi-directional** relationships, which refer to interactions where influence flows in both directions between variables. The **F-Test** will be introduced as a method for comparing the variances between groups to determine if they are statistically different. We will also discuss **R-Square**, a measure of how well data fits a statistical model, and delve into **causation**, which examines the cause-and-effect relationship between variables. Additionally, we'll cover **variability**, which looks at how much data points differ from each other, and the **p-value**, a crucial metric used to determine whether a result is **statistically significant**—that is, unlikely to have occurred by chance. Understanding these concepts is essential for interpreting research findings and making informed decisions based on statistical evidence. The definitions are as follows:

1. Bi-directional-influence flows in both directions between variables.
2. F-Test: In regression analysis, the P-Value is used to determine whether the overall regression model is useful. Suppose the P-Value is less than the chosen significance level. In that case, there is enough evidence to conclude that the regression model explains the data better than a model with no predictor variables (Sureiman & Mangera, 2020).
3. R-Square: See definition in Chapter 4.
4. Causation: In the context of Chinese infrastructure development aid and Foreign Direct Investment (FDI) in Nigeria, Kenya, and Ethiopia, causation describes how Chinese economic development aid and Chinese FDI lead to specific economic and developmental outcomes in these countries.
5. Variability: See definition in Chapter 4.

J. Guest, *China's Infrastructure Aid and Investment*, African Studies and Research Forum Series, https://doi.org/10.1007/978-3-032-11964-3_5

6. Statistically Significant: See definition in Chapter 4.

Correspondingly, this chapter explores the following query: Does Chinese infrastructure development aid affect economic growth? Similar to what was done in the preceding chapters, this one begins by providing a brief historical background of the Chinese-Ethiopian relationship. It then unfolds through a systematic exploration of several essential areas. The quantitative section presents empirical findings on Chinese infrastructure development aid and its impact on economic development in Ethiopia. Through statistical examinations, this chapter examines measurable correlations while providing insight into the relationship between Chinese infrastructure development aid and economic growth measured by GDP. Next, the non-quantifiable facets of Chinese infrastructure development aid and economic growth in Ethiopia are delineated.

Thereafter, the chapter conducts a comprehensive analysis of the results. This analytical exploration aims to draw meaningful conclusions and identify potential patterns or variations. The chapter also provides a concise and insightful summary by highlighting the key takeaways and implications of the study's findings, thereby setting the stage for a deeper understanding of the relationship between Chinese infrastructure development aid and economic growth in Ethiopia. Suitably, the chapter covers the following topics: (a) brief historical context of China-Ethiopia relations, (b) in-depth analysis of infrastructure aid projects, (c) quantitative analysis (economic impact) and qualitative analysis (social impact), (d) analysis of the findings, and (e) chapter summary.

5.1 Brief Historical Context of China-Ethiopia Relations

This section provides a concise exploration of the historical ties between China and Ethiopia, tracing the early interactions between the two nations pre- and post-Ethiopia's independence. Diplomatic relations between China and Ethiopia have a rich history dating back several decades. In the mid-twentieth century, Ethiopia played a pivotal role in supporting China's bid for admission into the United Nations, showcasing an early sign of solidarity and cooperation between the two countries.

The diplomatic relations between China and Ethiopia have deep historical roots dating back to ancient times that reflect their long-standing engagement and mutual respect. Formal diplomatic ties began solidifying in the 1960s, with significant visits by leaders such as China's Prime Minister Zhou Enlai and Ethiopian Emperor Haile Selassie. Nonetheless, during the Cold War (which started in 1947, two years after the end of World War II, and ended when the Soviet Union fell in 1991), Ethiopia's alignment with Western powers strained relations with China. It was not until the mid-1980s, following the end of the Sino-Soviet conflict and Mengistu Hailemariam's departure from power, that diplomatic relations between China and Ethiopia began to improve (Bilate & Zou, 2021).

During the Cold War, Ethiopia aligned with Western powers, which limited its relations with China. The Ethiopian Revolution of 1974 further strained ties as the country embraced Marxism-Leninism and aligned with the Soviet Union until 1991. Despite these challenges, the relationship evolved with agreements signed on bilateral trade, investment, and technical cooperation. The 50-year diplomatic history reflects a complex journey marked by shifting geopolitical dynamics and evolving economic priorities (Bilate & Zou, 2021).

The diplomatic relations between China and Ethiopia have strengthened since the 1970s and are built on equality, mutual benefit, and non-interference in internal affairs. Both countries prioritize economic cooperation and mutual interests, leading to deepening bilateral collaboration and fruitful outcomes. Chinese President Xi Jinping congratulated Ethiopia on the 50th anniversary of their diplomatic ties, highlighting their support for each other's core interests and cooperation in regional and international affairs (Bilate & Zou, 2021).

China has emerged as Ethiopia's largest foreign direct investor, fostering economic development since the 1970s. The relationship has increased trade, investment volume, and economic cooperation that benefit both nations. Ethiopia values China's financial aid, infrastructure projects, and involvement in economic development, while China sees Ethiopia's strategic location and regional influence as advantageous. The two countries have established a comprehensive strategic cooperation partnership which focuses on areas such as industrialization and the BRI (Bilate & Zou, 2021).

Ethiopia's economic growth and transformation and China's expanding global presence through initiatives like the BRI have further strengthened their cooperation. The histories of their diplomatic relations provide a basis for analyzing their partnership and understanding the factors shaping their collaboration. Their relationship has become increasingly strategic and mutually beneficial, thereby reflecting shared interests and goals in economic development and regional cooperation (Bilate & Zou, 2021).

Ethiopia serves as a notable case study within China-Africa relations, challenging the prevailing belief that China's engagement in Africa is solely driven by a quest for resources. Agriculture dominates Ethiopia's economy, with approximately 85% of its population relying on it, and contributing 41% to the GDP and 90% to export earnings. The Ethiopian government has identified rapid agricultural growth as crucial for poverty reduction and economic advancement, making it central to its "Growth and Transformation Plan" through agricultural development-led industrialization (Malancha, 2016).

To understand the foundation of the relationship between China and Ethiopia and Ethiopia's interest in collaborating on infrastructure development projects, it is essential to delve into the historical context of their relationship. To do so, I will first explore Ethiopia's GDP from 2000 to 2022 in the section that follows.

5.2 Quantitative Analysis

As shown in Fig. 5.1, the GDP of Ethiopia started with slight drops from 2000 to 2002, which could be due to various economic factors and challenges faced by the country during that time. Nonetheless, there was constant and notable growth in the per capita GDP from 2003 to 2009, indicating significant economic growth and development during this period. Between 2009 and 2010, there was a slight drop; but after 2010, the GDP continued to grow continuously until 2022. The per capita GDP continued to rise steadily throughout the 2010s, with some fluctuations. A particularly significant increase from 2013 to 2015 reflects strong economic growth during those years. In the early 2020s, despite the global economic challenges posed by the COVID-2019 pandemic, Ethiopia's per capita GDP grew and surpassed $900 in 2020 and more than $1,000 by 2022 (see Fig. 5.1 for details).

Based on the information in Fig. 5.2, the Multiple R-value indicates how well the independent variable (in this case, Chinese aid to Ethiopia) predicted the dependent variable (per capita GDP, 2000–2022). With an R-value of 0.16504083, the relationship between Chinese infrastructure aid to Ethiopia and it's per capita GDP is weak.

The sign of the R-value indicates the direction of the relationship. A positive value suggests a positive relationship (as one variable increases, the other also tends to increase). In contrast, a negative value suggests a negative relationship (as one variable increases, the other tends to decrease). Since the R-value is positive in this case, it indicates a positive but weak relationship between Chinese infrastructure aid to Ethiopia and its per capita GDP. Also, the multiple R-value of 0.16504083 suggests that approximately 16.5% of the variability in per capita GDP can be explained by Chinese infrastructure aid to Ethiopia. This means other factors not included in the analysis account for the remaining 83.5% of the variability in per capita GDP.

In addition, the Multiple R-value indicates a weak and positive relationship between Chinese infrastructure aid to Ethiopia and its per capita GDP. While there is some relationship between these variables, other factors not included in the analysis might have played a more significant role in determining Ethiopia's per capita GDP. It is imperative to repeat here what was noted earlier in this book that correlation does not imply causation and, thus, further study is needed to

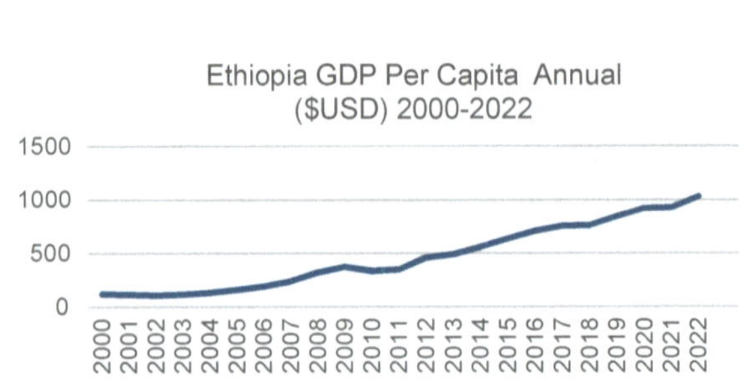

Fig. 5.1 Ethiopia's per capita GDP in US dollars, 2000–2022. Self-generated by the Author Using Data Obtained from the World Bank (2024)

SUMMARY OUTPUT

Regression Statistics	
Multiple R	0.165040826
R Square	0.027238474
Adjusted R Square	-0.019083503
Standard Error	305.0840625
Observations	23

ANOVA

	df	*SS*	*MS*	*F*	*Significance F*
Regression	1	54731.16954	54731.16954	0.58802486	0.4517192
Residual	21	1954601.989	93076.28518		
Total	22	2009333.158			

	Coefficients	*Standard Error*	*t Stat*	*P-value*	*Lower 95%*
Intercept	429.1984467	77.23922374	5.556742105	1.63038E-05	268.5706877
X Variable 1	2.50147E-08	3.2621E-08	0.76682779	0.4517192	-4.28244E-08

Fig. 5.2 Regression output Chinese infrastructure aid to Ethiopia, 2000–2022. *Source* Self-generated by the Author Using Data from https://www.bu.edu/gdp/chinese-loans-to-africa-database (2024) and aiddata.org (2023)

understand the nature and direction of the relationship between Chinese aid and the per capita GDP of Ethiopia.

Furthermore, the R-Square value of 0.027238474 means that approximately 2.72% of the variability in per capita GDP can be explained by Chinese infrastructure aid to Ethiopia. The remaining percentage of variance (100%–2.72% = 97.28%) is not explained by the model and may be due to other factors or variables not included in the analysis. As mentioned earlier in this book, a low R-Square value suggests that a model does not fit the data well. While a small proportion of the variability in per capita GDP is explained by Chinese aid to Ethiopia, much of the variability is attributed to other factors not included in the model.

Moreover, the R-Square value suggests that Chinese infrastructure aid to Ethiopia alone explains a small fraction (2.72%) of the variability in per capita GDP. This implies that other factors, such as domestic policies, global economic conditions, and other aid or investments, play a more substantial role in determining Ethiopia's per capita GDP. In essence, even though there is a relationship between Chinese aid and Ethiopia's per capita GDP, it does not mean that Chinese aid directly causes changes in the per capita GDP.

In terms of the Significance F, it indicates that there might not be a statistically significant linear relationship between Chinese infrastructure aid to Ethiopia and per capita GDP based on the model. Given the non-Significance F-test, the model, as it stands, does not provide strong evidence that Chinese infrastructure aid to Ethiopia has a significant impact on per capita GDP when considering all the data points. A Significance F value of 0.4517192 suggests that the regression model,

SUMMARY OUTPUT

Regression Statistics	
Multiple R	0.963471547
R Square	0.928277422
Adjusted R Square	0.924862061
Standard Error	82.84079804
Observations	23

ANOVA

	df	*SS*	*MS*	*F*	*Significance F*
Regression	1	1865218.604	1865218.604	271.7948294	1.71697E-13
Residual	21	144114.5542	6862.59782		
Total	22	2009333.158			

	Coefficients	*Standard Error*	*t Stat*	*P-value*	*Lower 95%*
Intercept	204.2220003	23.33154839	8.753041028	1.89045E-08	155.7013893
X Variable 1	2.65478E-07	1.61031E-08	16.48620118	1.71697E-13	2.3199E-07

Fig. 5.3 Chinese Foreign Direct Investment to Ethiopia Regression Output, 2000–2022. *Source* Self-generated by the Author Using Data from https://www.bu.edu/gdp/chinese-loans-to-africa-database/ (2024) and aiddata.org (2023)

which includes Chinese infrastructure aid to Ethiopia as a predictor of per capita GDP, is not statistically significant at the conventional 0.05 significance level. This indicates that the model might not represent the best relationship between Chinese aid and per capita GDP in Ethiopia or that the relationship could be more linear. Further investigation or additional years may be necessary to understand better the relationship between GDP and Chinese infrastructure aid to Ethiopia. Interpreting this result as evidence of no relationship might mean that the relationship is not linear or that other variables not included in the model could influence per capita GDP (see Fig. 5.3 for the results).

In reviewing the regression output in Fig. 5.3, Chinese foreign FDI to Ethiopia as the independent variable and per capita GDP as the dependent variable, the regression coefficient of 0.96347155 suggests a strong and positive correlation between Chinese FDI to Ethiopia and per capita GDP. Approximately 96.35% of the variability in per capita GDP can be explained by Chinese FDI to Ethiopia. The high Multiple R indicates a strong linear relationship between the two variables. This implies that as Chinese FDI increases, Ethiopia's per capita GDP also tends to increase. The multiple R value of 0.96347155 suggests a strong and positive linear relationship between Chinese FDI to Ethiopia and its per capita GDP. This indicates that Chinese FDI is a significant predictor of per capita GDP in Ethiopia based on this model.

The R-Square value of 0.92827742 indicates that approximately 92.83% of the variability in the per capita GDP can be explained by Chinese FDI to Ethiopia. The strong R-Square value also suggests that Chinese FDI to Ethiopia strongly predicts per capita GDP. The high R-Square also indicates that the model fits the data very well, thereby capturing a large portion of the variability in per capita GDP based on Chinese FDI to Ethiopia. According to the model, the R-Square value suggests that Chinese FDI to Ethiopia is a highly influential factor in explaining variations in per capita GDP in Ethiopia. While the R-Square indicates a strong relationship, it does not, however, imply causation. Other factors or potential reverse causality might be influencing the observed relationship. The R-Square value suggests that Chinese FDI to Ethiopia is a highly significant predictor of per capita GDP in Ethiopia vis-à-vis the model. Based on this predictor, the model explains approximately 92.83% of the variability in the per capita GDP.

The Significance *F* value of 0.0000000000001717 is much smaller than the conventional significance level of 0.05 (or 5%). This suggests that the model is statistically significant. Based on this information, we can reject the null hypothesis. The low significance *F* value also indicates that the model fits the data well and explains significant variability in the dependent variable (per capita GDP) based on the independent variable (Chinese FDI to Ethiopia). Given this result, the small P-Value further supports the idea that Chinese FDI to Ethiopia strongly predicts per capita GDP. The low Significance *F* value provides strong evidence that Chinese FDI to Ethiopia is a significant predictor of per capita GDP in Ethiopia. As aforementioned for previous models, significance does not imply causation; thus, other variables might have influenced the relationship between Chinese FDI and per capita GDP or be bi-directional. The Significance *F* value of 0.0000000000001717 strongly indicates that the relationship between Chinese FDI to Ethiopia and per capita GDP is statistically significant. This strengthens the validity of the findings and suggests that Chinese FDI is a crucial factor in predicting per capita GDP in Ethiopia based on the available data.

Essentially, the preceding analysis underscores the significant role of Chinese FDI in shaping Ethiopia's economic landscape, specifically its per capita GDP. The remarkably low significance *F* value highlights the statistical relevance of Chinese FDI as a predictor of Ethiopia's per capita GDP. While these findings are robust and indicative of a strong relationship, it is important to approach them cautiously by recognizing that correlation does not necessarily imply causation. Nevertheless, the results suggest that Chinese investment plays a critical role in Ethiopia's economic development, thereby emphasizing the importance of fostering and maintaining such foreign partnerships for sustained economic growth.

5.3 Qualitative Analysis

It is important to not only review the quantitative data but also the qualitative data to better understand the social impact Chinese infrastructure aid has had on the Ethiopian economy. Two projects are assessed. These projects are the Addis Ababa–Adama Expressway which is a significant infrastructure project in Ethiopia and Africa that reflects the country's commitment to enhancing its road networks to support its growing economy (ICS Global, 2015). According to China, the expressway is the country's first Chinese-built toll road and has garnered praise from the government for its economic impact since its launch. Managed by the Ethiopian Toll Roads Enterprise (ETRE), the expressway has facilitated the travel of over 30 million vehicles and generated approximately one billion Ethiopian birr (about 35 million United States dollars) in revenue. In the 2018 fiscal year alone, the road collected 245 million Ethiopian birr, with expectations to serve 8.8 million vehicles and earn 266 million Ethiopian birr that year. This infrastructure project was partly funded by China's Export–Import Bank and constructed by China Communications Construction Company. This road replaced an outdated one between Addis Ababa and Adama which was overburdened with over 16,000 vehicles daily (Xinhua, 2019).

Building on the success of the expressway, Ethiopia continues to invest in toll road infrastructure. The Ethiopian Roads Authority (ERA) has inaugurated a 220-km toll road linking Dire Dawa and Dewele constructed by the Chinese firm CGC Overseas Construction Group Ltd. This new road, financed 85% by China's Export–Import Bank and 15% by the Ethiopian government, aims to bolster Ethiopia's trade with Djibouti. The latter country handles about 95% of Ethiopia's import–export trade, making the new toll road a crucial asset in enhancing trade facilitation and economic growth for the country (Xinhua, 2023).

5.4 Analysis of Ethiopian Newspapers

According to Kidanemariam Alula, from *The Reporter*, article titled "Assessing Economic and Environmental Impacts of road pricing in Ethiopia." Ethiopia introduced toll roads like the Addis-Adama Expressway, Dire Dawa-Dewele, and Modjo-Batu Expressway, with the aim to balance economic and environmental impacts. These toll roads, strategically located in high-volume transportation areas, reduce travel time and congestion and benefit individuals and businesses. By enhancing transportation efficiency, businesses can reduce their operational costs, increase productivity, and improve domestic and international competitiveness. Additionally, improved transportation links help to facilitate trade, stimulate investment, and boost economic growth by connecting key economic centers and facilitating the movement of goods and services. Nevertheless, road pricing policies can disproportionately affect low-income individuals and businesses due to increased transportation costs (Kidanemariam Alula, 2023). This is important to understand in that while the toll roads generate revenue for maintaining and expanding current infrastructure, the roads can also impose additional costs on road users, particularly low-income individuals and small businesses. The increased transportation costs could lead to higher prices for goods and services, potentially impacting consumer spending and overall economic activity. Moreover, these policies may disproportionately affect low-income individuals who rely on their cars for transportation and cannot easily afford the additional costs, which could lead to the inability of low-income households to not be able to make it to their places of employment and potentially exacerbating income inequality.

5.5 Chapter Summary

The chapter has comprehensively examined the impact of Chinese infrastructure development aid on Ethiopia's economic growth within the broader context of China-Ethiopia relations. Beginning with a historical backdrop dating back to the 1960s, it traces the evolution of diplomatic ties and highlights the shift toward strategic economic cooperation despite Cold War tensions. The chapter employed quantitative and qualitative analyses to assess the effects of Chinese aid on Ethiopia's per capita GDP trends from 2000 to 2022 and reveal periods of growth and fluctuations that underscored significant economic development despite challenges and global setbacks such as the COVID-2019 pandemic.

The quantitative findings on Chinese infrastructure aid suggested a modest and positive relationship with Ethiopia's per capita GDP with a multiple R-value indicating that about 16.5% of the variability in the per capita GDP could be attributed to the aid. Nevertheless, the low R-Square and non-Significance *F* value indicated that other factors were more substantial in determining economic outcomes. In contrast, the analysis of Chinese FDI in Ethiopia showed a robust correlation with per capita GDP and explained approximately 96.35% of its variability. This funding highlighted FDI's significant role in Ethiopia's economic growth, supported by a strong R-Square value and a Significance *F* value.

Qualitatively, the social impact analysis focused on the Addis Ababa-Adama Expressway and the Dire Dawa-Dewele toll road. These projects have enhanced transportation efficiency, reduced congestion, and stimulated economic activity by connecting vital economic centers. Nevertheless, they also posed challenges such as increased transportation costs, potentially impacting low-income individuals and small businesses disproportionately and exacerbating income inequality. Addressing these socioeconomic implications is crucial for ensuring equitable benefits from infrastructure development while fostering sustainable economic growth in Ethiopia.

References

AidData. (2023). *Global Chinese Development Finance Dataset, Version 3.0.* 2023. Retrieved July 6, 2024, from https://www.aiddata.org/data/aiddatas-global-chinese-development-finance-dataset-version-3-0

Bilate, G. T., & Zou, X. (2021). 50-Year China-Ethiopia Diplomatic Relations: Achievements and Challenges. *Journal of African Foreign Affairs, 8*(1), 77–96. https://doi.org/10.31920/2056-5658/2021/v8n1a4

Boston University Global Development Policy Center. (2024). *Chinese Loans to Africa Database.* Retrieved from http://bu.edu/gdp/chinese-loans-to-africa-database

ICS Global. (2015). *Addis Ababa-Adama Expressway.* 2015. Retrieved July 6, 2024. https://www.icsglobal.com/addis-ababa-adama-expressway.html

Kidanemariam Alula. (2023). Assessing Economic and Environmental Impacts of Road Pricing in Ethiopia. *The Reporter,* October 21, 2023. Date Retrieved May 15, 2024, from https://www.thereporterethiopia.com/37003/

Malancha, C. (2016). Ethiopia–China Economic Relations: A Classic Win–Win Situation? *World Review of Political Economy*, *7*(2), 226–248. https://doi.org/10.13169/worlrevipoliecon.7.2.0226

Sureiman, Onchiri, and Callen Moraa Mangera. "F-test of Overall Significance in Regression Analysis Simplified." Journal of the Practice of Cardiovascular Sciences 6 (2020): 116. https://doi.org/10.4103/jpcs.jpcs_18_20

World Bank. (2024). *GDP per capita (current US$)—Ethiopia.* Retrieved May 12, 2024. https://data.worldbank.org/indicator/NY.GDP.PCAP.CD?end=2022&locations=ET&start=2000

Xinhua. (2019, June 21). News analysis: Chinese-built toll road wins acclaim for Ethiopia's economic achievements. Xinhuanet. Retrieved July 6, 2024, from https://www.xinhuanet.com/english/2019-06/21/c_138162531.htm

Xinhua. (2023). *Chinese-built Ethiopia-Djibouti railway wins acclaim for boosting integration on 5th anniversary.* Xinhuanet, March 11, 2023. Retrieved July 6, 2024. http://www.xinhuanet.com/english/201906/21/c_138162531.htm#:~:text=Some%20five%20years%20since%20the,its%20contribution%20to%20the%20economy

Theoretical Framework

6

In this chapter, we explore a range of key concepts fundamental to understanding the dynamics of global development and economic theory. These concepts, including Global North and Global South, help frame the geopolitical and economic distinctions between developed and developing regions. The chapter delves into various theoretical frameworks such as Knowledge-Based Economy, Infrastructure-Based Economic Theory, and Social Infrastructure Development Theory, which provide insights into how economics evolve and develop. Additionally, we examine models like the South-South Model and African Renaissance Theory, which emphasize alternative paths to development tailored to the Global South. The chapter also covers Modernization Theory, Classical Dependency Theory, and the perspectives of Neoclassical Theorists, offering a comprehensive view of different economic and social development strategies. Finally, concepts like Alternative Hypothesis and National Development Plan are discussed to highlight the methodological and policy-oriented approaches used in assessing and planning national growth. These definitions, adapted from multiple sources cited throughout this text, provide a foundational understanding of the complex interactions that shape global development. The definitions are as follows:

1. Infrastructure-Based Economic Theory—Argues that a large portion of a country's resources should be geared toward infrastructure development to promote long-term development.
2. Modernization Theory—International factors are the causes for underdevelopment in the Global South countries, dependency theorists argued that there are international factors and the Global South's dependence on the dominant great powers that affect development.
3. Social Infrastructure Development Theory—Emphasizes the importance of human development indicators in driving economic growth. It underscores the

J. Guest, *China's Infrastructure Aid and Investment*, African Studies and Research Forum Series, https://doi.org/10.1007/978-3-032-11964-3_6

significance of education and healthcare in fostering economic development. By investing in education and healthcare, countries can improve the well-being and productivity of their citizens, leading to overall economic progress.

4. Global South—See definition in Chapter 1.
5. Global North—See definition in Chapter 1.
6. South-South Model—cooperation within the countries of the Global South to work together to promote their political and economic development.
7. Periphery—The countries that are less developed than the countries on the semi-periphery. Nigeria, Kenya, and Ethiopia are considered periphery countries.
8. Classical Dependency Theory—Argues that wealthy countries have taken quality materials from poor countries, such as minerals and metals needed to produce automobiles and weapons. In addition, many agricultural products, such as coffee, tea, sugar, and cocoa, have been exported to wealthy countries and processed there.
9. Neoclassical Theorists—Argue that strong trade and investment between the North and South countries should lead to positive economic growth for both regions.
10. Knowledge-Based Economy—Emphasizes the importance of knowledge and technology as being the major engine for economic growth. KBE are economies that are "based on the production, distribution and use of knowledge and information."
11. African Renaissance Theory—Theory highlights the importance of community-based solutions and reliance on local resources for development. This theory also aims to incorporate Africans into the development process.
12. Alternative Hypothesis—At least one coefficient is not equal to zero (the model has explanatory power, or there is a linear relationship between the variables in the model).
13. National Development Plan—The National Development Plan 2021–2025 is a detailed plan created to boost the economy, improve social aspects, and enhance infrastructure. It aims to tackle challenges and maximize Nigeria's strengths in various areas. It aims to create a blueprint for upgrading Nigeria's infrastructure to a well-integrated, multi-modal transportation system that is economically efficient, socially equitable, and environmentally sustainable.

Duly, this chapter first presents the theoretical framework and research methodology used to guide the analysis. There needs to be more than just the discussions of the theoretical framework and research methodology to stand as independent chapters. The two sections are closely related, as the study is grounded upon both. Each aspect is discussed separately to ensure clarity.

This section covers alternative development theories, including Infrastructure-Based Economic Theory, Modernization Theory, and Social Infrastructure Development Theory, and explaining their relevance to this study. Additionally, it provides contending reviews of Dependency Theory to highlight debates among theorists regarding its relevance.

The Dependency Theory is being examined as it relates to Chinese infrastructure aid and FDI to Nigeria, Kenya, and Ethiopia. Dependency is as theorists say is a result of exploitation of the Global South by the Global North which results in the subordination of the Global South to the Global North. In addition, it results into vulnerabilities of the Global South to the Global North business cycles (Kegley & Blanton, 2010). **This study highlights the theory as it relates to South-South cooperation. In reviewing much of the literature on the theory, the common theme that resonates is that the world system favors the rich countries at the expense of the poor countries.**

The theoretical framework of this study is based mostly on Dependency Theory and its relevance to Chinese infrastructure development aid to Nigeria, Kenya, and Ethiopia by focusing on its impact on economic development. The disparity in development between the Global North and Global South has prompted various explanations from theorists. Some theorists attribute development gaps to internal factors, while others emphasize international influences.

According to Charles Kegley and Shannon Blanton (2010), modernization theorists emerged in the early post-World War II era and argued that internal characteristics are crucial for development in Global South countries. They believed that wealthy countries should supply the "missing components" of development through capital investment, foreign aid, or foreign direct investment.

Modernization theorists such as Walt W. Rostow (1960) posited that with sufficient capital accumulation, economic growth would generate widespread benefits. Rostow in his *The Stages of Economic Growth: A Non-Communist Manifesto* (1960) outlined five stages of economic development: (1) traditional society, (2) preconditions for take-off, (3) take-off, (4) drive to maturity, and (5) mass consumption. He suggested that Global South countries would follow a similar path to the Global North. Rostow's theory, however, faced criticism for its inability to replicate success in Latin America or Africa South of the Sahara and for neglecting the importance of external influences in development.

While modernization theorists argued that international factors are the causes for underdevelopment in the Global South, dependency theorists argued that there are international factors and the Global South's dependence on the dominant great powers that affect development (Kegley & Blanton, 2010).

There is no unified definition of Dependency Theory among its proponents. According to Theotonio Dos Santos, dependence is defined as "a condition where the world economy favors one country at the expense of the others" (1970, pp. 231–233). The author added that there are three kinds of dependencies that occur in the following sequence: (1) colonial dependency with the colonial powers, (2) financial-industrial dependence which is "the domination of big capital in the hegemonic centers, and its expansion abroad through investment in the production of raw materials and agricultural products for consumption in the hegemonic centers," and (3) technological-industrial dependence which is where technology monopolizes through multinational corporations (Dos Santos, 1970, pp. 231–233).

For Raul Prebisch in his *Economic Development of Latin America and Its Principal* Problems (Alusine et al., 2008), dependency is a condition whereby a relationship between two states evolve over time at the advantage of the dominant state and the expense of the other (Alusine et al., 2008).

Essentially, Dependency Theory suggests that the poorer states are powerless and are subjected to the policies that work in favor of the richer and more powerful states. I therefore posit that although Dependency Theory highlights the relationship between Global North and Global South countries, also called the North-South, it can also be applied to the Global South or South-South relationships. A major milestone for South-South cooperation began with the Bandung Conference of 1955. This conference marked a celebratory time when the Global South countries in attendance were no longer a part of the European colonies.

In his article titled "Deeping South-South Dependency? China's Cooperative Rhetoric and Economic Engagement in Zambia," William Mangimela pointed out that the rise of China as a major economic power has facilitated practical South-South cooperation and provided developing countries with new opportunities for economic growth. Unlike earlier aspirations for the struggle against imperialism during the League of Nations (which lasted from 1920 to 1946) until the Bandung Conference, today's South-South cooperation avoided establishing dependency within the Global South, unlike the historical dependency on the West (Guest, 2017; Mangimela, 2015).

South-South cooperation is rooted in the idea that countries within the Global South can collaborate to advance their collective political and economic development. This model of partnership is founded on core principles, including respect for national sovereignty, national ownership, equality among states, non-interference in internal affairs, and mutual benefit (United Nations, "United Nations Special Unit for South-South Cooperation," United Nations Development Programme 2024). As previously mentioned, this study applies the Dependency Theory to assess whether China's approach to foreign aid aligns with the guiding principles of South-South cooperation—particularly in instances where aid is exchanged for access to natural resources—to foster mutually beneficial outcomes.

The dependency paradigm emerged in response to two significant developments: the rise of neo-Marxist thought and critical analyses of development patterns in Latin America. Neo-Marxism emphasized the persistent underdevelopment of the Global South and critiqued the structural inequalities in the global economic system. Simultaneously, the Latin American "dependencia" school gained traction during the economic downturn of the 1930s, focusing on the unique developmental challenges facing Latin American countries (Alusine et al. 2008). Much of the foundational thinking behind Dependency Theory was cultivated within the United Nations Economic Commission for Latin America and the Caribbean (ECLAC), which served as a key institution for shaping the ideas of early dependency theorists (Alusine et al., 2008). A prominent voice in this discourse, Argentine economist Raúl Prebisch, conceptualized the world economy as divided between an industrialized core and a resource-dependent periphery. He asserted that the economic growth of wealthy nations often came at the expense of

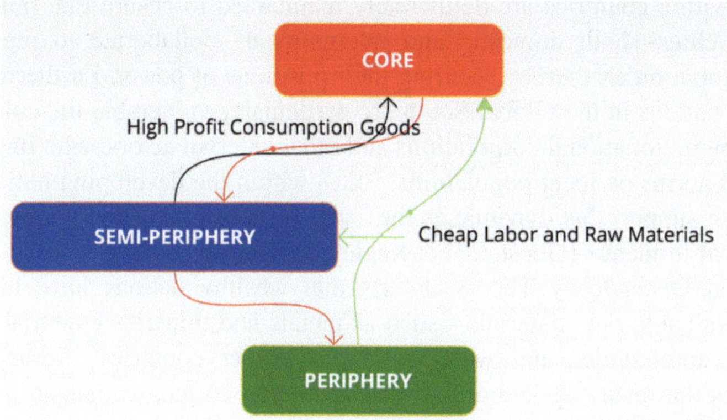

Fig. 6.1 Dependency Theory diagram. Self-generated by author based on Wallerstein's World System Theory Model based on text on Immanuel Wallerstein's World System Theory (Cosma, 2010; Guest, 2017). *Source* Self-generated by the Author based on the Literature on Dependency Theory

poorer countries due to unequal terms of trade between industrial and agricultural products—a dynamic particularly evident in North–South relations (Alusine et al., 2008; Guest, 2017).

Dependency theorists argue that a small group of industrialized nations sustains their prosperity by exploiting the resources and labor of less developed countries, often to the detriment of the latter's well-being. According to this perspective, developing nations resemble former colonial territories, as they continue to transfer wealth to developed countries while receiving little in return (Alusine et al., 2008). At its core, Dependency Theory maintains that powerful nations preserve this imbalance by imposing mechanisms such as economic sanctions or conditional trade agreements, often enforced through institutions like the International Monetary Fund and the World Bank (Guest, 2017).

Figure 6.1 represents the core concepts of Dependency Theory by illustrating how resources flow from less developed nations to more affluent states. The "core" or central zone of this global system includes wealthy, industrialized countries such as the United States, the United Kingdom, and France. In contrast, nations like Nigeria, Kenya, and Ethiopia are categorized as part of the "periphery," characterized by their reliance on resource extraction and low-cost labor. The "semi-periphery" comprises developing nations that have achieved a certain level of economic growth and are accumulating increasing wealth—examples include India, South Africa, Brazil, and China. According to the theory, core nations maintain their dominance through control of capital-intensive industries, technological advancements, and global markets, while peripheral nations remain structurally dependent on them (Guest, 2017).

According to dependency theorists, the structure of the current global system actively hinders economic advancement in developing nations while reinforcing the dominance of wealthier states. These scholars also contend that internal class divisions within countries are deliberately maintained to ensure that political and economic elites—both domestic and international—collaborate to preserve the existing global order, thereby securing their positions of power. Furthermore, they argue that nations in the Global South are particularly vulnerable to "cultural penetration" by multinational corporations and other external actors, who impose their values and norms on local populations. Elites within the developing nations themselves often support this dynamic as they seek to accumulate and retain economic and political influence (Guest, 2017; Kegley & Blanton, 2009–2010).

Classical Dependency Theory asserts that wealthy nations have historically extracted valuable raw materials—such as metals and minerals essential for manufacturing automobiles and weapons—from poorer countries. Additionally, it emphasizes that many agricultural goods, including coffee, tea, sugar, and cocoa, are cultivated in developing nations but are exported and processed in wealthier countries, thereby limiting the economic benefits for the producers (Boundless Sociology, 2014). This dynamic is powerfully illustrated in Adam Hochschild's King Leopold's Ghost: A Story of Greed, Terror, and Heroism in Colonial Africa (1998), which recounts how the King of Belgium exploited the Democratic Republic of the Congo for its abundant natural resources, including rubber and ivory (Guest, 2017).

Building on this historical context, modern aid dynamics reflect a continuation of the same structural imbalances outlined by classical dependency theory. While contemporary foreign aid, particularly infrastructure development aid from countries like China, is framed as mutually beneficial and rooted in South-South cooperation, the patterns often resemble earlier extractive relationships. Much like the historical export of unprocessed agricultural goods and natural resources, many developing nations today still send raw materials abroad while relying on external actors for industrial processing and technological advancement. This can limit the long-term economic transformation of aid-receiving countries, reinforcing their dependent status. For instance, in Nigeria, Kenya, and Ethiopia, although Chinese infrastructure aid has contributed to improvements in transportation and trade logistics, questions remain about whether these projects primarily serve external interests, such as facilitating resource extraction, expanding export routes, or empowering local industries. As with the example from King Leopold's Ghost, the concern is not just about the resources themselves but about who ultimately benefits from their extraction and how power dynamics are preserved through economic relationships that appear cooperative on the surface.

Advocates of Modern Dependency Theory contend that many low-income countries today remain economically constrained by heavy debt burdens, which hinder their ability to pursue meaningful development. These scholars argue that powerful nations and global financial institutions—such as the World Bank and the International Monetary Fund—issue loans that, rather than fostering growth, exacerbate the economic struggles of developing nations. As a result, these countries prioritize debt repayment over investments in infrastructure, health, education, or other developmental needs. Furthermore, theorists assert that providing substantial aid alone is insufficient to combat poverty; instead, they emphasize that meaningful debt relief offers a more viable path toward sustainable development (Boundless Sociology, 2014; Guest, 2017).

According to James C. W. Ahiakpor of the article titled "The Success and failure of dependency theory: the experience of Ghana." Dependency theory contends that global trade and monetary systems, combined with the cultural influences of developed nations, disadvantage less developed countries (LDCs). The theory suggests that LDCs are pushed into producing raw materials and labor-intensive products for export at low prices, while developed countries export capital- and skill-intensive goods at much higher prices. This results in an "unequal exchange" and creates unfavorable trade conditions for LDCs (Ahiakpor, 1985). Kegley, Jr. and Shannon contrast Dependency Theory with Classical Theory, in that Classical Theory argues that the causes of underdevelopment are from internal factors within the states, whereas Dependency Theory argues that international factors have an impact upon development and the Global South's dependence on the major powers (Kegley, Jr. and Shannon, 2009–2010).

Vincent H. Shie and Craig D. Meer, in their 2010 article "The Rise of Knowledge in Dependency Theory: The Experience of India and Taiwan," argue that the development and progress of individual nations are significantly shaped by the broader international system. As a result, they argue that Dependency Theory falls short in explaining the rise of newly industrialized countries. Their analysis suggests that with the advancement of various Global South nations in multiple areas of development, economic growth has become increasingly attainable, and the historical constraints that once hindered their progress are no longer as dominant (Guest, 2017).

During the 1980s and 1990s, the influence of Dependency Theory began to decline as several newly industrializing countries experienced significant economic growth. This development challenged the theory's core assumptions and cast doubt on its ability to explain the phenomenon of industrialization in what was traditionally considered the "Third World" (Shie & Meer, 2010). Classical dependency theorists, in effect, overlooked the potential for economic advancement in developing nations. However, despite its decline in popularity during that period, I contend in this book—and previously in my dissertation—that Dependency Theory remains relevant, especially as the global economy transitions toward a knowledge-based economy (KBE). According to the Organization for Economic Co-Operation and Development (OECD), a KBE is driven primarily by the production, distribution, and application of knowledge and information, which are now seen as central engines of economic growth (Guest, 2017; OECD, 1996).

What follows is a discussion of alternative development theories to determine their relevance to Chinese infrastructure development aid to Nigeria, Kenya, and Ethiopia and their applicability to this study. To begin with, Infrastructure-based Economic Development Theory, also called infrastructure-driven development, argues that a large portion of a country's resources should be geared toward infrastructure development in order to promote long-term development. The Aschauer's Model, for instance, argues that there is a positive and statistically significant correlation between investment in infrastructure and economic growth. The model also argues that investment in infrastructure not only improves quality of life but also positively impacts labor productivity (Aschauer, 1990; Guest, 2017). This theory supports the claim that investment in infrastructure—i.e. Chinese aid to Nigeria, Kenya, and Ethiopia for infrastructure projects promotes economic growth. These propositions were tested in the regression analyses conducted in preceding chapters.

Some scholars critical of Dependency Theory argue that no framework can fully address Africa's developmental challenges without recognizing the socio-historical impact of Western European expansion and colonial rule (Frank, 1981). J. Mantunhu, for example, contends that the West has turned Africa into a dumping ground for waste and surplus labor and a marketplace where trade terms favor developed countries. He highlights that Africa remains positioned as a supplier of raw materials, while industrialized nations dominate the export of finished goods (Matunhu, 2011, pp. 65–72). Mantunhu also critiques Dependency Theory for failing to address development models imposed by external actors. In response, he proposes the **African Renaissance Theory**, which is rooted in African cultural values and community-based solutions (Guest, 2017).

The African Renaissance Theory, as proposed by Mantunhu, offers an alternative by advocating for micro-level development tailored to local needs. It encourages nations to focus on poverty reduction through community-driven initiatives, build capacity using local resources, and ensure Africans play an active role in shaping and implementing development strategies (Matunhu, 2011, pp. 65–72). In practice, this could mean strengthening local entrepreneurship, investing in rural agriculture, and decentralizing development planning to reflect indigenous knowledge and priorities in Nigeria, Kenya, and Ethiopia (Guest, 2017).

In addition to the Infrastructure-based Economic Development Theory and the African Renaissance Theory, the Social Infrastructure Development Theory emphasizes the importance of human development indicators in driving economic growth. It underscores the significance of the development of assets that support social services such as education and healthcare (New Zealand Social Infrastructure fund, 2009). Strategic investments in education and healthcare not only enhance the immediate well-being of a population but also contribute significantly to long-term economic productivity. A healthier, more educated workforce is more capable of innovation, adaptation, and sustained output, which directly supports national development goals. The Social Infrastructure Development Theory underscores this interdependence between human capital development and economic growth. Without corresponding advancements in health and education, the benefits of large-scale physical infrastructure projects may be short-lived or inequitably distributed.

As this chapter presents the theoretical framework and research methodology guiding this study, Dependency Theory forms the basis of this framework for analyzing Chinese infrastructure development aid and foreign direct investment to Nigeria, Kenya, and Ethiopia and its effects on economic growth. Dependency theorists argue that the current global system hinders developing countries' economic development and benefits wealthy nations while maintaining class divisions within countries. They highlight how multinational corporations and external forces impose their values on the Global South, supported by local elites to maintain their wealth and power. Classical Dependency Theory focuses on resource exploitation by wealthy nations. At the same time, Modern Dependency Theory emphasizes the burden of debt on poor countries and suggests debt relief as a more effective solution than aid. Neoclassical theorists, however, advocate for strong trade and investment to foster mutual economic growth. Critics of Dependency Theory point to the emergence of newly industrialized countries and the importance of understanding the socio-historical context of Western colonization. Alternative theories such as Infrastructure-based Economic Development Theory, African Renaissance Theory, and Social Infrastructure Development Theory were briefly explored for their relevance to Chinese infrastructure aid and potential applicability to this study. I will examine the dependency relationship further by utilizing a regression equation as illustrated in the following paragraphs.

This study hypothesizes that a dependency relationship exists between Chinese infrastructure development aid and foreign direct investment to Nigeria and Ethiopia in that when Chinese infrastructure aid or foreign direct investment is excluded from the regression equation, per capita GDP decreases. It is further hypothesized, however, that a dependency relationship does not exist with Kenya.

A mixed methodology is used to test these hypotheses. The quantitative portion analyzes Nigeria, Kenya, and Ethiopia's overall gross GDPs and how they are impacted by Chinese infrastructure development aid and FDI. In addition to Chinese infrastructure development aid, other variables are included in the regression equation to determine how Chinese infrastructure development aid interacts with the different variables. The other variables included in the study are aid from China, the United Kingdom, the United States, Germany, France, the International Development Association (IDA), the African Development Bank, Japan, the Development Assistance Committee (DAC), consumption, FDI, expenditures, exports, and imports.

6.1 Infrastructure Aid

A regression study was conducted to determine if a dependency relationship exists between Chinese infrastructure development aid and FDI to Nigeria, Kenya, and Ethiopia. A variable, ChineseInfrastructureAid, was added to the regression equation along with other variables that represent infrastructure development aid from different countries to determine the effect Chinese aid has on per capita GDP. To determine if a dependency relationship exists, the ChineseInfrastructureAid variable was excluded from the regression equation to see if the GDPs for Nigeria, Kenya, and Ethiopia increased or decreased. The regression equations that measure dependency are as follows:

GDPpc = per capita GDP of Nigeria

Y is the impact on Nigeria (per capita GDP)
X_1 is Chinese infrastructure aid
X_2 is United States infrastructure aid
X_3 is France infrastructure aid
X_4 is United Kingdom infrastructure aid
X_5 is AFDB infrastructure aid

$$Y = \beta_0 + \beta_1 X_1 + \beta_2 X_2 + \beta_3 X_3 + \beta_4 X_4 + \beta_5 X_5 + \varepsilon$$

$$\text{Dependency Equation: } Y = Y = \beta_0 + \cancel{\beta_1} X_1 + \beta_2 X_2 + \beta_3 X_3 + \beta_4 X_4 + \beta_5 X_5 \ + \varepsilon$$

X_1 will be removed from the regression equation. If per capita GDP for Nigeria decreases as a result of this removal, a dependency relationship exists between Chinese infrastructure development aid and Nigeria's per capita GDP from 2000 to 2022, where

β_0 is the intercept term
$\beta_1$is the coefficient for Chinese infrastructure aid
$\beta_2$is the coefficient for United States infrastructure aid
β_3 is the coefficient for France infrastructure aid
β_4 is the coefficient for United Kingdom infrastructure aid
β_5 is the coefficient for AFDB infrastructure aid
ε is the error term.

The results from the multiple regression computation are summarized in Fig. 6.2.

Based on the results in Fig. 6.2, a Multiple R of 0.89 indicates a strong and positive linear relationship between the independent variables (infrastructure aid from China, the United States, the UK, France, and AFDB) and the dependent variable (per capita GDP). The Multiple R value suggests that the regression model fits the data well. The independent variables collectively explain much of the variability in the dependent variable. Other variables must be analyzed when examining data to determine whether the quantitative data adequately support the qualitative data. The regression testing is conducted here to determine whether there is a dependency relationship between Chinese infrastructure aid and per capita GDP in Nigeria. For policymakers, this strong correlation underlines the importance of continuing and possibly increasing infrastructure aid from these sources to sustain or improve Nigeria's economic performance. It suggests that such aid is crucial in driving economic growth as measured by per capita GDP.

In terms of the R-Square of 0.79, it means that the independent variables in the model explain 79% of the variance in the dependent variable. The value indicates a good fit of the model to the data. It also suggests that the model does a good job of capturing the relationship between the independent variables and the dependent variable. Nonetheless, it is important to mention that the model is imperfect. Since the value is 0.79, this also means that the independent variables in the model do not

SUMMARY OUTPUT

Regression Statistics	
Multiple R	0.89041148
R Square	0.79283261
Adjusted R Square	0.73190102
Standard Error	8.1287E+10
Observations	23

ANOVA

	df	*SS*	*MS*	*F*	*Significance F*
Regression	5	4.29881E+23	8.59761E+22	13.0118491	2.59889E-05
Residual	17	1.12328E+23	6.60752E+21		
Total	22	5.42208E+23			

	Coefficients	*Standard Error*	*t Stat*	*P-value*	*Lower 95%*	*Upper 95%*	*Lower 95.0%*	*Upper 95.0%*
Intercept	1.0161E+11	36222276781	2.805149141	0.01217275	25186564791	1.78031E+11	25186564791	1.78031E+11
X Variable 1	-21.353022	15.71881494	-1.358437136	0.192079639	-54.51682258	11.81077868	-54.51682258	11.81077868
X Variable 2	428.984101	82.4511025	5.202891022	7.18342E-05	255.0274805	602.9407215	255.0274805	602.9407215
X Variable 3	261.086342	170.120286	1.534716099	0.143254237	-97.83608785	620.0087711	-97.83608785	620.0087711
X Variable 4	-468.63609	254.7393632	-1.83966894	0.083346219	-1006.089171	68.8169824	-1006.089171	68.8169824
X Variable 5	762.42481	670.4343301	1.137210276	0.271226099	-652.0679837	2176.917603	-652.0679837	2176.917603

Fig. 6.2 Multiple Regression Analysis Result (Infrastructure Aid from China, the United States, the UK, France, and AFDB). *Source* Self-generated by the Author from Data Obtained from the World Bank (2024), OECD.org (2024), aiddata.org (2023), and China Africa Research Initiative (2024)

explain 21% of the variance in the dependent variable. This unexplained variance could be due to other factors not included in the model, such as random variation or measurement error.

The Significance F, or P-Value of 0.0000259, means that the overall regression model is statistically significant at the 0.01 level. It is important to explain the difference between the null hypothesis and the alternative hypothesis. The Significance F value (P-Value of 0.0000259) indicates that the combined infrastructure aid from China, the United States, the United Kingdom, France, and the AfDB statistically affects Nigeria's per capita GDP. This underscores the importance of international infrastructure aid in promoting economic growth and development in Nigeria and validates using these aid sources as key predictors in the regression model. The model's strong statistical significance and a high adjusted R-Square value suggest that infrastructure aid is a crucial driver of economic performance. Nevertheless, other factors also contribute to Nigeria's per capita GDP.

For the null hypothesis (H_0), all of the coefficients of the model are equal to zero; thus, the model has no explanatory power, or there is no relationship between the variables. In this case, this hypothesis would mean that the combination of the aid provided by each country in the model is not statistically significant and that a relationship does not exist between the per capita GDP and the aid provided by the countries in the model.

In regard to the alternative hypothesis (H_1), at least one coefficient is not equal to zero; therefore, the model has explanatory power, or there is a linear relationship between the variables in the model. In this case, this hypothesis would mean that the combination of the aid provided by each of the countries included in the model is statistically significant and that a relationship exists between the per capita GDP and the aid provided by the countries in the model. The P-Value of 0.0000259 indicates that the null hypothesis can be rejected as the alternative hypothesis is accepted.

An adjusted R-Square value of 0.73 indicates that the regression model explains 73% of the variance in the dependent variable, which is adjusted for the number of predictors in the model. This result supports the remainder of the results by suggesting a strong and reliable fit with this model, indicating that the independent variables collectively have significant and substantial explanatory power for the dependent variable (GDP). It is apparent that aid collectively aids in improving Nigeria's GDP. While 73% of the variance is explained by infrastructure aid, 27% of the variance remains unexplained by this model. This suggests that other factors also contribute to Nigeria's per capita GDP. These factors could include domestic policies, other forms of foreign aid, private sector investments, and broader economic conditions.

The next step of this analysis involves removing Chinese infrastructure aid from the equation to determine if the statistical significance decreases as a result of its removal. As a result of this removal, the revised regression equation is as follows:

Original Regression equation: $Y = \beta_0 + \beta_1 X_1 + \beta_2 X_2 + \beta_3 X_3 + \beta_4 X_4 + \beta_5 X_5 + \varepsilon$
Dependency Equation: $Y = \beta_0 + \beta_1 X_1 + \beta_2 X_2 + \beta_3 X_3 + \beta_4 X_4 + \beta_5 X_5 + \varepsilon$
Revised Equation: $Y = \beta_0 + \beta_1 X_1 + \beta_2 X_2 + \beta_3 X_3 + \beta_4 X_4 + \varepsilon$

Y is the impact on Nigeria (per capita GDP)
X_1 is United States infrastructure aid
X_2 is France infrastructure aid
X_3 is United Kingdom infrastructure aid
X_4 is AFDB infrastructure aid

where:

β_0 is the intercept term
β_1 is the coefficient for US infrastructure aid
β_2 is the coefficient for France infrastructure aid
β_3 is the coefficient for UK infrastructure aid
β_4 is the coefficient for AFDB infrastructure aid
ε is the error term.

The results yielded after the removal of Chinese infrastructure aid to Nigeria in the regression model appear in Fig. 6.3.

In comparing Figs. 6.2 and 6.3, it can be observed that the Multiple R decreased from 0.89 to about 0.88. This means that after removing Chinese infrastructure aid to Nigeria from the regression equation, there is a slight reduction in the strength of the relationship between the independent variables (US infrastructure aid, UK infrastructure aid, France infrastructure aid, and AfDB infrastructure aid) and the

SUMMARY OUTPUT

Regression Statistics	
Multiple R	0.877692753
R Square	0.770344568
Adjusted R Square	0.719310028
Standard Error	83173548903
Observations	23

ANOVA

	df	SS	MS	F	Significance F
Regression	4	4.17687E+23	1.04422E+23	15.09457247	1.40972E-05
Residual	18	1.24521E+23	6.91784E+21		
Total	22	5.42208E+23			

	Coefficients	Standard Error	t Stat	P-value	Lower 95%	Upper 95%	Lower 95.0%	Upper 95.0%
Intercept	1.04312E+11	37007115325	2.818705145	0.01137131	26563082130	1.8206E+11	2.6563E+10	1.8206E+11
X Variable 1	356.7482054	64.47477765	5.533143633	2.97262E-05	221.291724	492.204687	221.291724	492.204687
X Variable 2	316.5650847	168.9788271	1.873400888	0.077344043	-38.44625739	671.576427	-38.446257	671.576427
X Variable 3	-538.6721737	255.258387	-2.110301565	0.049088735	-1074.950145	-2.3942025	-1074.9501	-2.3942025
X Variable 4	796.2880246	685.522477	1.161578287	0.260578915	-643.9412563	2236.51731	-643.94126	2236.51731

Fig. 6.3 Summary Output Exclusion of Chinese Infrastructure Aid to Nigeria. Self-generated by author from Data obtained from World bank (2024), OECD.org (2024), aiddata.org (2023), and China Africa Research Initiative (2024)

dependent variable (per capita GDP). This result may also indicate that there are stronger predictors of Nigeria's per capita GDP Per from 2000 to 2022.

An R-Square value of 0.77 indicates that approximately 77% of the variance in the per capita GDP can be explained by the independent variables included in the regression model after removing Chinese infrastructure aid to Nigeria. In terms of the P-Value, the very low score of 0.0000141 calls for the rejection of the null hypothesis and concludes that there is a statistically significant relationship between the combined independent variables and Nigeria's per capita GDP.

In addition, for the null hypothesis test, all coefficients of the model are equal to zero, meaning that the model has no explanatory power, or there is no relationship between the variables. In this case, this hypothesis would mean that the combination of the aid provided by each of the countries, excluding China, included in the model is not statistically significant and that a relationship does not exist between the per capita GDP and the aid provided by the countries in the model.

As it pertains to the alternative hypothesis, at least one coefficient is not equal to zero. Thus, the model has explanatory power, or there is a linear relationship between the variables in the model. In this case, this hypothesis would mean that the combination of the aid, excluding China, provided by each of the countries included in the model is statistically significant and that a relationship does exist between the per capita GDP and the aid provided by the countries in the model. Also, a P-Value of 0.0000141 indicates that the null hypothesis can be rejected as the alternative hypothesis is accepted.

Based on the preceding findings, a dependency relationship between Chinese Infrastructure aid to Nigeria and Nigeria's per capita GDP is absent. Also, although the GDP slightly decreased, the slight change in the statistical relationship between the variables and Nigeria's GDP indicates that a dependency relationship does not exist.

In examining whether a dependency relationship exists between Chinese infrastructure aid and per capita GDP in Kenya, the regression equation is as follows:

GDPpc = per capita GDP of Kenya
Y is the impact on Kenya (per capita GDP)
X_1 is AfDB infrastructure aid
X_2 is France infrastructure aid
X_3 is United States infrastructure aid
X_4 is United Kingdom infrastructure aid
X_5 is Chinese infrastructure aid

$$Y = \beta_0 + \beta_1 X_1 + \beta_2 X_2 + \beta_3 X_3 + \beta_4 X_4 + \beta_5 X_5 + \varepsilon$$

$$\text{Dependency Equation: } Y = \beta_0 + \beta_1 X_1 + \beta_2 X_2 + \beta_3 X_3 + \beta_4 X_4 + \beta_5 X_5 + \varepsilon$$

X_5 will be removed from the preceding regression equation. If per capita GDP for Kenya decreases as a result of this removal, a dependency relationship exists between Chinese infrastructure development aid and Kenya's per capita GDP from 2000 to 2022, where

β_0 is the intercept term
β_1 is the coefficient for Chinese infrastructure aid
β_2 is the coefficient for United States infrastructure aid
β_3 is the coefficient for France infrastructure aid
β_4 is the coefficient for United Kingdom infrastructure aid
β_5 is the coefficient for AfDB infrastructure aid
ε is the error term

The results generated after the preceding multiple regression model was tested are summarized in Fig. 6.4.

GDPpc = per capita GDP of Kenya
Y is the impact on Kenya (per capita GDP)
X_1 is Chinese infrastructure aid
X_2 is United States infrastructure aid
X_3 is France infrastructure aid
X_4 is United Kingdom infrastructure aid
X_5 is AfDB infrastructure aid

$$Y = \beta_0 + \beta_1 X_1 + \beta_2 X_2 + \beta_3 X_3 + \beta_4 X_4 + \beta_5 X_5 + \varepsilon$$

SUMMARY OUTPUT

Regression Statistics	
Multiple R	0.947316754
R Square	0.897409032
Adjusted R Square	0.867235218
Standard Error	214.8187403
Observations	23

ANOVA

	df	SS	MS	F	Significance F
Regression	5	6862376.788	1372475.358	29.74131896	7.78463E-08
Residual	17	784500.5499	46147.09117		
Total	22	7646877.338			

	Coefficients	Standard Error	t Stat	P-value	Lower 95%	Upper 95%	Lower 95.0%	Upper 95.0%
Intercept	199.6105664	156.9123853	1.272114792	0.220458864	-131.4456285	530.666761	-131.44563	530.666761
X Variable 1	-5.053512971	1.250360063	-4.041646179	0.000847229	-7.691542109	-2.4154838	-7.6915421	-2.4154838
X Variable 2	0.488292728	1.720365531	0.283830802	0.779967886	-3.141361269	4.11794673	-3.1413613	4.11794673
X Variable 3	2.552466005	0.314383616	8.118953647	2.98371E-07	1.889174555	3.21575746	1.88917455	3.21575746
X Variable 4	-0.291904232	2.049745201	-0.142410009	0.888430361	-4.616488589	4.03268012	-4.6164886	4.03268012
X Variable 5	9.20854E-08	4.62992E-08	1.988920027	0.063051679	-5.59737E-09	1.8977E-07	-5.597E-09	1.8977E-07

Fig. 6.4 Summary of Output Multivariate Analysis Aid to Kenya from China, the United States, France, UK, and AfDB. *Source* Self-generated by the Author Using Data obtained from the World Bank (2024), OECD.org (2024), aiddata.org (2023), and China Africa Research Initiative (2024)

where:

β_0 is the intercept term
β_1 is the coefficient for Chinese infrastructure aid
β_2 is the coefficient for United States infrastructure aid
β_3 is the coefficient for France infrastructure aid
β_4 is the coefficient for United Kingdom infrastructure aid
β_5 is the coefficient for AfDB infrastructure aid
ε is the error term

Based on the results in Fig. 6.4, the Multiple R of 0.95 indicates a strong, positive, and linear relationship between the independent variables and the dependent variable. The Multiple R value suggests that the regression model fits the data well. The independent variables collectively explain much of the variability in the dependent variable. Other variables must be analyzed when examining data to determine whether the quantitative data adequately supports the qualitative data. The regression testing is conducted here to determine whether there is a dependency relationship between Chinese infrastructure aid and Kenya's per capita GDP. For policymakers, this strong correlation underlines the importance of continuing and increasing infrastructure aid from these sources to sustain or improve Kenya's economic performance. It also suggests that such aid is crucial in driving economic growth as measured by per capita GDP.

Vis-à-vis the R-Square value of 0.90, it indicates that the independent variables in the model explain 90% of the variance in the dependent variable. It also reveals a good fit of the model to the data. It in addition suggests that the model does a good job of capturing the relationship between the independent variables and the dependent variable. Nevertheless, it is also important to state that the model is imperfect, as the independent variables in the model do not explain 10% of the variance in the dependent variable. This unexplained variance could be due to other factors not included in the model, such as random variation or measurement error.

The Significance F, or P-Value of 0.0000000778, means that the overall regression model is statistically significant at the 0.01 level. It indicates that the combined infrastructure aid from China, the United States, the United Kingdom, France, and the AfDB statistically affects Kenya's per capita GDP. This underscores the importance of international infrastructure aid in promoting economic growth and development in Kenya and validates using these aid sources as key predictors in the regression model. The model's strong statistical significance and a high adjusted R-Square value suggest that infrastructure aid is a crucial driver of economic performance, albeit other factors also contribute to per capita GDP.

Apropos the null hypothesis, all of the coefficients for the model are equal to zero; as such, the model has no explanatory power, or there is no relationship between the variables. In this instance, this hypothesis would mean that the combination of the aid provided by each country in the model is not statistically significant and that a relationship does not exist between the per capita GDP and the aid provided by the countries.

In regard to the alternative hypothesis, at least one coefficient is not equal to zero; in other words, the model has explanatory power, or there is a linear relationship between the variables in the model. Accordingly, this hypothesis would mean that the combination of the aid provided by each of the countries included in the model is statistically significant and that a relationship exists between the per capita GDP and the aid provided by the countries in the model. A P-Value of 0.0000000778 indicates that the null hypothesis can be rejected as the alternative hypothesis is tenable.

Also, an Adjusted R-Square value of 0.87 indicates that the regression model explains 87% of the variance in the dependent variable, which is adjusted for the number of predictors in the model. This result supports the remainder of the results by suggesting a strong and reliable fit with this model, thereby indicating that the independent variables collectively have significant and substantial explanatory power for the dependent variable (GDP). It is apparent that aid collectively assists in improving Kenya's GDP. While 87% of the variance is explained by infrastructure aid, 13% of the variance remains unexplained by this model. This suggests that other factors also contribute to Kenya's per capita GDP. These factors could include domestic policies, other forms of foreign aid, private sector investments, and broader economic conditions.

The next step of this analysis involves removing Chinese infrastructure aid from the equation to determine if the statistical significance decreases as a result of the removal of the variable from the regression equation. Based on this removal, the revised regression equation is as follows:

Original Regression equation: $Y = \beta_0 + \beta_1 X_1 + \beta_2 X_2 + \beta_3 X_3 + \beta_4 X_4 + \beta_5 X_5 + \varepsilon$
Dependency Equation: $Y = \beta_0 + \beta_1 X_1 + \beta_2 X_2 + \beta_3 X_3 + \beta_4 X_4 + \beta_5 X_5 + \varepsilon$
Revised Equation: $Y = \beta_0 + \beta_1 X_2 + \beta_2 X_2 + \beta_3 X_3 + \beta_4 X_4 + \varepsilon$

Y is the impact on Kenya (per capita GDP)
X_1 is AfDB infrastructure aid
X_2 is France infrastructure aid
X_3 is United States infrastructure aid
X_4 is United Kingdom infrastructure aid

where:

β_0 is the intercept term
β_1 is the coefficient for AfDB infrastructure aid
β_2 is the coefficient for France infrastructure aid
β_3 is the coefficient for United States infrastructure aid
β_4 is the coefficient for United Kingdom infrastructure aid
ε is the error term

The results obtained after the removal of Chinese infrastructure aid to Kenya from the regression model are presented in Fig. 6.5.

Comparing Figs. 6.4 and 6.5, it can be seen that the Multiple R decreased from 0.94 to about 0.93. This means that after removing Chinese infrastructure aid to

SUMMARY OUTPUT

Regression Statistics	
Multiple R	0.93463185
R Square	0.8735367
Adjusted R Sq	0.84543374
Standard Err	231.786461
Observations	23

ANOVA

	df	*SS*	*MS*	*F*	*Significance F*
Regression	4	6679827.99	1669957	31.0834458	7.3317E-08
Residual	18	967049.346	53724.9637		
Total	22	7646877.34			

	Coefficients	*Standard Error*	*t Stat*	*P-value*	*Lower 95%*	*Upper 95%*	*Lower 95.0%*	*Upper 95.0%*
Intercept	118.157353	163.438131	0.72294851	0.47900092	-225.21342	461.528124	-225.21342	461.528124
X Variable 1	-4.4940051	1.31453278	-3.418709	0.00306194	-7.2557359	-1.7322742	-7.2557359	-1.7322742
X Variable 2	-1.4423979	1.53252292	-0.9411917	0.35906747	-4.6621091	1.77731327	-4.6621091	1.77731327
X Variable 3	2.71983983	0.32683722	8.32169562	1.3915E-07	2.03318032	3.40649935	2.03318032	3.40649935
X Variable 4	1.01950683	2.09409571	0.48684825	0.63224126	-3.380025	5.41903866	-3.380025	5.41903866

Fig. 6.5 Regression Output with the Exclusion of Chinese Infrastructure Aid, 2000–2022. *Source* Self-generated by the Author Using Data Obtained from the World Bank (2024), OECD.org (2024), aiddata.org (2023), and China Africa Research Initiative (2024)

Kenya from the regression equation, there is a slight reduction in the strength of the relationship between the independent variables and the dependent variable. This result may also indicate that there are stronger predictors of Kenya's per capita GDP from 2000 to 2022. Also, an R-Square value of 0.87 indicates that the independent variables explain 87% of the variance in the dependent variable after removing Chinese infrastructure aid to Kenya. In addition, with a very low P-Value of 0.0000000733, the null hypothesis is to be rejected and conclude that there is a statistically significant relationship between the combined independent variables and Kenya's per capita GDP.

As it pertains to the null hypothesis, all of the model's coefficients are equal to zero; hence, the model has no explanatory power or there is no relationship between the variables. In this regard, this hypothesis would mean that the combination of the aid provided by each of the countries, excluding China, included in the model is not statistically significant and that a relationship does not exist between the per capita GDP and the aid provided by the countries in the model.

Regarding the alternative hypothesis, at least one coefficient is not equal to zero, an indication that the model has explanatory power, or there is a linear relationship between the variables in the model. Accordingly, this hypothesis would mean that the combination of the aid, excluding that of China, provided by each of the countries included in the model is statistically significant and that a relationship does exist between the per capita GDP and the aid provided by the countries in the model. Also, a P-Value 0.0000733 indicates that the null hypothesis can be rejected as the alternative hypothesis is acceptable.

Given the aforementioned findings, it can be asserted that a dependency relationship does not exist between Chinese infrastructure aid to Kenya and Kenya's per capita GDP. Although the GDP slightly decreased, the slight change in the statistical relationship between the variables and Kenya's GDP indicates that a dependency relationship does not exist. In terms of equation for the case of Ethiopia, the following is suggested:

GDPpc = per capita GDP of Ethiopia
Y is the impact on Ethiopia (per capita GDP)
X_1 is Chinese infrastructure aid
X_2 is United Kingdom infrastructure aid
X_3 is USA infrastructure aid
X_4 is France infrastructure aid
X_5 is AfDB infrastructure aid

$$Y = \beta_0 + \beta_1 X_1 + \beta_2 X_2 + \beta_3 X_3 + \beta_4 X_4 + \beta_5 X_5 + \varepsilon$$

where:

β_0 is the intercept term
β_1 is the coefficient for Chinese infrastructure aid

β_2 is the coefficient for United Kingdom infrastructure aid
β_3 is the coefficient for United States infrastructure aid
β_4 is the coefficient for France infrastructure aid
β_5 is the coefficient for AfDB infrastructure aid
ε is the error term

The results of the preceding multiple regression equation appear in Fig. 6.7. In lieu of the results in Figs. 6.4 and 6.5, a multiple regression analysis was conducted that included per capita GDP as the dependent variable. A Multiple R of 0.91 indicates a strong and positive linear relationship between the independent and the dependent variable. A Multiple R value suggests that the regression model fits the data well. The independent variables collectively explain much of the variability in the dependent variable. Nonetheless, other variables must be analyzed when examining data to determine whether the quantitative data adequately support the qualitative data. The regression testing is conducted here to determine whether there is a dependency relationship between Chinese infrastructure aid and per capita GDP for Ethiopia. Thus, for policymakers, this strong correlation highlights the essence of continuing and possibly increasing infrastructure aid from these sources to sustain or improve Ethiopia's economic performance. It suggests that such aid is crucial in driving economic growth as measured by per capita GDP (Fig. 6.6).

The R-Square of 0.83 represents the proportion of the variance in the dependent variable that is predictable from the independent variables. It means that the independent variables in the model explain 83% of the variance in the dependent variable and also indicates a good fit of the model to the data. It further suggests that the model does a good job of capturing the relationship between the independent variables and the dependent variable. It is important to note, however, that the model is imperfect, as the R-Square value also indicates that the independent

SUMMARY OUTPUT

Regression Statistics	
Multiple R	0.913288303
R Square	0.834095524
Adjusted R Square	0.78530009
Standard Error	140.0330559
Observations	23

ANOVA

	df	SS	MS	F	Significance F
Regression	5	1675975.794	335195.1588	17.09372075	4.20422E-06
Residual	17	333357.3645	19609.25674		
Total	22	2009333.158			

	Coefficients	Standard Error	t Stat	P-value	Lower 95%	Upper 95%	Lower 95.0%	Upper 95.0%
Intercept	-45.05174066	83.71045175	-0.538185373	0.597425636	-221.6653558	131.5618745	-221.6653558	131.5618745
X Variable 1	8.2653E-09	2.08106E-08	0.397168098	0.696185614	-3.56412E-08	5.21718E-08	-3.56412E-08	5.21718E-08
X Variable 2	0.516276858	0.268317656	1.924125551	0.071245497	-0.049823913	1.082377629	-0.049823913	1.082377629
X Variable 3	0.409406797	0.138161387	2.963250487	0.00871046	0.117911751	0.700901843	0.117911751	0.700901843
X Variable 4	5.896011379	1.921542609	3.068373998	0.006960266	1.841910848	9.950111909	1.841910848	9.950111909
X Variable 5	-0.713366864	0.543460643	-1.312637583	0.206750963	-1.859968594	0.433234866	-1.859968594	0.433234866

Fig. 6.6 Multivariate Regression Analysis Inclusive of Chinese Infrastructure Aid to Ethiopia. *Source* Self-generated by the Author from Data Obtained from the World Bank (2024), OECD.org (2024), aiddata.org (2023), and China Africa Research Initiative (2024)

SUMMARY OUTPUT

Regression Statistics	
Multiple R	0.912445122
R Square	0.832556101
Adjusted R Square	0.795346346
Standard Error	136.7175876
Observations	23

ANOVA

	df	*SS*	*MS*	*F*	*Significance F*
Regression	4	1672882.581	418220.6452	22.37467287	8.7879E-07
Residual	18	336450.5776	18691.69876		
Total	22	2009333.158			

	Coefficients	*Standard Error*	*t Stat*	*P-value*	*Lower 95%*	*Upper 95%*	*Lower 95.0%*	*Upper 95.0%*
Intercept	-53.64691831	78.95012281	-0.679503925	0.505463752	-219.5149714	112.2211348	-219.5149714	112.2211348
X Variable 1	0.540183724	0.25528788	2.115978728	0.048544539	0.00384379	1.076523657	0.00384379	1.076523657
X Variable 2	0.415033737	0.134179152	3.093131327	0.006272844	0.1331338	0.696933674	0.1331338	0.696933674
X Variable 3	5.751356151	1.842039023	3.122277041	0.005885256	1.881375768	9.621336533	1.881375768	9.621336533
X Variable 4	-0.62415328	0.483150437	-1.291840453	0.212753811	-1.639214682	0.390908123	-1.639214682	0.390908123

Fig. 6.7 Multivariate Output: Exclusion of Chinese Infrastructure Aid to Ethiopia. *Source* Self-generated by the Author from Data Obtained from World Bank (2024), OECD.org (2024), aiddata.org (2023), China Africa Research Initiative (2024)

variables in the model do not explain 17% of the variance in the dependent variable. This unexplained variance could be due to other factors not included in the model—for instance, random variation or measurement error.

The Significance F, or P-Value of 0.00000420, means that the overall regression model is statistically significant at the 0.01 level. The value indicates that the combined infrastructure aid from China, the United States, the United Kingdom, France, and the AfDB statistically affects Ethiopia's per capita GDP. This finding underscores the importance of international infrastructure aid in promoting economic growth and development in Ethiopia and validates using these aid sources as key predictors in the regression model. The model's strong statistical significance and high adjusted R-Square suggest that infrastructure aid is an important promoter of economic performance, although other factors also contribute to per capita GDP.

In reference to the null hypothesis, all of model's coefficients are equal to zero; therefore, the model has no explanatory power or there is no relationship between the variables. In essence, this hypothesis means that the combination of the aid provided by each country in the model is not statistically significant and that a relationship does not exist between the per capita GDP and the aid provided by the countries in the model.

For the alternative hypothesis, at least one coefficient is not equal to zero; thus, the model has explanatory power, or there is a linear relationship between the variables in the model. Subsequently, this hypothesis means that the combination of the aid provided by each country in the model is statistically significant and that a relationship exists between the per capita GDP and the aid provided by the countries in the model. The P-Value of 0.00000420 indicates that the null hypothesis can be rejected as the alternative hypothesis is valid.

The adjusted R-Square value of 0.79 indicates that the regression model explains 79% of the variance in the dependent variable, which is adjusted for the number of predictors in the model. This result supports the remainder of the results by suggesting a strong and reliable fit with this model, indicating that the independent variables collectively have significant and substantial explanatory power for the dependent variable. It is therefore apparent that aid collectively contributes to improving the GDP of Ethiopia. While 79% of the variance is explained by infrastructure aid, 21% of the variance remains unexplained by this model. This suggests that other factors also contribute to Ethiopia's per capita GDP. These could include domestic policies, other forms of foreign aid, private sector investments, and broader economic conditions.

The next step of this analysis involves removing Chinese infrastructure aid from the equation to determine if the statistical significance decreases as a result of the removal of the Chinese infrastructure aid from the regression equation. As a result of this removal, the revised regression equation is the following:

Original Regression Equation: $Y = \beta_0 + \beta_1 X_1 + \beta_2 X_2 + \beta_3 X_3 + \beta_4 X_4 + \beta_5 X_5 + \varepsilon$
Dependency Equation: $Y = \beta_0 + \beta_1 X_1 + \beta_2 X_2 + \beta_3 X_3 + \beta_4 X_4 + \beta_5 X_5 + \varepsilon$
Revised Equation: $Y = \beta_0 + \beta_1 X_1 + \beta_2 X_2 + \beta_3 X_3 + \beta_4 X_4 + \varepsilon$

Y is the impact on Ethiopia (per capita GDP)
X_1 is United Kingdom infrastructure aid
X_2 is United States infrastructure aid
X_3 is France infrastructure aid
X_4 is AfDB infrastructure aid

where:

β_0 is the intercept term
β_1 is the coefficient for United Kingdom infrastructure aid
β_2 is the coefficient for United States infrastructure aid
β_3 is the coefficient for France infrastructure aid
β_4 is the coefficient for AfDB infrastructure aid
ε is the error term.

The results that emerged after the exclusion of Chinese infrastructure aid to Ethiopia from the regression model are presented in Fig. 6.7.

Looking at Figs. 6.6 and 6.7, it can be observed that the Multiple R decreased from 0.913 to about 0.912. This result means that after removing Chinese infrastructure aid to Ethiopia from the regression equation, there is a slight reduction in the strength of the relationship between the independent variables and the dependent variable. This result may also indicate that there are stronger predictors of Ethiopia's per capita GDP from 2000 to 2022.

The R-Square value of 0.83 indicates that the independent variables included in the regression model can explain approximately 83% of the variance in the dependent variable after removing Chinese infrastructure aid to Ethiopia. The very low P-Value of 0.000000878 calls for rejecting the null hypothesis and conclude that there is a statistically significant relationship between the combined independent variables and Ethiopia's per capita GDP.

Vis-à-vis the null hypothesis, all of the coefficients of the model are equal to zero, meaning that the model has no explanatory power, or there is no relationship between the variables. Thus, this hypothesis would mean that the combination of the aid provided by each of the countries, excluding China, included in the model is not statistically significant and that a relationship does not exist between the per capita GDP and the aid provided by those countries.

Apropos the alternative hypothesis, at least one coefficient is not equal to zero; accordingly, the model has explanatory power, or there is a linear relationship between the variables in the model. In tandem, this hypothesis would mean that the combination of the aid, excluding China, provided by each of the countries included in the model is statistically significant and that a relationship does exist between the per capita GDP and the aid provided by the countries in the model. The P-Value of 0.000000878 indicates that the null hypothesis can be rejected since the alternative hypothesis is valid.

Considering the preceding findings, a dependency relationship does not exist between Chinese infrastructure aid to Ethiopia and Ethiopia's per capita GDP. Although the GDP slightly decreased due to the subtle change in the statistical relationship between the variables and Ethiopia's GDP, it is determined that a dependency relationship does not exist. When conducting the regression analysis that initially included infrastructure aid from multiple sources—specifically China, the United Kingdom, the United States, France, and the AfDB, the removal of Chinese infrastructure aid from the regression equation had significant implications for the observed relationship between infrastructure aid and per capita GDP.

The aforementioned finding that a dependency relationship does not exist between Ethiopia's per capita GDP and Chinese infrastructure development aid, after its removal from the equation, indicates several important points. First, there is the statistical insignificance that the Chinese infrastructure aid variable did not contribute significantly to explaining variations in per capita GDP. When Chinese aid data are excluded, the model's ability to predict per capita GDP remains largely unaffected. While the impact is minimal in all three countries, Ethiopia sees the slightest change in Multiple R compared to Kenya and Nigeria. This implies that Chinese infrastructure aid does not have a statistically significant impact on per capita GDP per in the context of the overall regression model.

Second, in reviewing the results, the robustness of the regression results to the exclusion of Chinese aid shows that other sources of infrastructure aid from the United Kingdom, the United States, France, and AFDB might be more influential or have more detectable effects on per capita GDP. The dependency of per capita GDP on infrastructure aid therefore appears to be driven by these other sources rather than Chinese aid.

Third, concerning context-specific factors, the lack of a dependency relationship may also reflect unique contextual factors of Chinese infrastructure aid. Chinese aid often comes with different conditionalities, structures, or target projects compared to aid from Western countries and multilateral organizations. This difference might mean that its effects on per capita GDP are not captured effectively by the same model that includes Western and AfDB aid.

From a policy standpoint, the preceding findings could inform aid recipients and policymakers about the relative effectiveness of different sources of infrastructure aid. They also suggest a need to scrutinize the terms and implementation of Chinese infrastructure projects to understand better why they do not exhibit the same relationship with per capita GDP as aid from other donors.

In sum, the removal of Chinese infrastructure aid from the regression equation and the subsequent finding of no dependency relationship with per capita GDP suggest that within the scope of this analysis, Chinese infrastructure aid does not significantly influence the per capita GDPs of Nigeria, Kenya, and Ethiopia. This outcome highlights the importance of examining the unique characteristics and implementation strategies of different aid sources when assessing their economic impact.

6.2 Foreign Direct Investment

As aforementioned, the removal of Chinese infrastructure aid from the regression equation and the subsequent finding of no dependency relationship with per capita GDP suggest that within the scope of this analysis, Chinese infrastructure aid does not significantly influence the per capita GDPs of Nigeria, Kenya, and Ethiopia. This outcome highlights the importance of examining different aid sources' unique characteristics and implementation strategies when assessing their economic impacts on recipient countries.

It is essential to delve into another critical dimension of China's economic engagement with these countries: i.e. FDI. Unlike infrastructure aid, which is typically state-led and project-focused, Chinese FDI involves private sector investments that can drive different economic dynamics. Examining Chinese FDI in Nigeria, Kenya, and Ethiopia will help to gain a broader understanding of China's economic influence and its potential role in shaping the economic trajectories of these nations. Data obtained from Bea.gov (2024) on FDI to Nigeria led to the delineation of the following equations:

GDPpc = per capita GDP of Nigeria
Y is the impact on Nigeria (per capita GDP)
X_1 is Chinese FDI
X_2 is United States FDI
X_3 is United Kingdom FDI
X_4 is France FDI

$$Y = \beta_0 + \beta_1 X_1 + \beta_2 X_2 + \beta_3 X_3 + \beta_4 X_4 + \varepsilon$$

$$\text{Dependency Equation: } Y = \beta_0 + \beta_1 X_1 + \beta_2 X_2 + \beta_3 X_3 + \beta_4 X_4 + \varepsilon$$

X_1 will be removed from the regression equation. Thus, if per capita GDP for Nigeria decreases as a result of this removal, a dependency relationship exists between Chinese FDI and Nigeria's per capita GDP from 2000 to 2022, where

β_0 is the intercept term
β_1 is the coefficient for Chinese FDI
β_2 is the coefficient for United States FDI
β_3 is the coefficient for United Kingdom FDI
β_4 is the coefficient for France FDI
ε is the error term

The results obtained from the multiple regression are summarized in Fig. 6.8.

As can be seen in Fig. 6.8, the multiple R of 0.93 indicates a strong and positive linear relationship between the independent variables and the dependent variable and also suggests that the regression model fits the data well. The independent variables collectively explain much of the variability in the dependent variable. Nonetheless, other variables must be analyzed when examining data to determine whether the quantitative data adequately supports the qualitative data. The regression testing is conducted here to determine whether there is a dependency relationship between Chinese FDI and Nigeria's per capita GDP.

SUMMARY OUTPUT

Regression Statistics	
Multiple R	0.930496509
R Square	0.865823753
Adjusted R Square	0.836006809
Standard Error	63574754553
Observations	23

ANOVA

	df	*SS*	*MS*	*F*	*Significance F*
Regression	4	4.69457E+23	1.17364E+23	29.03797782	1.23934E-07
Residual	18	7.27515E+22	4.04175E+21		
Total	22	5.42208E+23			

	Coefficients	*Standard Error*	*t Stat*	*P-value*	*Lower 95%*	*Upper 95%*	*Lower 95.0%*	*Upper 95.0%*
Intercept	93843351333	28416657397	3.302406403	0.003960214	34142169498	1.5354E+11	3.4142E+10	1.5354E+11
X Variable 1	26.4661347	18.64443244	1.419519462	0.172834425	-12.70436434	65.6366337	-12.704364	65.6366337
X Variable 2	48.82925606	10.10894936	4.830299799	0.000134226	27.59114155	70.0673706	27.5911415	70.0673706
X Variable 3	-6.335088685	7.360769623	-0.860655748	0.400746777	-21.79949182	9.12931445	-21.799492	9.12931445
X Variable 4	7.110102293	3.994140319	1.780133326	0.091941215	-1.281275136	15.5014797	-1.2812751	15.5014797

Fig. 6.8 Multivariate Regression Result: Inclusive of FDI from China, United States, UK, and France to Nigeria. *Source* Self-generated by the Author Using Data from https://data.worldbank.org (2024), Trading Economics, UN Trade & Development (2024), and Bea.gov (2024)

For policymakers, the strong correlation underlines the importance of continuing and possibly increasing infrastructure aid from these sources to sustain or improve Nigeria's economic performance. It also suggests that such aid is crucial in pursuing economic growth as measured by per capita GDP.

The R-Square of 0.87 indicates that the independent variables in the model explain 87% of the variance in the dependent variable. It also shows a good fit of the model to the data. It further suggests that the model does a good job of capturing the relationship between the independent variables and the dependent variable. Nevertheless, it is imperative to note that the model is imperfect, as it also means that the independent variables in the model do not explain 13% of the variance in the dependent variable. This unexplained variance could be due to other factors that are not included in the model, most commonly random variation or measurement error.

The Significance F, or P-Value of 0.000000124, means that the overall regression model is statistically significant. It is important to explain the difference between the null hypothesis and the alternative hypothesis. The Significance F value indicates that the combined FDI from China, the United States, the United Kingdom, and France statistically affects Nigeria's per capita GDP. This finding underscores the importance of FDI in promoting economic growth and development in Nigeria and validates using these investment sources as key predictors in the regression model. The model's strong statistical significance, coupled with a high adjusted R-Square, suggests that FDI is a significant catalyst for economic performance, albeit other factors also contribute to per capita GDP.

About the null hypothesis, all of the coefficients of the model are equal to zero, meaning that the model has no explanatory power, or there is no relationship between the variables. In this respect, this hypothesis would mean that the combination of the FDI provided by each country in the model is not statistically significant and that a relationship does not exist between the per capita GDP and the aid provided by the countries.

As for the alternative hypothesis, at least one coefficient is not equal to zero; therefore, the model has explanatory power, or there is a linear relationship between the variables in the model. In this case, the hypothesis would mean that the combination of the FDI provided by each country in the model is statistically significant and that a relationship exists between the per capita GDP and the aid provided by the countries. A P-Value of 0.000000124 indicates that the null hypothesis can be rejected as the alternative hypothesis is tenable.

An adjusted R-Square value of 0.84 indicates that the regression model explains 84% of the variance in the dependent variable, which is adjusted for the number of predictors in the model. This result supports the remainder variance by suggesting a strong and reliable fit with this model, indicating that the independent variables collectively have significant and substantial explanatory power for the dependent variable. It is apparent that FDI collectively aids in improving Nigeria's GDP. While 84% of the variance is explained by FDI, 16% of the variance remains unexplained by this model. This suggests that other factors also contribute to Nigeria's per capita GDP. These factors could include domestic policies, other forms of foreign aid, FDI, private sector investments, and broader economic conditions.

The next step of this analysis involves removing Chinese FDI from the equation to determine if the statistical significance decreases as a result of its removal. As a result of this removal, the revised regression equation is as follows:

Original Regression Equation: $Y = \beta_0 + \beta_1 X_1 + \beta_2 X_2 + \beta_3 X_3 + \beta_4 X_4 + \varepsilon$
Dependency Equation: $Y = \beta_0 + \cancel{\beta_1} X_1 + \beta_2 X_2 + \beta_3 X_3 + \beta_4 X_4 + \varepsilon$
Revised Equation: $Y = \beta_0 + \beta_1 X_1 + \beta_2 X_2 + \beta_3 X_3 + \beta_4 X_4 + \varepsilon$

Y is the impact on Nigeria's (per capita GDP)
X_1 is China FDI
X_2 is United States FDI
X_3 is United Kingdom FDI
X_4 is France FDI

where:

β_0 is the intercept term
β_1 is the coefficient for China FDI
β_2 is the coefficient for United States FDI
β_3 is the coefficient for United Kingdom FDI
β_4 is the coefficient for France FDI
ε is the error term

Presented in Fig. 6.9 are the results generated after the exclusion of Chinese FDI to Nigeria in the regression model. In comparing the two figures, it can be noticed that the Multiple R decreased from 0.93 to about 0.922. This means that after removing Chinese FDI to Nigeria from the regression equation, there is a slight reduction in the strength of the relationship between the independent variables and the dependent variable. This result may also indicate that there are stronger predictors of Nigeria's per capita GDP from 2000 to 2022.

Also, the R-Square value of 0.85 indicates that the independent variables included in the regression model can explain approximately 85% of the variance in the dependent variable after removing Chinese FDI to Nigeria. In addition, the very low P-Value of 0.0000000475 warrants the rejection of the null hypothesis and to conclude that there is a statistically significant relationship between the combined independent variables and Nigeria's per capita GDP.

In terms of the null hypothesis, every coefficient of the model is equal to zero, indicating that the model has no explanatory power, or there is no relationship between the variables. In this regard, this hypothesis would mean that the combination of the aid provided by each of the countries, excluding China, in the model is not statistically significant and that a relationship does not exist between the per capita GDP and the aid provided by the countries.

SUMMARY OUTPUT								
Regression Statistics								
Multiple R	0.922389941							
R Square	0.850803203							
Adjusted R Square	0.827245814							
Standard Error	65250835067							
Observations	23							
ANOVA								
	df	*SS*	*MS*	*F*	*Significance F*			
Regression	3	4.61313E+23	1.53771E+23	36.11619274	4.7544E-08			
Residual	19	8.08958E+22	4.25767E+21					
Total	22	5.42208E+23						
	Coefficients	*Standard Error*	*t Stat*	*P-value*	*Lower 95%*	*Upper 95%*	*Lower 95.0%*	*Upper 95.0%*
Intercept	94445705938	29162580270	3.238592232	0.004323118	33407723945	1.55484E+11	33407723945	1.55484E+11
X Variable 1	54.03461342	9.668766305	5.588573735	2.17283E-05	33.79765297	74.27157387	33.79765297	74.27157387
X Variable 2	-3.892166146	7.345443603	-0.529874893	0.602336364	-19.2663563	11.48202401	-19.2663563	11.48202401
X Variable 3	8.268990274	4.012893552	2.060605438	0.053300635	-0.130092458	16.66807301	-0.130092458	16.66807301

Fig. 6.9 Exclusion of Chinese FDI to Nigeria Multivariate Regression Summary. *Source* Self-generated by the Author Using Data from https://data.worldbank.org (2024), UN Trade & Development (2024), Trading Economics, and Bea.gov (2024)

In regard to the alternative hypothesis, at least one coefficient is not equal to zero, implying that the model has explanatory power, or there is a linear relationship between the variables in the model. In this case, this hypothesis would mean that the combination of the FDIs, excluding that of China, provided by each of the countries included in the model is statistically significant and that a relationship does exist between the per capita GDP and the FDI supplied by the countries in the model. The P-Value of 0.0000000475 indicates that the null hypothesis can be rejected as the alternative hypothesis is kosher.

Taking the preceding findings into account, it can be asserted that a dependency relationship does not exist between Chinese FDI to Nigeria and Nigeria's per capita GDP. Even though the GDP decreased slightly, the small change in the statistical relationship between the variables and Nigeria's GDP indicates that a dependency relationship does not exist.

Indeed, removing Chinese FDI from the regression equation had significant implications for the observed relationship between FDI and per capita GDP. Thus, the finding that a dependency relationship does not exist between the per capita GDP and Chinese FDI after its removal from the equation indicates several important aspects. One aspect is that of limited dependency. In this case, the slight decrease in Multiple R indicates that Chinese FDI explains some variance in Nigeria's per capita GDP, although it is not the sole determinant. The dependency relationship between Chinese FDI and per capita GDP therefore appears weak.

Another aspect is partial influence—i.e. while Chinese FDI explains the per capita GDP of Nigeria, its removal from the regression equation only marginally affects the model's ability to predict per capita GDP. This finding suggests that other factors besides Chinese FDI significantly influence Nigeria's GDP per capita.

The other aspect concerns other factors at play. This aspect refers to the decrease in the Multiple R which implies that other important variables or factors beyond Chinese FDI influence Nigeria's per capita GDP. These factors could include domestic economic policies, education, healthcare, infrastructure, and other investment forms.

Yet, another aspect is in regards to a complex relationship. Stated succinctly, even though removing Chinese FDI leads to a slight decrease in the Multiple R, this does not necessarily imply a lack of interdependence between Chinese FDI and Nigeria's per capita GDP. There may still be economic connections between Chinese FDI and Nigeria's overall economic performance, but these connections may be more nuanced and not fully captured by the regression model.

In terms of examining the FDI to Kenya from 2000 to 2022, the following regression equation is established:

GDPpc = per capita GDP of Kenya
Y is the impact on Kenya (per capita GDP)
X_1 is Chinese FDI
X_2 is United Kingdom FDI
X_3 is United States FDI
X_4 is France FDI

$$Y = \beta_0 + \beta_1 X_1 + \beta_2 X_2 + \beta_3 X_3 + \beta_4 X_4 + \beta_5 X_5 + \varepsilon$$

where:

β_0 is the intercept term
β_1 is the coefficient for Chinese FDI
β_2 is the coefficient for United Kingdom FDI
β_3 is the coefficient for United States FDI
β_4 is the coefficient for France FDI
ε is the error term

Entailed in Fig. 6.11 are the results for the multiple regression of the preceding equation. As can be gleaned from the figure, the Multiple R of 0.98 indicates a strong and positive linear relationship between the independent variables and the dependent variable. The value also suggests that the regression model fits the data well. In addition, the independent variables collectively explain much of the variability in the dependent variable. For policymakers, this strong correlation underlines the importance of continuing and possibly increasing infrastructure aid from these sources in order to sustain or improve Kenya's economic performance. It further suggests that such aid is crucial in advancing economic growth as measured by per capita GDP (Fig. 6.10).

The R-Square of 0.96 indicates that the independent variables together explain 96% of the variance in the dependent variable. It also suggests that there exists a

SUMMARY OUTPUT								
Regression Statistics								
Multiple R	0.97892083							
R Square	0.958285991							
Adjusted R Square	0.949016211							
Standard Error	133.1210624							
Observations	23							
ANOVA								
	df	*SS*	*MS*	*F*	*Significance F*			
Regression	4	7327895.428	1831973.857	103.3774278	3.6806E-12			
Residual	18	318981.9105	17721.21725					
Total	22	7646877.338						
	Coefficients	*Standard Error*	*t Stat*	*P-value*	*Lower 95%*	*Upper 95%*	*Lower 95.0%*	*Upper 95.0%*
Intercept	464.2312942	63.50106992	7.310605865	8.62898E-07	330.8204968	597.642092	330.820497	597.642092
X Variable 1	6.462E-07	4.63469E-08	13.94269503	4.3511E-11	5.48829E-07	7.4357E-07	5.4883E-07	7.4357E-07
X Variable 2	-3.02098E-08	2.39377E-07	-0.126201896	0.900971095	-5.33122E-07	4.727E-07	-5.331E-07	4.727E-07
X Variable 3	1.41349E-07	3.08522E-07	0.458149887	0.652327515	-5.06831E-07	7.8953E-07	-5.068E-07	7.8953E-07
X Variable 4	4.4915E-06	1.06512E-06	4.216882703	0.00051841	2.25376E-06	6.7292E-06	2.2538E-06	6.7292E-06

Fig. 6.10 Multiple Regression Summary Table FDI (China, United States, UK, and France). *Source* Self-generated by the Author Using Data from https://data.worldbank.org (2024), Trading Economics, UN Trade & Development (2024), Bea.gov, (2024)

SUMMARY OUTPUT								
Regression Statistics								
Multiple R	0.712585154							
R Square	0.507777602							
Adjusted R Square	0.430058276							
Standard Error	445.0880635							
Observations	23							
ANOVA								
	df	*SS*	*MS*	*F*	*Significance F*			
Regression	3	3882913.037	1294304.346	6.533479226	0.00319979			
Residual	19	3763964.301	198103.3843					
Total	22	7646877.338						
	Coefficients	*Standard Error*	*t Stat*	*P-value*	*Lower 95%*	*Upper 95%*	*Lower 95.0%*	*Upper 95.0%*
Intercept	346.7534977	210.4374873	1.647774368	0.115837384	-93.69722523	787.204221	-93.697225	787.204221
X Variable 1	3.482E-07	7.95192E-07	0.437881536	0.666409634	-1.31616E-06	2.0126E-06	-1.316E-06	2.0126E-06
X Variable 2	2.7384E-06	8.22326E-07	3.330064779	0.003518624	1.01725E-06	4.4595E-06	1.0173E-06	4.4595E-06
X Variable 3	1.09856E-06	3.46703E-06	0.316859272	0.754805561	-6.15802E-06	8.3551E-06	-6.158E-06	8.3551E-06

Fig. 6.11 Multiple Regression Summary Table FDI (US, UK, and France) Exclusion of Chinese FDI to Kenya. *Source* Self-generated by the Author Using Data from https://data.worldbank.org, Trading Economics, (2024), UN Trade & Development (2024), and Bea.gov (2024)

good fit of the model to the data. It in addition reveals that the model does a good job of capturing the relationship between the independent variables and the dependent variable. Despite all this, it is essential to know that the model is imperfect, as the R-Square value also means that the independent variables in the model do not explain 4% of the variance in the dependent variable. This unexplained variance could be due to other factors not included in the model, particularly random variation or measurement error.

The Significance F, or P-Value of 0.00000000000368, means that the overall regression model is statistically significant. This result underscores the importance of FDI in promoting economic growth and development in Kenya and validates using these investment sources as key predictors in the regression model. The model's strong statistical significance, coupled with a high adjusted R-Square, suggests that FDI is an important driver of economic performance, albeit other factors also contribute to Kenya's per capita GDP.

For the null hypothesis, all coefficients of the model are equal to zero; as such, the model has no explanatory power, or there is no relationship between the variables. Accordingly, this hypothesis means that the combination of the FDI provided by each country in the model is not statistically significant and that a relationship does not exist between Kenya's per capita GDP and the FDI provided by the countries in the model.

About the alternative hypothesis, at least one coefficient is not equal to zero; thus, the model has explanatory power, or there is a linear relationship between the variables in the model. Therefore, this hypothesis means that the combination of the FDI provided by each country in the model is statistically significant and that a relationship exists between Kenya's per capita GDP and the FDI supplied by the countries in the model. The P-Value of 0.00000000000368 indicates that the null hypothesis is to be rejected since the alternative hypothesis is tenable.

The adjusted R-Square value of 0.95 indicates that the regression model explains 95% of the variance in the dependent variable, which is adjusted for the number of predictors in the model. This result supports the remainder by suggesting a strong and reliable fit with this model, indicating that the independent variables collectively have a significant explanatory power for the dependent variable. It is therefore apparent that FDI collectively aids in improving Kenya's GDP. While FDI explains 95% of the variance, 4% remains unexplained by this model. This suggests that other factors also contribute to Kenya's per capita GDP. These factors could include domestic policies, other forms of foreign aid, FDI, private sector investments, and broader economic conditions.

The next step of this analysis involves removing Chinese FDI from the equation to determine if the statistical significance decreases with the removal of the variable from the regression equation. As a result of this removal, the revised regression equation is as follows:

Original Regression Equation: $Y = \beta_0 + \beta_1 X_1 + \beta_2 X_2 + \beta_3 X_3 + \beta_4 X_4 + \varepsilon$
Dependency Equation: $Y = \beta_0 + \beta_1 X_1 + \beta_2 X_2 + \beta_3 X_3 + \beta_4 X_4 + \varepsilon$
Revised Equation: $Y = \beta_0 + \beta_1 X_1 + \beta_2 X_2 + \beta_3 X_3 + \varepsilon$

Y is the impact on Nigeria (per capita GDP)
X_1 is United Kingdom FDI
X_2 is United States FDI
X_3 is France FDI

where:

β_0 is the intercept term
β_1 is the coefficient for United Kingdom FDI
β_2 is the coefficient for United States FDI
β_3 is the coefficient for France FDI
ε is the error term

Presented in Fig. 6.11 are the results obtained for the regression model after the exclusion of Chinese FDI to Nigeria.

Glancing at Figs. 6.10 and 6.11, it can be noticed that the Multiple R decreased from 0.98 to 0.71. This means that after removing Chinese FDI to Kenya from the regression equation, there is a significant reduction of 0.27 in the strength of the relationship between the independent variables and the dependent variable. This result indicates stronger predictors of Kenya's per capita GDP from 2000 to 2022. After removing Chinese FDI, the Multiple R value drops to 0.71, indicating a weaker, although still substantial, linear relationship between the combined FDI inflows from the United Kingdom, the United States, and France and the dependent variable. The significant decrease also highlights the critical role that Chinese FDI plays in explaining the variation in the dependent variable. This suggests that Chinese FDI significantly contributes to the overall relationship observed when considering all four countries' FDI inflows. In addition, the lower Multiple R value without Chinese FDI implies that the other three countries' FDIs alone can only explain the variation in the dependent variable when Chinese FDI is included.

The R-Square value of 0.51 indicates that approximately 51% of the variance in the dependent variable can be explained by the independent variables included in the regression model after removing Chinese FDI to Kenya. This means that while the model provides valuable insights, decisions based on it should consider that nearly half of the variance is not explained. The P-Value of 0.003 is very low; thus, the null hypothesis is to be rejected and conclude that there is a statistically significant relationship between the combined independent variables and Kenya's per capita GDP.

In terms of the null hypothesis, every coefficient of the model is equal to zero; appropriately, the model has no explanatory power, or no relationship exists between the variables. In this case, the hypothesis would mean that the combination of the aid provided by each of the countries, excluding China, included in the model is not statistically significant and that a relationship does not exist between the per capita GDP and the aid provided by the countries in the model.

Regarding the alternative hypothesis, at least one coefficient is not equal to zero; thus, the model has explanatory power, or there is a linear relationship between the variables in the model. Accordingly, the hypothesis would mean that the combination of the FDIs, excluding that of China, provided by each of the countries included in the model is statistically significant and that a relationship does exist between the per capita GDP and the FDIs supplied by the countries in the model. Also, the P-Value of 0.003 indicates that the null hypothesis is to be rejected and the alternative hypothesis is to be accepted.

Considering the preceding findings, it can be postulated that a dependency relationship does not exist between Chinese FDI to Kenya and Kenya's per capita GDP. In essence, the GDP significantly declined, and a strong dependency relationship existed between Chinese FDI to Kenya and its GDP from 2000 to 2022.

The marked decrease in the Multiple R from 0.98 to 0.71 after removing Chinese FDI from the regression equation indicates that the variable is a critical factor in the model. This suggests a strong dependency relationship, whereby Chinese FDI substantially influences the all FDIs to Kenya. Without Chinese FDI, the model's explanatory power is significantly reduced, thereby highlighting the importance of Chinese investments in Kenya's financial landscape. The overall results of examining Chinese FDI along with the other variables indicate that the strong influence of Chinese FDI on per capita GDP highlights an economic dependency. Kenya's financial performance, as measured by its per capita GDP, is significantly influenced by the level of Chinese investments.

The dependency suggests that fluctuations in Chinese FDI could have a pronounced impact on Kenya's economic stability and growth. A reduction in Chinese investments could lead to lower per capita GDP. In addition, while Chinese FDI is crucial, the dependency indicates a need for diversification. Relying too heavily on one country for FDI could expose the economy to risks. Efforts to attract FDIs from a broader range of countries might reduce vulnerability. The Kenyan government must recognize this dependency to focus on FDI-related diversification. Policies should be developed to ensure that no one country significantly impacts the Kenyan economy. Regarding FDI in Kenya's infrastructure, the country must focus on policies that enhance the overall investment climate to attract more FDIs from various sources while leveraging the existing solid relationship with China, which could foster long-term sustainable economic growth.

In order to investigate FDI to Ethiopia from 2000 to 2022, the following regression equation is proffered:

GDPpc = per capita GDP of Ethiopia
Y is the impact on Ethiopia (per capita GDP)
X_1 is Chinese FDI
X_2 is United States FDI
X_3 is United Kingdom FDI
X_4 is France FDI

$$Y = \beta_0 + \beta_1 X_1 + \beta_2 X_2 + \beta_3 X_3 + \beta_4 X_4 + \beta_5 X_5 + \varepsilon$$

where:

β_0 is the intercept term
β_1 is the coefficient for Chinese FDI
β_2 is the coefficient for United States FDI
β_3 is the coefficient for United Kingdom FDI

SUMMARY OUTPUT

Regression Statistics	
Multiple R	0.970525785
R Square	0.941920299
Adjusted R Square	0.929013698
Standard Error	80519655.86
Observations	23

ANOVA

	df	SS	MS	F	Significance F
Regression	4	1.89263E+18	4.73158E+17	72.97973732	7.12694E-11
Residual	18	1.16701E+17	6.48341E+15		
Total	22	2.00933E+18			

	Coefficients	Standard Error	t Stat	P-value	Lower 95%	Upper 95%	Lower 95.0%	Upper 95.0%
Intercept	180666892.5	30315694.42	5.959516875	1.22455E-05	116975981.9	244357803	116975981.9	244357803
X Variable 1	0.250441216	0.037644769	6.652749357	3.04469E-06	0.17135249	0.329529942	0.17135249	0.329529942
X Variable 2	0.010202674	0.027070973	0.376886098	0.710664568	-0.046671331	0.067076678	-0.046671331	0.067076678
X Variable 3	8.53558E-05	5.71973E-05	1.492303982	0.152939199	-3.48113E-05	0.000205523	-3.48113E-05	0.000205523
X Variable 4	0.043105245	0.059563212	0.723689062	0.478557057	-0.08203242	0.168242911	-0.08203242	0.168242911

Fig. 6.12 Multiple Regression Summary Table FDI (China, United States, UK, and France). *Source* Self-generated by the Author Using Data from https://data.worldbank.org (2024), UN Trade & Development (2024), and (Bea.gov (2024), & Trading Economics

β_4 is the coefficient for France FDI
ε is the error term

Appearing in Fig. 6.12 are the results generated from the preceding multiple regression equation. Based on the results, the Multiple R of 0.97 indicates a strong and positive linear relationship between the independent variables and the dependent variable. The Multiple R value suggests that the regression model fits the data well, and the independent variables collectively explain much of the variability in the dependent variable. Accordingly, policymakers must recognize that the strong correlation underlines the importance of continuing and possibly increasing infrastructure aid from these sources to sustain or improve Ethiopia's economic performance. The finding also suggests that such aid is crucial in driving economic growth as measured by per capita GDP.

The R-Square of 0.94 represents the proportion of the variance in the dependent variable that is predictable from the independent variables and indicates a good fit of the model to the data. In addition, it suggests that the model does a good job of capturing the relationship between the independent variables and the dependent variable. Nevertheless, the finding also means that the independent variables in the model do not explain 6% of the variance in the dependent variable. This unexplained variance could be due to other factors not included in the model, most notably random variation or measurement error.

The Significance F, or P-Value of 0.00000000007127, means that the overall regression model is statistically significant. This underscores the importance of FDI in promoting economic growth and development in Ethiopia and validates using these investment sources as key predictors in the regression model. The model's strong statistical significance, coupled with a high adjusted R-Square, suggests that FDI is a crucial promoter of economic performance, although other factors also contribute to per capita GDP.

As it concerns the null hypothesis, each coefficient of the model is equal to zero; hence, the model has no explanatory power, or there is no relationship between the variables. Given this result, this hypothesis would mean that the combination of the FDI provided by each country in the model is not statistically significant and that a relationship does not exist between the per capita GDP and the FDIs provided by the countries in the model.

In terms of the alternative hypothesis, at least one coefficient is not equal to zero; essentially, the model has explanatory power, or there is a linear relationship between the variables in the model. Accordingly, this hypothesis means that the combination of the FDIs provided by the countries in the model is statistically significant and that a relationship exists between the per capita GDP and the FDIs supplied by the countries in the model. The P-Value of 0.0000000007127 indicates that the null hypothesis ought to be rejected as the alternative hypothesis is valid.

The adjusted R-Square value of 0.93 indicates that the regression model explains 93% of the variance in the dependent variable, which is adjusted for the number of predictors in the model. This result supports the remainder of the value which suggests a strong and reliable fit with this model and indicates that the independent variables collectively have significant and substantial explanatory power for the dependent variable. It is apparent that FDI collectively aids in improving Ethiopia's GDP. While FDI explains 93% of the variance, 7% remains unexplained by this model. This suggests that other factors also contribute to Ethiopia's per capita GDP. These could include domestic policies, different forms of foreign aid, FDI, private sector investments, and broader economic conditions.

The next step of this analysis involves removing Chinese FDI from the equation to determine if the statistical significance decreases due to its removal from the regression equation. As a result of this removal, the revised regression equation is the following:

Original Regression Equation: $Y = \beta_0 + \beta_1 X_1 + \beta_2 X_2 + \beta_3 X_3 + \beta_4 X_4 + \varepsilon$
Dependency Equation: $Y = \beta_0 + \beta_1 X_1 + \beta_2 X_2 + \beta_3 X_3 + \beta_4 X_4 + \varepsilon$
Revised Equation: $Y = \beta_0 + \beta_1 X_1 + \beta_2 X_2 + \beta_3 X_3 + \varepsilon$

Y is the impact on Ethiopia's (per capita GDP)
X_1 is United States FDI
X_2 is United Kingdom FDI
X_3 is France FDI

where:

$\beta_{0=}$ β_0 is the intercept term
β_1 is the coefficient for United States FDI
β_2 is the coefficient for United Kingdom FDI
β_3 is the coefficient for France FDI
ε is the error term

SUMMARY OUTPUT								
Regression Statistics								
Multiple R	0.893930509							
R Square	0.799111754							
Adjusted R Square	0.767392558							
Standard Error	145755998.9							
Observations	23							
ANOVA								
	df	*SS*	*MS*	*F*	*Significance F*			
Regression	3	1.60568E+18	5.35227E+17	25.19331629	7.80489E-07			
Residual	19	4.03651E+17	2.12448E+16					
Total	22	2.00933E+18						
	Coefficients	*Standard Error*	*t Stat*	*P-value*	*Lower 95%*	*Upper 95%*	*Lower 95.0%*	*Upper 95.0%*
Intercept	155554802.2	54450158.46	2.856829192	0.010090305	41589310.75	269520293.6	41589310.75	269520293.6
X Variable 1	0.173415629	0.020715563	8.371272927	8.48834E-08	0.130057458	0.2167738	0.130057458	0.2167738
X Variable 2	-1.03742E-05	0.000100208	-0.103526728	0.918629887	-0.000220112	0.000199364	-0.000220112	0.000199364
X Variable 3	0.132002882	0.105072517	1.256302657	0.224234204	-0.087916423	0.351922186	-0.087916423	0.351922186

Fig. 6.13 Multiple Regression Summary Table FDI (US, UK, and France) Exclusion of Chinese FDI to Ethiopia. *Source* Self-generated by the Author Using Data from https://data.worldbank.org (2024), UN Trade & Development (2024), and Bea.gov (2024), & Trading Economics

The results derived after the exclusion of Chinese FDI to Ethiopia from the regression model are presented in Fig. 6.13.

Looking at Figs. 6.12 and 6.13, it is obvious that the Multiple R decreased from 0.97 to 0.89. This means that after removing Chinese FDI to Ethiopia from the regression equation, there is a slight reduction of 0.08 in the strength of the relationship between the independent variables and the dependent variable. This result indicates stronger predictors of Kenya's per capita GDP from 2000 to 2022. This indicates a weaker, although still a substantial and linear relationship between the combined FDI inflows from the United Kingdom, the United States, and France, and the dependent variable. The slight decrease in Multiple R also highlights the critical role that Chinese FDI plays in explaining the variation in the dependent variable. This suggests that Chinese FDI significantly contributes to the overall relationship observed when considering all four countries' FDI inflows. In addition, the lower multiple R value without Chinese FDI implies that the other three countries' FDIs can only explain the variation in the dependent variable when Chinese FDI is included.

The R-Square value of 0.80 indicates that approximately 80% of the variance in the dependent variable can be explained by the independent variables included in the regression model after removing Chinese FDI to Ethiopia, while 20% of the variance is not explained. The very low P-Value of 0.003 requires the rejection of the null hypothesis and to conclude that there is a statistically significant relationship between the combined independent variables and Kenya's per capita GDP.

Apropos the null hypothesis, every coefficient in the model is equal to zero, meaning that the model has no explanatory power, or no relationship exists between the variables. Justifiably, this hypothesis means that the combination of the aid provided by each of the countries, excluding China, included in the model is not statistically significant and that a relationship does not exist between the per capita GDP and the aid provided by the countries in the model.

Regarding the alternative hypothesis, at least one coefficient is not equal to zero; this means that the model has explanatory power, or there is a linear relationship between the variables. In this case, this hypothesis would mean that the combination of the FDIs, excluding China's, provided by each of the countries included in the model is statistically significant and that a relationship does exist between the per capita GDP and the FDIs supplied by the countries in the model. The P-Value of 0.00000078 indicates that the null hypothesis can be rejected as the alternative hypothesis is valid.

Based on the preceding finding, it can be proffered that a slight dependency relationship exists between Chinese FDI to Ethiopia and the country's per capita GDP. As a result, there was a slight reduction in the GDP, and a slight dependency relationship exists between Chinese FDI to Ethiopia and its GDP from 2000 to 2022.

The marked decrease in the Multiple R from 0.97 to 0.89 after removing Chinese FDI from the regression equation indicates that Chinese FDI is a critical factor in the model. This finding also suggests a slight dependency relationship, whereby Chinese FDI substantially influences the dependent variable. Without Chinese FDI, the model's explanatory power is slightly reduced, highlighting the importance of Chinese investments in Ethiopia's financial landscape. The overall results of examining Chinese FDI along with the other variables indicate that the strong influence of Chinese FDI on per capita GDP highlights a slight economic dependency. In essence, Ethiopia's financial performance, as measured by per capita GDP, is significantly influenced by the level of Chinese investments.

This slight dependency suggests that fluctuations in Chinese FDI could have a pronounced impact on Ethiopia's economic stability and growth. A reduction in Chinese investments could potentially lead to lower per capita GDP. In addition, while Chinese FDI is crucial, the dependency indicates a need for diversification. Relying too heavily on one country for FDI could expose the economy to risks. Efforts to attract FDI from a broader range of countries might reduce vulnerability. The Ethiopian government must recognize this slight dependency and focus on diversification related to FDI. Policies should be developed to ensure that no one country significantly impacts the Ethiopian economy. Regarding FDIs in Ethiopia's infrastructure, the country must focus on policies that enhance the overall investment climate to attract more FDIs from various sources while leveraging the existing solid relationship with China, which could foster long-term sustainable economic growth.

This relationship may indicate that Ethiopia's economy may be diversified enough not to be solely dependent on Chinese FDI. Other domestic or international factors could also be influencing economic outcomes.

Overall, in examining Chinese FDIs to Nigeria, Kenya, and Ethiopia, the key takeaway from the results is that each country conducts regular assessments of the impact of FDIs on the economy to ensure that policies remain effective and are adjusted as necessary based on changing economic conditions and investor feedback. It is also essential that the leaders of the three countries engage with stakeholders, including foreign investors, local businesses, and civil society, to continually gather insights and improve the investment environment. Doing all this will ensure that the needs of everyday citizens are considered when making decisions with investors, and it is essential to develop policies that also consider the concerns of the citizens and local businesses. By implementing these recommendations, Nigeria, Kenya, and Ethiopia can attract and retain diverse FDIs, reduce economic vulnerability, and foster sustainable economic growth while at the same time making sure that the local communities have a say in who and how country investments are made.

6.3 Chapter Summary

The chapter has delved into the theoretical framework underpinning the study of Chinese infrastructure aid in Nigeria, Kenya, and Ethiopia by emphasizing Dependency Theory alongside alternative development paradigms. Dependency Theory is shown to generally posit that underdevelopment in the Global South results from exploitative relationships perpetuated by the Global North, characterized by unequal exchange and economic dependency. This theory serves as a critical lens through which the study examined how Chinese infrastructure aid influences economic development in these African nations, contrasting with traditional development theories like Modernization Theory. By integrating Dependency Theory, the chapter aimed to determine whether Chinese aid fosters mutual benefit or perpetuates dependency dynamics, especially in South-South cooperation.

The theoretical framework critiqued classical development paradigms prioritizing internal factors over global economic relations. It underscored the importance of examining how infrastructure aid from China intersects with local economic contexts and development pathways. The chapter highlighted the evolution of Dependency Theory from its origins in Latin American economic debates to its current application in African contexts by emphasizing its relevance in critiquing global economic structures that marginalize developing countries. Tables and figures illustrating global economic hierarchies and resource flows underscore how dependency perpetuates economic inequalities and cultural hegemony, shaping discussions on economic development in Nigeria, Kenya, and Ethiopia.

Overall, the theoretical framework informed the chapter's approach to analyzing the impacts of Chinese infrastructure aid on economic development and South-South relations. It provided a basis for understanding the complexities of economic dependency and resource exploitation in the context of foreign aid. By integrating Dependency Theory with empirical analysis of infrastructure aid's effects, the study aimed to contribute nuanced insights into sustainable development pathways for Nigeria, Kenya, and Ethiopia. These insights highlighted the need for policies that promote economic resilience and local capacity building amidst global economic dynamics.

References

African Development Bank Group. *Africa Must Tackle Huge Infrastructure Gap to Unlock Opportunities for Transformation - Report*. African Development Bank Group. Accessed July 6, 2024. https://www.AfDB.org/en/news-and-events/press-releases/africa-must-tackle-huge-infrastructure-gap-unlock-opportunities-transformation-report-65734#:~:text=As%20of%202022%2C%20the%20African,16%20bridges%20for%20%2413.5%20billion

Ahiakpor, J. C. W. (1985). The Success and Failure of Dependency Theory: The Experience of Ghana. *International Organization, 39*(3), 535–552. http://www.jstor.org/stable/2706689

AidData. (2023). *Global Chinese Development Finance Dataset, Version 3.0*. Accessed July 6, 2024. https://www.aiddata.org/data/aiddatas-global-chinese-development-finance-dataset-version-3-0

AidData. *Project 1112*. Accessed July 6, 2024. https://china.aiddata.org

Aschauer, D. A. (1990). January/February). Why Is Infrastructure Important? Conference Series; [Proceedings]. *Federal Reserve Bank of Boston, 34*, 21–68.

Assessing Economic and Environmental Impacts of Road Pricing in Ethiopia. (2023, October 21). Accessed July 6, 2024. https://www.thereporterethiopia.com/37003/#

Boundless Sociology. (2014). *Dependency Theories*. Accessed November 14, 2014. https://www.boundless.com/sociology/textbooks/boundless-sociology-textbook/global-stratification-and-inequality-8/sociological-theories-and-global-inequality-72/dependency-theories-428-8541/

China Africa Research Initiative. *Data: Chinese Global Foreign Aid*. Accessed July 1, 2024. http://www.sais-cari.org/data-chinese-global-foreign-aid

Cosma, S. (2010). *Immanuel Wallerstein's World System Theory*. Annals of the University of Oradea: Economic Science. 1. Accessed July 2, 2024. https://www.researchgate.net/publication/49615339_IMMANUEL_WALLERSTEIN'S_WORLD_SYSTEM_THEORY

Frank, A. G. (1967/1981). *Crisis in the Third World*. Holmes & Meier Publishers. 1981.

Guest, J. (2017). *Chinese Infrastructure Development Aid and Its Effect on Economic Growth and Productivity: The Nigerian Case, 2000–2015* (Unpublished doctoral dissertation). Howard University.

Hochschild, A. (1998). *King Leopold's Ghost: A Story of Greed, Terror, and Heroism in Colonial Africa*. Houghton Mifflin Harcourt.

Jalloh, A., & Falola, T. (Eds.). (2008). *The United States and West Africa: Interactions and Relations* (NED-New edition). Boydell & Brewer. http://www.jstor.org/stable/https://doi.org/10.7722/j.ctt81vt5

Kegley, C., & Blanton, S. (2010). *World Politics Trend and Transformation* (p. 141). Twelfth Edition. 2009–2010 Update. Wadsworth, Cengage Learning.

Mangimela, W. (2015, June 15). *Deeping South-South Dependency? China's Cooperative Rhetoric and Economic Engagement in Zambia* (M.A. Central European University School of Public Policy). Budapest, Hungary.

Matunhu, J. (2011, June). A Critique of Modernization and Dependency theories in Africa: Critical Assessment. *African Journal of History and Culture, 3*(5), 65–72. https://academicjournals.org/article/article1381858116_Matunhu.pdf.

New Zealand Social Infrastructure Fund. (2009). *What Is Social Infrastructure?* Retrieved June 22, 2024, from: https://www.nzsif.co.nz/Social-Infrastructure/What-is-Social-Infrastructure/

OECD. *Foreign Direct Investment (FDI)*. OECD-iLibrary. Accessed February 3, 2024. https://www.oecd-ilibrary.org/finance-and-investment/foreign-direct-investment-fdi/indicator-group/english_9a523b18-en

OECD. *FDI Stocks*. Accessed February 5, 2024. https://www.oecd.org/en/data/indicators/fdi-stocks.html

OECD. (1996). *Knowledge Based Economy*. Accessed July 6, 2024. https://one.oecd.org/document/OCDE/GD(96)102/en/pdf

Santos, T. D. (1970). The Structure of Dependence. *The American Economic Review, 60*(2), 231–236. http://www.jstor.org/stable/1815811

Shie, V. H., & Meer, C. D. (2010). The Rise of Knowledge in Dependency Theory: The Experience of India and Taiwan. *Review of Radical Political Economics, 42*(1), 81–99. https://doi.org/10.1177/0486613409357182

Trading Economics. *France - Foreign Direct Investment.* Trading Economics. Accessed June 8, 2024. https://tradingeconomics.com/france/foreign-direct-investment

Trading Economics. *Ethiopia Foreign Direct Investment.* Trading Economics. Accessed July 6, 2024. https://tradingeconomics.com/ethiopia/foreign-direct-investment

Trading Economics. *Kenya Foreign Direct Investment.* Trading Economics. Accessed July 6, 2024. https://tradingeconomics.com/kenya/foreign-direct-investment

Trading Economics. *Nigeria Foreign Direct Investment.* Trading Economics. Accessed July 6, 2024. https://tradingeconomics.com/nigeria/foreign-direct-investment

UNCTAD. *US FDI Flows and Stock.* UNCTADStat. https://unctadstat.unctad.org/datacentre/dataviewer/US.FdiFlowsStock

United Nations. (2024). *About South-South and Triangular Cooperation.*

United Nations Development Programme. https://unsouthsouth.org/about/about-sstc/

U.S. Bureau of Economic Analysis. *Direct Investment by Country and Industry.* Accessed August 19, 2024. https://www.bea.gov/data/intl-trade-investment/direct-investment-country-and-industry

World Bank. *GDP Per Capita (Current US$) - Ethiopia.* Accessed May 12, 2024. https://data.worldbank.org/indicator/NY.GDP.PCAP.CD?end=2022&locations=ET&start=2000

World Bank. *GDP (Current US$) - Kenya.* Accessed May 12, 2024. https://data.worldbank.org/indicator/NY.GDP.MKTP.CD?end=2022&locations=KE&start=2000

World Bank. *GDP (Current US$) - Nigeria.* Accessed May 12, 2024. https://data.worldbank.org/indicator/NY.GDP.MKTP.CD?end=2022&locations=NG&start=2000

World Bank. (2018). *Ethiopia (Excludes Eritrea) Product Exports to China 2018.* World Integrated Trade Solution. Accessed June 12, 2025. https://wits.worldbank.org/CountryProfile/en/Country/ETH/Year/2018/TradeFlow/EXPIMP/Partner/CHN/Product/all-groups

Alusine Jalloh and Toyin Falola. (2008) *The United States and West Africa. Rochester Studies in African History and the Diaspora.* University of Texas at Austin, 280.

Comparative Analysis 7

It is important to do a comparative analysis of Nigeria, Kenya, and Ethiopia to understand the overall impact of Chinese infrastructure aid and FDI on these economies. The chapter will first summarize the colonial histories of all three countries and how this information plays into the impact of Chinese infrastructure aid and FDI on the countries studied. Next, this chapter will review geographical differences related to access to the flow of goods and services and the role this plays in the economies. Then, there will be a comparison of the quantitative results of Chinese infrastructure aid to each country and its GDP. There will be a comparative analysis of the quantitative and qualitative data to understand better how the results play into the analysis. Policies each country has established for Chinese infrastructure aid and FDI to the country will be examined to assess which strategies have been most influential in attracting Chinese FDI and maximizing its positive impact on the economy. This includes evaluating economic development, infrastructure development, job generation, and technology transfer. Understanding the successful elements of different countries' policies can help identify best practices that others can adopt or adapt to improve their investment climates.

7.1 Historical Comparison and Infrastructure Development

Two countries, Nigeria and Kenya, were colonized by the British and shaped by European imperialism, resistance, and eventual paths to independence. These histories offer insights into the broader narrative of colonialism in Africa and highlight the enduring impacts on the continent's development and political landscapes, which impact these countries even today. The colonial histories of Nigeria, Kenya, and Ethiopia offer distinct insights into the impact of European imperialism on

J. Guest, *China's Infrastructure Aid and Investment*, African Studies and Research Forum Series, https://doi.org/10.1007/978-3-032-11964-3_7

infrastructure development in these African countries. British colonial strategies in Nigeria and Kenya involved substantial infrastructural projects primarily aimed at economic exploitation, whereas Ethiopia's brief Italian occupation led to a different type of infrastructural influence. These histories highlight the diverse legacies of colonialism on Africa's infrastructure development.

The primary motive of colonialism in Africa was predominantly economic. To realize these economic objectives, it was necessary to establish basic infrastructure. The Berlin Conference of 1884–1885 initiated the Scramble for Africa during which European powers arbitrarily divided and colonized the continent. Seventy years later, they left behind significantly altered countries, many of which remain among the poorest in the world today (Heldring, 2013). The colonial histories of Nigeria, Kenya, and Ethiopia illustrate the diverse experiences of African nations under European rule. In Nigeria and Kenya, British colonialism exploited and intensified ethnic divisions, implemented exploitative economic policies, and laid the groundwork for post-independence challenges related to national unity and economic development.

Nigeria was colonized by the British in 1901 and divided into the Colony of Lagos and the Protectorates of Southern and Northern Nigeria. The Colony of Lagos was merged with the Southern Protectorate and, subsequently, the Northern and Southern Protectorates were combined to form Nigeria. The country gained independence on October 1, 1960. During colonial rule, the government focused on establishing basic infrastructure like roads and railways primarily to facilitate the extraction of natural resources for Britain, rather than developing the Nigerian economy. Today, the country faces significant developmental challenges, particularly in physical and social infrastructure, which threaten its socioeconomic progress (Ewetan & Urhie, 2014). There were a series of military coups and counter-coups that spanned from 1966 to 1999 in Nigeria. The poor condition of Nigeria's infrastructure is attributed to poor governance, corruption, and years of neglect which characterized both the civilian and military governments.

Kenya was officially colonized by the British in 1920, although British influence in the country began earlier with the establishment of the British East African Company in 1888. The colonization process involved substantial land expropriation and the implementation of forced labor systems to meet the needs of British settlers and support the colonial economy (Black History Month, 2020).

Also, Kenya's colonial infrastructure development was primarily driven by the needs of White settlers and the British colonial administration. The British constructed railways, roads, and urban infrastructure to support the settler economy, particularly in the fertile highlands occupied by Europeans. The renowned Uganda Railway, extending from the port of Mombasa to Kisumu on Lake Victoria, facilitated the movement of goods and settlers, playing a crucial role in the economic exploitation of the region (Lesutis, 2021).

In terms of Ethiopia, the Italian invasion, beginning in October of 1935, encountered fierce Ethiopian resistance and went far less smoothly than Italy had anticipated. Italian forces committed numerous atrocities, including the use of mustard gas and the massacre of civilians. The Italian occupation faced relentless resistance from Ethiopian fighters and ordinary citizens, which severely hampered Italy's colonization efforts. The attempted Italianization of Ethiopia was marred by logistical issues, economic challenges, and the brutal repression of the Ethiopian population. Ultimately, the Italian occupation ended during World War II with the help of British forces and Ethiopian resistance fighters, leading to Haile Selassie's return in 1941(Hallee, 2020).

The long-term impact of the Italian occupation on Ethiopia was devastating. The destruction of Ethiopia's elite, infrastructure, and social fabric led to enduring political instability, economic hardship, and violence. Despite reparations from Italy, Ethiopia struggled to rebuild and has remained one of the poorest and most unstable nations facing challenges such as ethnic tensions and external influence. The Italian occupation, intended to enhance Italy's prestige, instead proved disastrous for both Ethiopia and Italy (Hallee, 2020).

Understanding the histories of Nigeria, Kenya, and Ethiopia is essential in comprehending the colonial past and how it significantly influenced the infrastructure developments in these countries. The Colonial powers built infrastructure primarily to extract resources, leading to uneven development and regional disparities. Often, after the countries gained their independence, conflict began from the artificial borders established by the colonial powers to conflict over the management of natural resources and the fight over who would remain in power. While this list is not all why Nigeria, Kenya, Ethiopia, and many other African countries are struggling with infrastructure challenges, these are key factors that must be considered.

In addition to conflict and challenges with governance, the policies and governance structures established post-independence have shaped infrastructure growth. Political stability, economic strategies, and government priorities influence planning and executing infrastructure projects. Historical conflicts and political instability have impacted infrastructure development. War and internal strife often destroy existing infrastructure and hinder new projects. Furthermore, many businesses are reluctant to engage in countries plagued by internal conflict and turmoil. Such instability deters FDIs and discourages nations from providing aid for infrastructure projects, fearing that these initiatives may be destroyed or left incomplete.

Given the complex interplay of conflict, governance, and post-independence policies shaping infrastructure development, it is also imperative to consider geographical factors. The diverse landscapes of Nigeria, Kenya, and Ethiopia significantly influence their infrastructure needs and challenges. For instance, Nigeria's coastal access, Kenya's strategic location as an East African hub, and Ethiopia's landlocked position lead to distinct infrastructural demands and opportunities. Analyzing these geographical differences provides further insight into the unique infrastructural trajectories of each nation, highlighting how their physical environments impact development strategies and outcomes.

In examining the geographical differences, coastal and inland shipping are vital to Nigeria's transportation network because of its extensive Atlantic coastline and numerous rivers. This sector is crucial for trade and economic development. Significant ports like Lagos, Tin Can Island, Port Harcourt, Calabar, and Onne are key gateways for international trade. Nigeria's inland waterways, including the Niger and Benue rivers, offer cost-effective transportation alternatives. Challenges such as inadequate infrastructure, limited access to deep-water ports, and security concerns hinder efficiency (Scholar, 2024). Enhancing coastal and inland shipping infrastructure is essential for Nigeria's economic growth and trade facilitation.

In Nigeria, several regulatory bodies oversee coastal and inland shipping operations, each with distinct roles and responsibilities. The Nigerian Ports Authority (NPA) is pivotal in managing and advancing the country's ports, facilitating their development and efficient operation. Concurrently, the Nigerian Maritime Administration and Safety Agency (NIMASA) is tasked with regulating and facilitating shipping activities across Nigerian waters, ensuring safety standards and promoting industry growth. Working with these entities, the Nigeria Customs Service (NCS) plays a crucial role in implementing and enforcing customs regulations and procedures pertinent to shipping operations. Moreover, the Shipping and Transportation Committee (STC) operates as a governing body, spearheading policies and laws to optimize the shipping industry's performance and foster sustainable growth. These regulatory bodies collectively contribute to effectively managing and regulating coastal and inland shipping activities within Nigeria, which is vital for the nation's maritime sector's integrity and development (Scholar, 2024). At the same time, the shipping industry in Nigeria is governed by various policies and regulations aimed at ensuring its smooth operation and promoting indigenous participation. Collaborative efforts among Nigeria and its neighboring nations, including Benin, Niger, Cameroon, and other coastal ports, are crucial for mitigating various challenges that hinder optimal utilization of geographical advantages. These challenges encompass piracy, deficient infrastructure, cumbersome bureaucratic processes, and more. By fostering synergy, these nations can collectively address these hurdles and pave the way for Nigeria and other African countries to fully harness the inherent benefits their strategic geographical positioning bestowed upon them. Such cooperation fosters regional stability and economic growth and facilitates seamless trade and navigation across borders, ultimately contributing to the holistic development of the African continent. Furthermore, this change encourages heightened appeal for foreign direct investments and garners assistance from influential donor nations like China, the United States, the United Kingdom, and France. It also sparks a keen interest among private enterprises seeking to establish ventures within Nigeria's vibrant economic landscape.

The diverse landscapes of Nigeria, Kenya, and Ethiopia significantly influence their infrastructure needs and challenges. Nigeria, which is situated on the western coast of Africa along the Atlantic Ocean, benefits from substantial port access, thereby facilitating the transportation of goods across the continent via waterways. This coastal advantage is a significant asset for trade and economic development. Kenya, which is located on the eastern coast of Africa, also enjoys port access via the Indian Ocean. Its strategic position as an East African hub enhances its role in regional trade and connectivity, thereby linking it to major shipping routes.

Ethiopia, in contrast, is a landlocked country bordered by Somalia, Eritrea, and Djibouti. This lack of direct access to the sea presents unique challenges for its infrastructure development, particularly regarding trade logistics and transportation. Ethiopia relies on its neighbors' ports for maritime access, influencing its economic strategies and infrastructural planning. Analyzing these geographical differences provides further insight into the unique infrastructural trajectories of each nation and highlights how their physical environments impact development strategies and outcomes. Figure 7.1 of a map of Africa depicts the geographical locations and differences of Nigeria, Kenya, and Ethiopia.

Fig. 7.1 Map of Africa depicting the geographical differences of Nigeria, Kenya, and Ethiopia. *Source* Self-generated by the Author Using Canva.com

7.2 Quantitative Comparison

Given their distinct geographical contexts, it is essential to quantitatively compare the impact of Chinese infrastructure aid on Nigeria, Kenya, and Ethiopia from 2000 to 2022. Regression analysis provides a robust statistical method to evaluate how Chinese investments have influenced infrastructural development across these countries, considering their unique geographical and logistical challenges. This comparative approach allows for a nuanced understanding of how Chinese aid and FDI have been tailored in order to address the specific needs of each nation and the resulting economic outcomes (see Tables 7.1 and 7.2) for the results from the regression analysis.

The comparison of the Multiple R values for Nigeria, Kenya, and Ethiopia indicates the strength of the relationship between Chinese infrastructure aid and infrastructural development outcomes in each country. Based on the Multiple R comparison in Table 7.1, Kenya had the highest value of 0.428, followed by Nigeria with 0.213, and Ethiopia with 0.165. Kenya having the highest Multiple R value suggests that Chinese infrastructure aid has a relatively stronger relationship with infrastructure development outcomes in Kenya compared to Nigeria and Ethiopia. This higher correlation might reflect the effective utilization of aid, the strategic significance of Kenya's location, more efficient implementation of infrastructure projects, or a combination of all the factors working together.

Nigeria's Multiple R value indicates a moderate relationship between Chinese aid and infrastructural development. This value also suggests that while Chinese aid does have an impact, other factors also significantly influence infrastructural development in Nigeria. These could include internal governance, corruption, diverse economic sectors, and existing infrastructure. Ethiopia has the lowest Multiple R value, indicating a weaker relationship between Chinese infrastructure aid and development outcomes. This could be due to Ethiopia's landlocked geography, which complicates infrastructure projects, reliance on neighboring countries

Table 7.1 Chinese Infrastructure Aid Comparison: Nigeria, Kenya, and Ethiopia, 2000–2022

Regression result	Nigeria	Kenya	Ethiopia
Multiple R	0.213	0.428	0.165
R-Square	0.045	0.183	0.027
Significance F	0.33	0.042	0.452

Source Self-generated by the Author

Table 7.2 Chinese FDI Regression Comparison: Nigeria, Kenya, and Ethiopia, 2000–2022

Regression result	Nigeria	Kenya	Ethiopia
Multiple R	0.863	0.93	0.9613
R-Square	0.746	0.86	0.928
Significance F	3.89E-06	2.1 E-10	1.7 E-13

Source Self-generated by the Author

for port access, less effective implementation of aid projects, or a combination of these factors.

As discussed in the previous chapters, the R-Square value measures the proportion of the variance in a dependent variable that is predictable from the independent variable(s). In this context, it reflects how much of the variability in infrastructural development outcomes can be explained by Chinese infrastructure aid in each country. In terms of evaluating the R-Square for Nigeria, Kenya, and Ethiopia from 2000 to 2022, the value of 0.183 suggests that approximately 18.3% of the variance in Kenya's infrastructural development can be explained by Chinese infrastructure aid. This indicates a moderate explanatory power, meaning that Chinese aid is a relatively significance factor in Kenya's infrastructure development, but other factors also play a substantial role. Nigeria's R-Square value of 0.045 indicates that only 4.5% of the variance in its infrastructural development is explained by Chinese infrastructure aid. This low value suggests that while Chinese aid has some impact, it is a minor factor compared to other influences on Nigeria's infrastructure development. Other factors such as internal policies, corruption, and existing infrastructure conditions likely play a more significant role. Ethiopia's R-Square value of 0.027 means that just 2.7% of the variance in its infrastructural development is accounted for by Chinese infrastructure aid. This very low value indicates that Chinese aid has a minimal explanatory power in Ethiopia's infrastructure development. The country likely faces other significant challenges and factors that overshadow the impact of Chinese aid, such as its landlocked geography, reliance on neighboring ports, and possibly less effective project management.

Overall, the R-Square values suggest that Chinese infrastructure aid has the most substantial impact on infrastructural development in Kenya. Nonetheless, it still leaves a significant portion of variance unexplained, indicating the presence of other influential factors. In Nigeria, Chinese aid explains only a small fraction of the variance in infrastructure development, highlighting the limited influence of this aid amid other predominant factors. Ethiopia shows the most negligible impact of Chinese aid on its infrastructure development, showing substantial challenges and other potential variables that affect its infrastructural outcomes.

In comparing the significance of F vis-à-vis Nigeria, Kenya, and Ethiopia from 2000 to 2022, the low significance supports the interpretation that Chinese infrastructure aid significantly impacts Kenya's infrastructural development. This aligns with the higher R-Square value, suggesting that a considerable portion of Kenya's infrastructure improvements can be attributed to Chinese aid. The high Significance F value indicates that the relationship between Chinese aid and infrastructure development is not statistically significant. This finding complements the low R-Square value, highlighting that Chinese aid plays a minor role in Nigeria's infrastructure development, with other factors being more influential. The very high Significance F value confirms no significant relationship exists between Chinese aid and infrastructure development in Ethiopia. This and the low R-Square value suggest that other factors heavily influence Ethiopia's infrastructural outcomes and Chinese aid's impact is negligible. These statistical results underscore the varying degrees of impact that Chinese infrastructure aid has on these three countries, with Kenya showing a significant positive relationship. At the same time, Nigeria and Ethiopia exhibit weak and statistically insignificant relationships.

Building on the analysis of the impact of Chinese infrastructure aid on infrastructural development in Nigeria, Kenya, and Ethiopia, it is also crucial to examine the role of Chinese FDI in these countries over the same period from 2000 to 2022. As we delve into the analysis, it is important to keep in mind that the focus is on the economic outcomes of Nigeria, Kenya, and Ethiopia. The comparison of the Multiple R values for these countries, as previously discussed, sheds light on the strength of the relationship between Chinese FDI and these economic outcomes.

Ethiopia has the highest Multiple R value of 0.96, which suggests an extremely strong relationship between Chinese FDI and economic outcomes. This high correlation indicates that Chinese FDI is a highly significant predictor of economic development in Ethiopia and likely reflects the investments' effective utilization and substantial impact. Kenya's Multiple R value of 0.93 indicates a strong relationship between Chinese FDI and economic outcomes. Like Ethiopia's, this high correlation suggests that Chinese investments are a major driver of economic development in Kenya, thereby highlighting the importance of these investments in the country's economic trajectory.

Nigeria's Multiple R value of 0.863, while slightly lower than those of Ethiopia and Kenya, still indicates a very strong relationship between Chinese FDI and economic outcomes. This strong correlation suggests that Chinese FDI significantly influences economic development in Nigeria, although slightly less so than in Ethiopia and Kenya. The high Multiple R values across all three countries indicate that Chinese FDI is a critical factor in their economic development. Ethiopia benefits the most from Chinese FDI, with the strongest correlation, suggesting that these investments are closely tied to the country's economic progress. Kenya also shows a very high correlation, underscoring the significant role of Chinese FDI in driving economic outcomes there. Nigeria, while slightly lower in comparison, still shows a very strong relationship, highlighting the importance of Chinese FDI in its economic development. Overall, these results demonstrate that Chinese FDIs play a pivotal role in the economic development of Ethiopia, Kenya, and Nigeria, albeit with varying degrees of influence.

Regarding the comparison of the R-Square, Ethiopia's high value of 0.928 implies that Chinese FDI is crucial to Ethiopia's economic outcomes, making it a key player in the country's development strategy. Kenya, with a high R-Square value of 0.86, indicates that Chinese FDI is also vital for Kenya's economic growth and shows robust dependency on these investments for economic progress. Nigeria's R-Square value of 0.746 reflects a strong but slightly less dominant influence of Chinese FDI on its economic outcomes and suggests that while important, other factors also significantly impact Nigeria's economic development. These R-Square values highlight the critical role that Chinese FDIs play in the economic development of these countries, with the influence being strongest in Ethiopia, followed by Kenya, and then Nigeria.

In comparing the Significance F values of Chinese FDI to Nigeria, Kenya, and Ethiopia, that for Ethiopia of 1.7e-13 means there is an extremely low probability (essentially zero) that the observed relationship between Chinese FDI and economic outcomes in Ethiopia is due to chance. This indicates a very strong and statistically significant relationship, affirming that Chinese FDI is a highly significant predictor of economic outcomes in Ethiopia. Kenya's Significance F value of 2.1e-10 also indicates an exceptionally low probability that the observed relationship is due to chance. This value signifies a strong and statistically significant relationship between Chinese FDI and economic outcomes in Kenya, underscoring the importance of Chinese investments in economic development. Nigeria's Significance F value of 3.89e-06, while higher than those of Ethiopia and Kenya, is still extremely low. This value suggests a very low probability that the relationship between Chinese FDI and economic outcomes in Nigeria is due to chance. It also indicates a strong and statistically significant relationship, confirming that Chinese FDI plays a crucial role in Nigeria's economic development.

What overall implications do the preceding findings have for the three countries? For **Ethiopia**, the Significance F value of 1.7e-13 reflects an extraordinarily strong and statistically significant relationship between Chinese FDI and economic outcomes, reinforcing the critical impact of Chinese investments on Ethiopia's economy. With Kenya having a Significance F value of 2.1e-10, the relationship between Chinese FDI and economic outcomes is also extremely strong and statistically significant, highlighting the major role of Chinese FDI in Kenya's economic growth. In the case of Nigeria, the Significance F value of 3.89e-06, while comparatively higher, still indicates a very strong and statistically significant relationship. This suggests that Chinese FDI is a significant factor in Nigeria's economic outcomes, although slightly less dominant compared to those of Ethiopia and Kenya. These Significance F values confirm that the relationship between Chinese FDIs and economic development is highly significant in all three countries, with the impact being most pronounced in Ethiopia, followed closely by Kenya, and then Nigeria.

In assessing whether a relationship exists between China and Nigeria, Kenya, and Ethiopia, a multiple regression analysis was conducted to evaluate whether Chinese aid, United Kingdom aid, United States aid, and French infrastructure aid result in a dependency relationship. Also, there is a question of which countries studied exhibit more of a dependency relationship with China. To further investigate the presence of a dependency relationship, the variable ChineseInfrastructureAid was removed from the regression equation to observe changes in Nigeria's GDP. This analysis measured ChineseInfrastructureAid using GDP data. Examining per capita GDP was crucial for understanding whether a dependency relationship influences Nigeria, Kenya, and Ethiopia's economic development.

A multiple regression analysis was conducted to account for the various sources of infrastructure development aid in Nigeria, Kenya, and Ethiopia. This approach helps to understand better the effect of Chinese infrastructure development aid on Nigeria's economic growth, measured by GDP. The multiple regression equations aimed to determine if a relationship exists between Chinese infrastructure aid and Nigeria's economic growth, as measured by GDP per capita. The analysis excludes Chinese infrastructure aid from the regression equation to test the

Table 7.3 Comparative results of the Exclusion of Chinese Infrastructure Aid from the Multiple Regression Analysis

Regression result	Nigeria	Kenya	Ethiopia
Multiple R	0.878 (0.89)	0.93 (0.88)	0.912 (0.95)
R-Square	0.770 (0.79)	0.87 (0.77)	0.833 (0.897)
Significance F	1.409E-05 (2.599E-05)	7.331E-08 (1.409E-05)	8.788E-07 (7.78E-08)

Note The numbers in the parentheses represent the results including Chinese Infrastructure Aid
Source Self-generated by the Author

tenability of the Dependency Theory. If Nigeria, Kenya, or Ethiopia's economic development decreases after removing Chinese infrastructure aid, it indicates a dependency relationship. The results from the regression analysis are illustrated in Table 7.3.

In the case of Nigeria, the Multiple R value decreases by 0.012 when Chinese infrastructure aid is excluded. Interestingly, the value increases by 0.05 when Chinese infrastructure aid is excluded. This unusual result might suggest that other variables in the model become more explanatory when Chinese aid is removed, indicating that the initial model with Chinese aid might not be the best fit for Kenya's economic outcomes. For Ethiopia, the Multiple R value decreases by 0.038 when Chinese infrastructure aid is excluded. Thus, Ethiopia shows the highest dependence on Chinese infrastructure aid as the value decreases by 0.038 when Chinese aid is excluded, indicating a significant reliance on this aid for its economic outcomes. Nigeria also shows some dependence, with a decrease of 0.012 in the Multiple R value when Chinese aid is excluded. Kenya appears to be the least dependent on Chinese infrastructure aid. The Multiple R value increases when Chinese aid is excluded, suggesting that the other variables in the model are more effective in explaining the economic outcomes without including Chinese aid. Ethiopia has the highest dependency on Chinese infrastructure aid from 2000 to 2022, followed by Nigeria. Conversely, Kenya appears to be less dependent, and the model performs better without including Chinese infrastructure aid, which indicates a more complex relationship or better explanatory power of other factors.

In comparing the R-Square results, the value decreases by 0.02 when Chinese infrastructure aid is excluded, indicating a moderate reliance on Chinese aid. For Kenya, The value increases by 0.10 when Chinese infrastructure aid is excluded, suggesting that the model explains more variability in the data without Chinese aid. This implies that the other factors in the regression model are more significance for Kenya's economic outcomes when Chinese aid is removed, indicating less dependency on Chinese infrastructure aid. The R-Square value decreases for Ethiopia by 0.064 when Chinese infrastructure aid is excluded, showing a significant reliance on Chinese aid for explaining economic outcomes. Ethiopia shows the highest dependency on Chinese infrastructure aid, with a substantial decrease in the R-Square value when this aid is excluded. This indicates that Chinese infrastructure aid plays a significant role in explaining the economic development in

Ethiopia. Nigeria shows a moderate level of dependency, with a slight decrease in the R-Square value when Chinese infrastructure aid is excluded.

7.3 Qualitative Analysis Comparison

It is not enough to do just a quantitative analysis in order to understand the impact Chinese infrastructure aid and FDI have on the economic development measured by per capita GDP in Nigeria, Kenya, and Ethiopia from 2000 to 2022. Quantitative analysis must be supplemented by qualitative analysis. As done earlier, this book conducted a content analysis of multiple online newspapers within these countries to obtain varying perspectives on the impact of Chinese aid and FDI. Qualitative content analysis of newspapers in Nigeria, Kenya, and Ethiopia also provides a rich, contextual layer of understanding that complements the quantitative analyses. It helps to explain the nuances behind the data, captures public and expert opinions, and identifies specific challenges and opportunities related to Chinese infrastructure aid and FDIs. This comprehensive approach is essential for a holistic assessment of the impact of Chinese investments on these countries' economic development. Some examples of the benefits of this analysis can reveal how cultural attitudes and political dynamics influence the reception and effectiveness of Chinese aid and FDIs. In addition, it offers more profound insights into the reasons behind these relationships. For instance, it can uncover factors like governance quality, corruption, or specific project implementation challenges. This analysis was also used to understand social acceptance and potential sociopolitical challenges of these investments and obtain feedback from policymakers, stakeholders, and the public that will aid in refining policies and improving the implementation of future projects.

In reviewing the newspapers for each country, the overall sentiment was that each country was excited about doing business with China and its impact on changing the lives of citizens in the country. Still, many observers seemed cautious about the potential debt implications of China's loans to the countries in this study. Each country has a right to be cautious about the debt implications, especially as one reflects on the 1970s and 1980s when many African countries were saddled with debt from structural adjustment programs from the International Monetary Fund and the World Bank. Many newspapers frequently highlighted the potential benefits of Chinese infrastructure projects such as improved transportation networks, enhanced trade capabilities, and job generation. For instance, some articles often reported about the transformative nature of new railways, roads, and ports, which catalyzes economic growth and modernization. There was a recurrent theme of cautious optimism, whereby concerns over the sustainability of debt tempered the potential economic benefits. Journalists and opinion pieces drew parallels between current Chinese loans and the historical experiences with IMF and World Bank loans and emphasized the need for prudent financial management.

In many reports, it was pointed out that government officials strongly supported Chinese investments and viewed them as critical to achieving national development goals. Nevertheless, there was also an undercurrent of political debate with opposition parties and civil society groups voicing concerns about transparency, sovereignty, and long-term economic independence.

In reviewing the newspapers, the public sentiment, as captured in letters to editors, opinion polls, and social media excerpts quoted in newspapers, showed a mixture of hope and skepticism. Many citizens appreciated the immediate benefits of improved infrastructure but worried about the potential long-term costs and the fairness of the loan agreements.

In addition, the newspapers portrayed Chinese infrastructure aid as "neocolonial in nature." For example, in a *Premium Times* article titled "Nigeria Must Lead Africa against Neocolonialism—NDA Commandant" (2023) written by Suleiman Qosim, Major General John Ochai, Commandant of the Nigeria Defence Academy (NDA), is reported to have emphasized that Nigeria must lead African countries in resisting neocolonialism from developed nations. Speaking at a leadership lecture series, Ochai is said to have argued that countries like the United States, China, Russia, France, and Saudi Arabia are engaging in a new scramble for Africa by exploiting the continent through multinational companies, big tech, and foreign investments. He is noted to have highlighted that these actions, including China's infrastructure projects and United States FDIs, constitute neocolonialism (Qosim, 2023).

Other articles looked at the relationships between China and Nigeria, Kenya, and Ethiopia as mutually beneficial and a shared partnership. A *Premium Times* article titled "What a Shared Day Means for China-Nigeria Relations" (2023) by Olalekan A. Babatunde focused on the shared partnership between the two countries. The article emphasized the mutual benefits of Nigeria-China relations, noting that Nigeria gains manufactured goods, expertise, funding, and aid from China while offering a favorable business climate and natural resources. Nonetheless, it also acknowledged the disparity in development between industrialized China, which has eradicated absolute poverty, and Nigeria, which still faces challenges like poverty, unemployment, and corruption (Babatunde, 2023). Reflecting on their cooperation, both nations were encouraged to draw lessons from each other in order to address these issues. Others argued that for China's security cooperation to be beneficial, it must deliver on its commitments and support "African solutions" while addressing governance challenges. This includes involving civil society in discussions and ensuring that security projects complement existing peace and security strategies. The article also suggested that a nuanced definition of sovereignty, which provides for protecting human rights, is essential (see also Kluiver, 2023).

Kenyan newspapers also presented a balanced view of Chinese investments, while recognizing the significant benefits and the challenges. They acknowledged the positive impact of projects on connectivity, regional integration, and economic growth. As mentioned in Nigeria's case, concerns about the long-term financial health of the nation due to extensive loans from China were also highlighted in the case of Kenya. As reflected in the newspapers of all three countries, the coverage noted an appreciation of economic benefits while being mindful of the financial risks involved.

Just as it was reflected in the newspapers in Nigeria and Kenya, Ethiopian newspapers also covered Chinese infrastructure development aid with optimism and caution by reflecting on both the positive impacts and potential concerns associated with these investments. Ethiopian newspapers highlighted the significant role of Chinese-funded infrastructure projects in boosting the country's economic growth. Projects like the Addis Ababa-Adama Expressway and the Dire Dawa-Dewele toll road were praised for enhancing connectivity and trade facilitation, particularly with Djibouti, which handles most of Ethiopia's import-export trade. In addition, articles often focused on the transformative impact of Chinese infrastructure aid in modernizing Ethiopia's road networks, railways, and other critical infrastructure. This included the construction of modern highways, railways, and industrial parks, which are essential for the country's development agenda. Specific projects, such as the Addis Ababa Light Rail and the Ethiopia-Djibouti Railway, are examples of successful collaborations that have significantly improved transportation infrastructure. Some articles, however, expressed concerns about the socioeconomic disparities that infrastructure projects might exacerbate.

For instance, while beneficial for overall economic growth, toll roads might impose additional costs on low-income individuals and small businesses, potentially leading to increased economic inequality. The increased cost of transportation due to tolls can impact consumer prices and spending, which could have broader implications for the economy. There were also some reports on the quality and durability of Chinese-built infrastructure projects. Some articles raised concerns about whether these projects meet the necessary standards and long term sustainability. Also, Ethiopian newspapers often discussed the strategic partnership between Ethiopia and China and emphasized mutual benefits and long-term cooperation. The strong political and economic ties are a cornerstone for continued development and collaboration. Kenya is the least dependent on Chinese infrastructure aid, with the R-Square value increasing when the aid is excluded. This suggests that the other variables in the model have a stronger explanatory power for Kenya's economic outcomes without including Chinese infrastructure aid. The analysis of R-Square values aligns with the previous conclusions based on the Multiple R values, reaffirming that Ethiopia has the highest dependency on Chinese infrastructure aid, followed by Nigeria, with Kenya being the least dependent.

For Nigeria, with and without Chinese infrastructure aid, the Significance F values are very low, indicating that the regression models are statistically significant in explaining the variation in the country's per capita GDP. Nevertheless, the F value is slightly higher when Chinese infrastructure aid is included, suggesting that the model with Chinese aid considered as a factor may have a more robust overall fit. In the case of Kenya, the Significance F value is notably higher when Chinese infrastructure aid is included than when it is excluded. This indicates that the regression model is more statistically significant in explaining Kenya's per capita GDP variation when considering Chinese infrastructure aid. When excluding Chinese aid, the Significance F value decreases significantly, suggesting a weaker overall fit of the model. Vis-à-vis Ethiopia, similar to Kenya, the Significance F value is higher when Chinese infrastructure aid is included in the model. This indicates that the model with Chinese aid considered is more statistically significant in explaining Ethiopia's per capita GDP variation. Nevertheless, even when excluding Chinese aid, the Significance F value remains relatively low, suggesting that the model without Chinese aid is still statistically significant, although to a lesser extent.

Given the varying degrees of dependency, it is necessary to evaluate the policies of each country regarding Chinese infrastructure aid and FDI from 2000 to 2022. This evaluation will consider how each nation has managed Chinese investments and the strategic decisions to leverage these funds for national development. In Nigeria, policies aimed at diversifying foreign investment sources and mitigating over-reliance on a single country have been pivotal. Conversely, Kenya's high dependency suggests that its policies may have been more aligned with maximizing the immediate benefits of Chinese FDI and infrastructure projects, potentially at the cost of increased economic vulnerability. Ethiopia's moderate dependency reflects a balanced approach, incorporating Chinese aid while seeking other international partnerships. Analyzing these policies will provide deeper insights into the long-term sustainability and impact of Chinese infrastructure aid and FDIs in these countries.

Chinese infrastructure aid has become a crucial element of development strategies in many African countries, including Nigeria, Kenya, and Ethiopia. Each of these nations has implemented specific policies and frameworks tailored to its unique contexts and development priorities to manage and optimize the benefits of this aid.

7.4 Comparison of Policies

The distinct policies adopted by Nigeria, Kenya, and Ethiopia to manage Chinese infrastructure aid have had profound impacts on their development trajectories, economic landscapes, and sociopolitical environments. In Nigeria, The National Development Plan 2021–2025 (2021) is a detailed blueprint developed to boost the economy, improve social aspects, and enhance infrastructure. It aims to tackle challenges and maximize Nigeria's strengths in various areas. It also seeks to establish a plan for upgrading Nigeria's infrastructure to a well-integrated, multi-modal transportation system that is economically efficient, socially equitable, and environmentally sustainable. The government's transport policy focuses on establishing an integrated system in which people and freight can use multiple transportation modes to reduce costs and travel time while improving service quality. This includes incentivizing private sector investment, promoting reforms for increased private sector participation and enhancing all transport modes—railways, roads, aviation, and maritime—to support economic growth and improve quality of life.

In Nigeria's development plan, the goal is to upgrade the transport infrastructure system in order to enhance transport service quality and reduce infrastructure strain by improving operational efficiencies across aviation, maritime, rail, and road sectors. To address these aspects, the plan establishes clear, non-duplicative regulations to attract private sector investment by harmonizing policies and accelerating the passage of critical transport bills, including the Railway Bill (National Development Plan, 2021). In terms of FDIs, the plan aims to grow Nigeria's FDIs to $5 billion by 2025 in order to enhance the country's attractiveness to international investors. The plan's focus is not only to improve the infrastructure of Nigeria but also on overall economic growth, infrastructure development, human capital improvement, social and regional development, investment, and governance; the NDP aims to launch a sustainable and inclusive future for Nigeria (National Development Plan, 2021).

For Kenya, Kenya Vision 2030 emphasizes infrastructure development as a key pillar to achieve its goal of transforming the country into a newly industrializing, middle-income country by 2030. This comprehensive blueprint outlines several major infrastructure projects designed to spur economic growth and improve the quality of life for all Kenyans. Kenya Vision 2030 was developed in 2008 and outlines infrastructure development as a critical driver to unlock additional benefits for Kenyans through various pillars. This approach aligns with the African Union Agenda 2063 and the United Nations Sustainable Development Goal No. 9, which aims to build resilient infrastructure, promote inclusive and sustainable industrialization, and foster innovation. The ongoing infrastructure initiative has solidified infrastructure development as a paramount concern for both present and past administrations in Kenya. Over the past 15 years, substantial investments of funds, time, and focus have been dedicated to this objective (Kluiver, 2023).

Consequently, Kenya has experienced commendable economic advancement over the past decade, primarily driven by the growth of both traditional and modern service sectors. Sectors like financial intermediation and mobile communications have witnessed significant expansion, spurring demand for ancillary services such as commerce (Kluiver, 2023). This development was also reflected in the results of both the qualitative and quantitative data examined in this study.

Some Notable projects developed under Kenya's plan are the Thika Superhighway and the Nairobi Expressway, which have transformed the transportation landscape and showcased Kenya's commitment to becoming a regional economic powerhouse. The standard gauge railway (SGR) initiative has further bolstered economic growth by generating jobs and improving regional integration within the East African community (Kluiver, 2023).

Additionally, the Lamu Port-South Sudan-Ethiopia Transport (Lapsset) Corridor project is a pivotal component of Kenya's Vision 2030; it is aimed at boosting cross-border trade with neighboring countries and solidifying Kenya's position as the gateway to Greater Eastern Africa (Ndwaru, 2022). The continued implementation of this plan promises to further enhance Kenya's development trajectory and achieve the long-term goal of becoming a middle-income country by 2030.

Regarding Ethiopia, the Growth and Transformation Plans (GTP I and II) outline the country's development priorities and emphasize infrastructure development as a critical driver of economic growth. Chinese aid has been strategically aligned with these plans. Ethiopia's GTP I and II are crucial strategies to help the country become a low-middle-income nation by 2025. These plans aim to maintain fast, widespread, and fair economic growth, which will speed up economic change and move the country toward its renewal (United Nations Ethiopia, 2019). The plans emphasize sectors such as agriculture, industry, infrastructure, social development, governance, and gender empowerment.

The Ethiopian government has initiated a ten-year development plan rooted in its 2019 Home-Grown Economic Reform Agenda from 2020/21 to 2029/30. This strategy aims to preserve the significant growth achieved under the previous decade's Growth and Transformation Plans while transitioning toward a more private sector-focused economy. It also intends to boost efficiency; foster competition in critical sectors like energy, logistics, and telecommunications; enhance the business environment; and resolve macroeconomic disparities (Federal Democratic Republic of Ethiopia, 2020).

During GTP I, Ethiopia experienced an average annual GDP growth rate of approximately 10%, positioning it among the world's fastest-growing economies. This expansion was fueled by significant public investments in infrastructure and capital development. In addition, the GTP 1 & II Plans increased investment for infrastructure projects such as roads, railways, and energy; and boosted economic efficiency and connectivity. Notable initiatives included the Grand Ethiopian Renaissance Dam and the extensive development of road networks. In addition, the GTP plans were responsible for increased FDIs. Efforts to draw FDIs were effective especially in the manufacturing and infrastructure sectors, which in turn spurred industrial growth and generated employment opportunities (Federal Democratic Republic of Ethiopia, 2020; World Bank, 2024).

Among the three countries' plans, Kenya's Vision 2030 is the most effective in driving development, evidenced by its successful implementation of large-scale infrastructure projects that have stimulated economic growth and regional integration. Ethiopia's GTPs also show impressive results with rapid GDP growth and increased FDI, while Nigeria's plan is more recent and its outcomes remain to be fully assessed. Kenya's focused approach to infrastructure and integration within the East African community, coupled with a continuous political commitment, gives it an edge in achieving sustained development. Since corruption has been highlighted by many observers that it hinders infrastructure development in the three countries investigated in this book, the issue is examined in the ensuing section within the scope of the Corruption Perception Index.

7.5 Corruption Perception Index

According to the Corruption Perception Index (CPI), it assesses 180 countries and territories worldwide based on their perceived levels of public sector corruption, using a scale from 0 (extremely corrupt) to 100 (very clean). Nigeria's score is 25/100 which indicates a high level of perceived public sector corruption (Transparency International Nigeria, 2023). This aspect is important as it relates to high corruption levels which deter foreign investment, as businesses are wary of the risks associated with corrupt practices such as bribery and opaque regulatory frameworks.

Kenya's 31/100 score also signifies considerable corruption within its public sector. Like Nigeria, corruption in Kenya affects infrastructure development, public service delivery, and economic reforms (Transparency International Kenya, 2023).

Ethiopia's score is 37/100 (Transparency International Ethiopia, 2023), which indicates significant corruption but is relatively less severe than Nigeria's and Kenya's. Although Ethiopia faces challenges of corruption, its lower level suggests comparatively better governance and potentially more effective public sector management. This finding is essential because a less corrupt environment can foster a more favorable investment climate and attracts FDIs and boost economic growth. Ethiopia's highest anti-corruption score among the three suggests relatively better corruption control than Nigeria and Kenya. High corruption levels in Nigeria and Kenya can impede economic development, governance, and social equity. Ethiopia's relatively lower corruption suggests that it might be better positioned to achieve sustainable development goals if it continues to address corruption effectively.

Corruption severely hinders development, with the most profound impact on the poor and vulnerable by escalating costs and limiting access to vital services such as healthcare, education, and justice. It deepens inequality, discourages private investment, and weakens emergency responses, thereby eroding public confidence in leadership and institutions, and potentially leading to heightened social unrest and conflict (Gatti, 2023).

Enhancing anti-corruption frameworks, strengthening institutions, promoting transparency, and encouraging public participation in governance are critical to improving the three countries' CPI scores and overall development outcomes. In sum, while all three countries face significant corruption challenges, Ethiopia's higher CPI score indicates better public sector integrity than those of Nigeria and Kenya. Continued efforts to combat corruption are essential for fostering economic growth, attracting investment, and ensuring equitable development in these nations.

7.6 Chapter Summary

The chapter has presented a comprehensive analysis of the impact of Chinese infrastructure aid and FDIs on Nigeria, Kenya, and Ethiopia through a comparative approach. It began by outlining the colonial histories of these nations and their relevance to understanding current economic dynamics influenced by Chinese investments. The analysis considered geographical factors affecting trade flows and economic development across the countries. Quantitative assessments of Chinese infrastructure aid relative to GDP in each nation are compared alongside qualitative data to provide a holistic view. Additionally, the chapter examined policy frameworks implemented by each country to attract and manage Chinese investments by focusing on economic and infrastructure development, job generation, and technology transfer. By identifying successful policies, the chapter aimed to inform best practices that can enhance investment climates across the three economies.

In addition, this chapter discussed the historical context and infrastructure developments in Nigeria, Kenya, and Ethiopia, which were shaped by colonial legacies and geographical factors. Nigeria and Kenya experienced British colonization focused on economic exploitation through infrastructure projects like railways and roads. Ethiopia, resisting Italian occupation, faced devastation and economic challenges post-colonization. These histories underscore how colonialism's economic motives led to uneven development and enduring challenges in governance and infrastructure. Geographically, Nigeria's coastal access, Kenya's strategic position, and Ethiopia's landlocked status influenced their infrastructure needs and development strategies, thereby highlighting the diverse impacts of physical environments on economic outcomes.

The comparison of Chinese infrastructure aid and FDIs in Nigeria, Kenya, and Ethiopia from 2000 to 2022 revealed distinct patterns in their impacts on infrastructural and economic development. Regarding Chinese infrastructure aid, Kenya exhibited the strongest correlation and explanatory power, with a Multiple R of 0.428 and an R-Square value of 0.183, indicating significant influence on infrastructural outcomes attributed to efficient implementation and strategic location. Nigeria followed with moderate impacts (Multiple R = 0.213, R-Square = 0.045), while Ethiopia showed the least impact (Multiple R = 0.165, R-Square = 0.027) due to geographic constraints and project management challenges. Conversely, for Chinese FDIs, Ethiopia demonstrated the highest correlation (Multiple R = 0.9613) and explanatory power (R-Square = 0.928), indicating substantial influence on economic outcomes despite infrastructural limitations. Kenya and Nigeria also showed strong relationships (Multiple R = 0.93 and 0.863, respectively), underscoring the significant role of Chinese FDIs in their economic development. These findings underscore the varied impacts of Chinese investments in these countries shaped by their unique geographical contexts and economic conditions.

The comparison of Chinese infrastructure aid and FDIs in Nigeria, Kenya, and Ethiopia from 2000 to 2022 revealed distinct patterns in their impacts on infrastructural and economic development. Regarding Chinese infrastructure aid, Kenya exhibited the strongest correlation and explanatory power, with a Multiple R of 0.428 and an R-Square value of 0.183, indicating significant influence on infrastructural outcomes attributed to efficient implementation and strategic location. Nigeria followed with moderate impacts (Multiple R = 0.213, R-Square = 0.045), while Ethiopia showed the least impact (Multiple R = 0.165, R-Square = 0.027) due to geographic constraints and project management challenges. Conversely, for Chinese FDIs, Ethiopia demonstrated the highest correlation (Multiple R = 0.9613) and explanatory power (R-Square = 0.928), indicating substantial influence on economic outcomes despite infrastructural limitations. Kenya and Nigeria also showed strong relationships (Multiple R = 0.93 and 0.863, respectively), underscoring the significant role of Chinese FDIs in their economic development. These findings highlighted the varied impacts of Chinese investments in these countries shaped again by their unique geographical contexts and economic conditions.

The qualitative analysis conducted alongside quantitative assessments shed light on the complex impact of Chinese infrastructure aid and FDIs on Nigeria, Kenya, and Ethiopia from 2000 to 2022. It revealed nuanced perspectives from local newspapers that captured optimism and caution among citizens and policymakers. Across all three countries, there was a shared appreciation for the immediate benefits of Chinese investments, particularly in infrastructure development like roads and railways. These were seen as catalysts for economic growth and modernization. Nonetheless, concerns about long-term debt sustainability and the transparency of loan agreements were prevalent. Nigerian and Kenyan newspapers highlighted debates over sovereignty and economic independence amid solid governmental support for Chinese investments. Ethiopian coverage emphasized the transformative impact of Chinese-funded projects on connectivity and trade facilitation, albeit with concerns about socioeconomic disparities and project quality. Overall, the qualitative analysis underscored the need for balanced policies that maximize benefits while mitigating risks associated with Chinese aid and FDIs tailored to each country's unique economic and developmental challenges.

Nigeria, Kenya, and Ethiopia have each implemented distinct policies to manage Chinese infrastructure aid, significantly shaping their economic landscapes and development trajectories. Nigeria's National Development Plan 2021–2025 (2021) emphasized upgrading transport infrastructure to establish an integrated, efficient system across railways, roads, aviation, and maritime sectors. It emphasized regulatory harmonization to attract private sector investment and aimed to boost FDIs to $5 billion by 2025 and support broader economic growth, human capital improvement, and social development (Nigeria National Development Plan 2021–2025).

Kenya's Vision 2030 positioned infrastructure development as pivotal for transforming into a middle-income country by 2030. Emphasizing resilience and sustainable industrialization, it has seen significant investments in projects like the Thika Superhighway and the Nairobi Expressway, along with the Standard Gauge Railway (SGR) and the Lamu Port-South Sudan-Ethiopia Transport (Lapsset) Corridor. These initiatives underscored Kenya's commitment to regional integration and economic advancement through enhanced transportation and trade capabilities (Kenya Vision 2030).

Ethiopia's Growth and Transformation Plans (GTP I and II) prioritized infrastructure alongside agriculture, industry, and social development; this was done to achieve a low-middle-income status by 2025. The plans have catalyzed into rapid economic growth, supported by substantial investments in projects like the

Grand Ethiopian Renaissance Dam and extensive road networks. The country's ten-year Development Plan builds on these successes and transitioning toward a more private sector-focused economy while enhancing competitiveness in the energy, logistics, and telecommunications sectors (United Nations, 2019).

The aforementioned policy frameworks demonstrate each country's strategic approach to leveraging Chinese infrastructure aid in order to promote economic growth, improve connectivity, and foster sustainable development over the coming years. Indeed, Nigeria, Kenya, and Ethiopia have distinct development plans influenced by Chinese infrastructure aid, each uniquely shaping its economic and sociopolitical landscapes.

References

Babatunde, O. A. (2023, October 2). What a Shared National Day Means for Nigeria-China Relations. *Premium Times*. Accessed January 15, 2024. https://www.premiumtimesng.com/opinion/629981-what-a-shared-national-day-means-for-nigeria-china-relations-by-olalekan-a-babatunde.html

Black History Month. (2020). The Colonisation of Kenya. *Black History Month 2020*. Accessed January 22, 2024. https://www.blackhistorymonth.org.uk/article/section/african-history/the-colonisation-of-kenya/

de Kluiver, J. (2023, September 25). Can China Be a More Attractive Security Partner for Africa? *Premium Times*. Accessed November 14, 2023. https://www.premiumtimesng.com/foreign/africa/628127-can-china-be-a-more-attractive-security-partner-for-africa.html

Ewetan, O. O., & Urhie, E. (2014). Insecurity and Socio-Economic Development in Nigeria. *Journal of Sustainable Development, 5*(1), 40–63. Accessed April 15, 2024. http://eprints.covenantuniversity.edu.ng/2323/1/Insecurity%20and%20development.pdf

Federal Democratic Republic of Ethiopia. (2020). *The Home-Grown Economic Reform Agenda*. Retrieved June 20, 2024, from https://www.dpgethiopia.org/resources/the-home-grown-economic-reform-agenda/

Federal Ministry of Finance, Budget and National Planning, Nigeria. (2021). *National Development Plan 2021–2025*. https://nationalplanning.gov.ng/wp-content/uploads/2021/12/NDP-2021-2025_AA_FINAL_PRINTING.pdf

Gatti, R. (2023, June 13). Corruption Is a Global Problem for Development: To Fight It, We All Have a Role to Play. *The World Bank*. https://www.worldbank.org/en/news/opinion/2023/06/13/corruption-is-a-global-problem-for-development-to-fight-it-we-all-have-a-role-to-play

Government of Kenya. (n.d.). *Kenya Vision 2030*. Retrieved June 18, 2024, from https://vision2030.go.ke/

Hallee, C. (2020, July 16). The Italian Occupation of Ethiopia: Failure and Consequences. *Medium*. https://clayhallee.medium.com/the-italian-occupation-of-ethiopia-failure-and-consequences-4949663be6a0

Heldring, L. (2013, January 10). Colonialism and Development in Africa. *VoxEU*. https://cepr.org/voxeu/columns/colonialism-and-development-africa

Lebrand, M., World Bank. (2024). *Better Transport Can Bring African Countries Closer Together and Support Their Economies*. World Bank Blogs. Accessed May 12, 2024. https://blogs.worldbank.org/transport/better-transport-can-bring-african-countries-closer-together-and-support-their-economies

Lesutis, G. (2021). Infrastructural Territorialisations: Mega-Infrastructures and the (Re)Making of Kenya. *Political Geography, 90*, Article 102459. https://doi.org/10.1016/j.polgeo.2021.102459

National Planning Commission of Nigeria. (2021). *National Development Plan 2021–2025* (Final Printing). Federal Government of Nigeria. Retrieved June 27, 2025, from https://nationalplanning.gov.ng/wp-content/uploads/2021/12/NDP-2021-2025_AA_FINAL_PRINTING.pdf

Ndwaru, J. (2022, July 7). *Infrastructure Development Accelerates Kenya's Economic Revolution.* The Exchange. Retrieved June 7, 2024, from https://theexchange.africa/industry-and-trade/infrastructure-development-accelerates-kenyas-economic-revolution/

Qosim, S. (2023, November 19). Nigeria Must Lead Africa Against Neocolonialism - NDA Commandant. *Premium Times.* Accessed July 6, 2024. https://www.premiumtimesng.com/news/top-news/644519-nigeria-must-lead-africa-against-neocolonialism-nda-commandant.html

Republic of Kenya. (n.d.). *Kenya Vision 2030.* Retrieved June 27, 2024, from https://vision2030.go.ke/

Scholar, N. (2024). *A Deep Dive into Nigeria's Coastal and Inland Shipping.* Retrieved June 27, 2024, from https://disciplines.ng/coastal-and-inland-shipping/

Transparency International. (2023). *Corruption Perceptions Index 2022: Ethiopia.* Accessed June 23, 2024. https://www.transparency.org/en/cpi/2022/index/eth

Transparency International. (2023). *Corruption Perceptions Index 2022: Nigeria.* Accessed June 23, 2024. https://www.transparency.org/en/cpi/2022/index/nga

Transparency International. (2023). *Corruption Perceptions Index 2022: Kenya.* Accessed June 23, 2024. https://www.transparency.org/en/cpi/2022/index/ken

United Nations Ethiopia. (2019, August 28). *Growth and Transformation Plan II.* Accessed July 6, 2024. https://ethiopia.un.org/en/15231-growth-and-transformation-plan-ii

8 Conclusion and Policy Recommendations

This book focuses on a comparative analysis of Chinese infrastructure development aid to Nigeria, Kenya, and Ethiopia. The analysis is essential because countries often compete to attract FDIs. Understanding how other nations successfully attract Chinese FDIs can help a country refine its strategies to become a more attractive investment destination. In addition, comparing policies allows countries to benchmark their performance against peers and identify areas for improvement to stay competitive in attracting FDIs. Understanding the policies and outcomes of other countries can also strengthen a country's position in negotiations with Chinese investors. It provides insights into what terms and conditions are favorable and how to negotiate for better deals. Overall, by comparing the policies established by Nigeria, Kenya, and Ethiopia for Chinese infrastructure aid and FDIs, other countries can learn valuable lessons to enhance their investment climates, mitigate risks, and promote sustainable and inclusive economic growth. This comparative approach fosters a deeper understanding of leveraging Chinese investment for national development objectives.

The book hypothesized that a dependency relationship exists between Chinese infrastructure development aid to Nigeria and Ethiopia in that when Chinese infrastructure aid is excluded from the regression equations, the two countries' per capita GDPs are affected. It was also hypothesized that a dependency relationship does not exist with Kenya. As a result of the findings, however, it was determined that a dependency relationship exists between Chinese FDI and Kenya's per capita GDP from 2000 to 2020 because the Multiple R decreased from 0.98 (inclusion of Chinese FDI) to 0.71 (exclusion of Chinese FDI). It was also noted that the Multiple R decreased from 0.971 (inclusive of Chinese FDI) to 0.89 (exclusive of Chinese FDI) in Ethiopia. A dependency relationship did not exist vis-à-vis Chinese FDI to Nigeria as the Multiple R decreased slightly from 0.93 to 0.922. In terms of Chinese infrastructure aid, there was a slight reduction in the Multiple R in Chinese

J. Guest, *China's Infrastructure Aid and Investment*, African Studies and Research Forum Series, https://doi.org/10.1007/978-3-032-11964-3_8

aid to Nigeria, which decreased from 0.89 (inclusion of Chinese infrastructure aid) to 0.88 (exclusion of Chinese infrastructure aid). In Kenya, the Multiple R decreased from 0.93 (inclusion of Chinese infrastructure aid) to 0.88 (exclusion of Chinese infrastructure aid). There was also a slight reduction in Multiple R in Ethiopia; the value decreased from 0.95 to 0.912.

When examining Chinese infrastructure aid to Africa, it is essential to understand key terms such as "concessional" and "non-concessional loans." Many of the loans issued by China are bilateral agreements, whereby both parties must agree to the terms and the degree of "concessionality" is based on the projects being implemented. The World Bank's Debtor Reporting System shows that Chinese loans typically have an average interest rate of 3.1%, a grace period of four years, and a maturity of 13 years. Nevertheless, there is significant variation: interest rates range from 1% to 6%, grace periods from two to ten years, and maturities from five to 25 years. According to OECD and IMF definitions, these loans are generally considered non-concessional, with an average grant element of only 18% relative to a concessional threshold of 35%. Despite this, some loans exceed the concessional threshold due to the variation in terms (Horn et al., 2021) (World Bank 2008) (International Monetary Fund, 2021).

The non-concessional loans imply that they come with less favorable terms than concessional loans. This means that African countries incur higher debt burdens due to higher interest rates and shorter grace periods. The cost of servicing these debts is relatively high, which can strain national budgets and limit fiscal space for other essential expenditures such as healthcare, education, and infrastructure maintenance. To meet the repayment obligations of these loans, African governments may need to cut spending on vital public services or increase taxes. This could lead to economic and social trade-offs, potentially hindering poverty reduction efforts and exacerbating inequality. So, in this instance, while the loans may be for infrastructure development, which may allow for better transport of goods and services, it may hurt other aspects of a country by not having enough funding for healthcare, education, or other vital services that are needed to support of the citizens of the country.

It is also important to note that high levels of non-concessional debts could negatively impact the credit ratings of African countries, making it more difficult and expensive to borrow in the future from other sources, including international financial markets and multilateral institutions. Borrowing countries must therefore balance their financing needs with the terms of the loans they accept. While concessional loans are more manageable, non-concessional loans can provide substantial funding but require careful consideration of repayment capabilities and project viability.

Why is infrastructure development so important? It's not just a matter of economic growth, but also a testament to the crucial role of policymakers and financial professionals. Policymakers' decisions on infrastructure development can enhance intra-country connectivity, strengthen regional and global production and distribution networks, and shape the future of our nations.

Thus, infrastructure development remains a crucial driver of FDIs due to the essential role efficient logistics play in global business operations. This is particularly evident in the E-commerce sector, which relies heavily on robust infrastructure for timely delivery and effective supply chain management. The growth of E-commerce has become a significant source of income and job generation both domestically and internationally. Moreover, well-developed infrastructure attracts multinational companies seeking reliable transportation networks, energy supply, and communication systems, which further boost economic growth and competitiveness. Thus, investing in infrastructure enhances a country's attractiveness for FDI and fosters sustainable economic development through improved global trade integration and increased productivity.

According to the African Development Bank, a 1% increase in infrastructure investment corresponds to a 2% increase in economic development. This relationship underscores the significant impact that infrastructure has on economic growth. Walt W. Rostow supports this viewpoint by arguing that investment in social overhead capital, such as electricity and transportation, is essential for a country to transition from the pre-condition for take-off stage to actual economic take-off (noted by Ndwaru, 2022).

Investments in infrastructure have a multiplier effect on an economy by generating jobs during the construction and post-construction maintenance phase and attracting further investments, in addition to generating additional jobs after the infrastructure project is completed for maintenance or operation of that service; for instance, railways or jobs generated for airports or roads. In addition, well-developed ports and railways can attract multinational companies that rely on efficient logistics for their operations, thereby increasing FDIs. This can lead to establishing new industries and fostering economic diversification and resilience, in turn leading to long-term economic growth and development.

Thus, the first policy recommendation is that the governments of Nigeria, Kenya, and Ethiopia should make a concerted effort to analyze the impact infrastructure development aid and FDIs will continue to have on their economies, considering per capita GDP. Examining the impact of assistance on individual variables will help the governments to negotiate better deals. In addition, as this study has shown, other factors greatly influence economic development other than Chinese infrastructure aid or infrastructure development aid overall.

Furthermore, there is a critical need to assess the dependency aspect of Chinese infrastructure aid and FDIs. While these investments have undeniably bolstered economic growth and improved infrastructure, they have also led to a dependency that could have long-term financial and political implications. Dependency on Chinese aid and FDIs may limit the recipient countries' ability to diversify their sources of investment and technology, potentially stifling local entrepreneurship and innovation. Additionally, the terms of Chinese loans and investments often include high interest rates and require the use of Chinese contractors and labor, which can lead to debt sustainability issues and limit job generation for local populations.

For instance, in Nigeria, the reliance on Chinese financing has led to concerns about increasing debt levels and the sovereignty implications of debt repayment terms, including potential asset seizures. Similarly, Kenya's significant borrowings for projects like the Standard Gauge Railway have raised questions about debt sustainability and economic autonomy. While benefiting from rapid infrastructure growth and industrialization, Ethiopia faces challenges related to the long-term impacts of these investments on local industries and economic diversification.

To mitigate these risks, the governments of Nigeria, Kenya, and Ethiopia should prioritize establishing policies that foster sustainable and inclusive growth and ensure that infrastructure projects are aligned with national development goals and do not lead to unsustainable debt levels. Diversifying investment sources and promoting local infrastructure projects can help build more resilient economies. Moreover, strengthening institutional capacities to manage and negotiate foreign investments effectively will be crucial in leveraging these opportunities for long-term development benefits.

To mitigate the risks associated with rising debt levels, Kenya, Nigeria, and Ethiopia should negotiate for a greater emphasis on concessional loans or alternative financing methods while limiting the issuance of non-concessional loans. Although both concessional and non-concessional loans have significantly contributed to infrastructure development, the reliance on non-concessional loans, characterized by higher interest rates and shorter repayment periods, can lead to increased debt service burdens. This can adversely affect fiscal stability and potentially result in a debt trap.

Addressing the preceding challenges requires a strategic approach: in essence, it is crucial for these countries to meticulously manage their debt portfolios, diversify their sources of funding, and ensure that borrowed funds are allocated to projects with high economic returns. Such projects not only promise financial gains but also inspire and motivate further investment. Additionally, by strengthening institutional capacities to negotiate better terms and enhancing debt transparency, the long-term impacts of Chinese infrastructure aid and FDIs can be managed more effectively.

The second policy recommendation is for Nigeria, Kenya, and Ethiopia to critically examine their political and economic stability, corruption, and negative perceptions. These factors are significant deterrents to foreign investment and need to be addressed. The analysis should lead to the identification of policies that can improve these conditions and make the countries more attractive to foreign investors. A key focus should be on good governance, which is essential for promoting economic growth and development.

Additionally, addressing political and economic stability is not just a recommendation, but a crucial necessity for establishing an environment that is conducive for investors. Political instability, such as frequent changes in government or civil unrest, can deter investors due to the uncertainty it generates. Economic instability, including high inflation rates and volatile exchange rates, can also undermine investor confidence. Implementing policies that ensure political stability and sound economic management will not only attract foreign investors but also safeguard the future of these countries.

Another crucial aspect is the battle against corruption. It can significantly impede economic development by inflating the cost of business and establishing an unfair playing field. Corruption can be reduced by establishing robust anti-corruption measures, ensuring utmost transparency in government dealings, and holding public officials accountable. This, in turn, will instill investor confidence and foster more FDIs.

Furthermore, improving the overall business climate is essential. This includes simplifying regulatory frameworks, reducing bureaucratic red tape, and protecting property rights. By establishing a more business-friendly environment, these countries can attract and retain investors looking for stable and predictable investment climates.

Negative perceptions can also be a significant barrier to attracting FDIs. These perceptions may arise from human rights abuses, political repression, or poor governance. By addressing these concerns and improving their international image, Nigeria, Kenya, and Ethiopia can enhance their attractiveness to foreign investors. This could involve engaging in public diplomacy, promoting success stories, and demonstrating commitment to international norms and standards.

Infrastructure investment is another critical area that can boost economic stability and attract investment. Reliable infrastructure, such as roads, ports, and telecommunications, is vital for efficient business operations. Improving infrastructure can reduce operational costs for businesses and enhance overall economic productivity.

Finally, fostering good governance is essential. Good governance involves ensuring accountability, transparency, and inclusiveness in decision-making processes. It also involves protecting the rule of law and ensuring institutions function effectively and impartially. By promoting good governance, these countries can establish a stable and predictable environment conducive to economic growth and development.

In terms of recommendations for individual countries, based on the research conducted, when examining the regression analysis for Nigeria from 2000 to 2022, it was found that a stronger linear relationship exists between Chinese FDI and per capita GDP than between Chinese infrastructure aid and per capita GDP; this finding suggests that Chinese FDI has a more significant impact on Nigeria's economic growth. This could be because FDIs typically involve not only capital investment but also the transfer of technology, management skills, and other forms of knowledge that can enhance productivity and economic development more effectively than infrastructure aid alone. Based on this finding, it is recommended that Nigeria focuses on establishing a more conducive environment for attracting FDIs. This could involve improving the business climate by reducing bureaucratic red tape, reducing perceived and actual corruption, enhancing legal frameworks for investment protection, and offering incentives to foreign investors. In addition, to fully leverage the benefits of FDIs, Nigeria needs a skilled workforce. Investing in education and vocational training can ensure that the local population can take advantage of the job opportunities and skill transfers that FDIs bring.

Also, while FDI is crucial, complementary infrastructure development remains important. The Nigerian government should prioritize projects directly supporting FDI initiatives, such as building industrial zones and improving transportation networks. In addition, the government should work to develop policies that encourage linkages between foreign investors and local businesses in order to enhance the benefits of FDIs. This will ensure that foreign investors do not run the local businesses out of business and instead establish an environment where all interested businesses can succeed. Furthermore, the Nigerian government must establish robust mechanisms for monitoring and evaluating the impact of FDIs and infrastructure development aid on economic development, which is essential. As discussed earlier, many concerns about the loans that China supplies to Nigeria are a debt trap; a thorough analysis must therefore be conducted on the true benefits of not only FDIs but also infrastructure development aid. This can help fine-tune policies and ensure that aid and investments are aligned with national development goals. Moreover, policymakers should continue to explore diversifying sources of infrastructure funding—for example, investments from other countries, multilateral development banks, or private investors. Policymakers should prioritize transparency and accountability in negotiating and implementing infrastructure projects financed by Chinese loans. This may involve conducting thorough cost-benefit analyses, ensuring fair and competitive procurement processes, and promoting public disclosure of project details and financial terms.

As it relates to the policy prescriptions for Nigeria and Dependency Theory, it was determined that a dependency relationship does not exist between Chinese infrastructure development aid and Nigeria's per capita GDP; accordingly, several recommendations can be made to enhance the effectiveness of infrastructure aid and overall economic development.

First, since the dependency on Chinese infrastructure aid does not significantly influence its per capita GDP, Nigeria should seek to diversify its sources of infrastructure funding. This can include attracting investments from other countries, international organizations, and private sector partnerships. Second, Nigeria should focus on improving the effectiveness of infrastructure aid by ensuring projects are well-planned, efficiently executed, completed, operational, and aligned with national development priorities. Establishing rigorous monitoring and evaluation frameworks can help assess the impact of aid on economic growth and make necessary adjustments. Third, robust institutions are crucial for maximizing the benefits of infrastructure development. Nigeria should strengthen its governance, reduce corruption as previously discussed, and enhance transparency to ensure that infrastructure projects are completed on time and contribute to sustainable development. Fourth, more than infrastructure is needed to drive economic growth. Complementary policies in education, healthcare, and technology can enhance the productivity of infrastructure investments. For example, improving educational outcomes can lead to a more skilled workforce that better leverages new infrastructure or education received, which can generate more local entrepreneurs that contribute to the overall growth and development of the country. Building local capacity to manage and maintain infrastructure projects is essential for their long-term success.

This includes training local engineers, managers, and workers and developing local supply chains and industries related to infrastructure development. Fifth, Nigeria can benefit from regional cooperation in infrastructure development. Working with neighboring countries on cross-border projects can enhance regional connectivity and economic integration, leading to greater economic opportunities and growth. Sixth, utilizing modern technology and innovative infrastructure solutions can improve efficiency and impact. Smart infrastructure, green technologies, and sustainable practices should be integrated into project planning and implementation. By implementing these recommendations, Nigeria can enhance the effect of infrastructure development aid and support broader economic growth and development goals.

Furthermore, since Chinese FDI does not significantly impact Nigeria's per capita GDP, it is advisable for Nigeria to diversify its sources of foreign investment. Encouraging investments from a broader range of countries could help mitigate dependency on a single source.

For Kenya, the following recommendations and policy prescriptions are offered as a result of this research. Chinese infrastructure aid to Kenya has a minor impact on the strength of the relationship between the independent and dependent variables in the regression model. The Multiple R decreased from 0.94 to about 0.93. This slight reduction of 0.01 suggests that while Chinese infrastructure aid does have an influence, its impact on the overall strength of the relationship between the variables is minimal. Although the effect is minor, Chinese infrastructure aid still contributes positively. Kenya should continue to attract and effectively utilize this aid by ensuring projects are well-managed, transparent, and aligned with national development priorities. In addition, Kenya should explore and secure additional sources of infrastructure funding, such as public-private partnerships, aid from other countries, and funding from international financial institutions. Diversifying funding sources will reduce reliance on a single donor and enhance infrastructure development. It is also recommended that domestic investment in infrastructure be increased through budget allocations and incentives for private sector participation. Strengthening domestic investment can complement foreign aid and ensure sustained infrastructure development because local economies will contribute to the country's economic growth while providing jobs and enhancing overall financial stability. It is also important to ensure that infrastructure projects funded by Chinese aid or other sources are efficient, sustainable, and provide high economic and social returns. Kenya must also implement robust project evaluation and monitoring mechanisms to assess impact and improve project outcomes.

Infrastructure aid can build local capacity in project planning, implementation, and maintenance. Training local professionals and transferring knowledge can enhance the long-term sustainability of infrastructure investments. This recommendation is critical because it allows the local population to develop skill sets that will generate lasting impacts on the local economy, and they will be able to continue maintenance on the infrastructure projects after the Chinese companies complete them. Additionally, this will help keep the money within the local communities and aids in successful local businesses. Establishing a stronger local workforce and entrepreneurship will also help to reduce the country's poverty rates. Engaging in regional and international collaborations is also important in sharing best practices and to learn from successful infrastructure projects in other countries. This can help improve the effectiveness and impact of infrastructure development efforts. Studies such as this are important because they allow countries within Africa to identify what is working in some countries and what is not. It is crucial to take the lessons learned and use them got their benefit, thereby enabling policymakers to make informed decisions, adapt successful strategies to their contexts, and avoid repeating the same mistakes.

In addition, Kenya must ensure that high standards of transparency and accountability govern all infrastructure projects. This can attract more aid and investment by building confidence among donors and investors. Finally, it is essential to align infrastructure projects with broader economic and social development goals, such as reducing poverty, improving health and education, and fostering economic diversification. Integrated planning can maximize the developmental impact of infrastructure investments.

Furthermore, since Chinese FDI significantly strengthens the economic relationship, it is vital to establish and maintain a favorable investment climate to attract and retain such investments. This includes ensuring political stability, reducing bureaucratic hurdles, and providing attractive incentives for foreign investors. Incentives may be in the form of tax reductions. In addition, Kenya must offer streamlined procedures for obtaining business licenses and permits. Also, regional stability and cooperation can attract more substantial and diversified investment flows. Lastly, it is important to put in place mechanisms to continuously monitor and evaluate the impact of FDIs on the economy. This can help make informed policy adjustments and ensure that investments contribute positively to national development goals. Studies such as this one will assist Kenyan leaders in making informed decisions before executing FDI and aid agreements.

An additional recommendation for Kenya is that while the country is making efficient use of the infrastructure aid and FDI that China is loaning to it, it is essential to consider the Kenyan residents' opinions before making infrastructure decisions. As Adam Welz points out in his article titled "How Kenya's Push for Development Is Threatening Its Famed Wild Lands" (Welz, 2019), an area of concern with the new infrastructure projects in Kenya is that many of the infrastructure projects are kept a secret to avoid feedback from the community or to prevent involvement from the community in the decision-making process. For example, Kenya Wildlife Service (KWS) has been allocated approximately $90 million in compensation for routing the Standard Gauge Railway and highways through the national parks. Conservationists criticize the government for withholding infrastructure location details until the last moment, hindering meaningful participation in decision-making. The government defends this secrecy, citing the need to prevent land speculation and corruption, as demonstrated by the failed Kinangop wind power project. The government must consider the protection of these lands, which are crucial for biodiversity and the long-term sustainability of Kenya's ecotourism industry. By incorporating community input and ensuring transparent decision-making, Kenya can balance development needs with environmental preservation and foster a more inclusive and sustainable growth model.

In terms of recommendations and policy prescriptions for Ethiopia, the result indicates that removing Chinese infrastructure aid from the regression equation caused the Multiple R value to decrease from 0.913 to 0.912. This slight reduction suggests that Chinese infrastructure aid has a minimal effect on the strength of the relationship between the independent and dependent variables in the regression model. In other words, the overall relationship among the independent variables is still strong and almost unchanged, implying that Chinese infrastructure aid is not a significant contributing factor to this relationship. Since Chinese infrastructure aid has a minimal impact on the overall relationship, Ethiopia should consider diversifying its sources of infrastructure aid. Engaging with multiple countries and international organizations can provide a broader support base and reduce dependency on a single source. The slight change in Multiple R suggests that other factors play a significant role in the regression model. Ethiopia should therefore focus on strengthening domestic investment in infrastructure to ensure sustained growth and development that are independent of foreign aid. This could encourage the development of local companies that provide infrastructure development services. Once local businesses are developed, these companies will also be able to provide maintenance services for infrastructure projects developed by Chinese companies. Local companies can compete with Chinese companies for infrastructure development projects. This will ensure that the Ethiopian government receives the benefits and the best prices for infrastructure projects.

Ethiopia should improve its planning and implementation processes to maximize the benefits of infrastructure aid. This includes better coordination between various aid projects and ensuring that they align with the country's long-term development goals. It is essential to also engage a wide range of stakeholders, including government agencies, private sector representatives, civil society, and international donors, in reviewing the planning process to incorporate diverse perspectives and expertise. It is also important to collaborate with neighboring countries on regional infrastructure projects. This can lead to more efficient use of resources and establish synergies that benefit multiple countries simultaneously. It is in addition important that the Ethiopian government implements robust economic policies that support infrastructure development, such as favorable tax policies for infrastructure investments, streamlined regulatory processes, and incentives for private sector participation.

In terms of recommendations and policy prescriptions for Chinese FDI to Ethiopia, based on the result which indicates that the Multiple R decreased from 0.97 to 0.89 after removing Chinese FDI to Ethiopia from the regression equation, this represents a reduction of 0.08 in the strength of the relationship between the independent variables and the dependent variable. It is therefore important that the Ethiopian government offers attractive incentives such as tax breaks, streamlined regulatory processes, and investment guarantees to attract FDIs from a variety of countries. In addition, the government must negotiate and strengthen bilateral investment agreements with a broader range of countries in order to diversify the sources of FDIs and prevent a dependency relationship with one country.

Also, the Ethiopian government should encourage investments in diverse sectors beyond those traditionally dominated by Chinese FDI. This includes technology, healthcare, education, and renewable energy. Diversification can spur innovation and enhance economic resilience. For instance, investing in technology can lead to the development of a robust digital economy, foster entrepreneurship, and generate high-quality jobs. In the healthcare sector, increased investment can improve public health infrastructure, leading to better health outcomes and increased productivity. Education sector investments can enhance the quality of education, equipping the workforce with necessary skills to compete in a globalized economy. Renewable energy investments can reduce dependence on fossil fuels, promote environmental sustainability, and ensure energy security. By promoting sectoral diversification, Ethiopia can build a more balanced and sustainable economic foundation that is less vulnerable to external shocks and more capable of long-term growth.

Next, Ethiopia ought to implement policies to support and grow local businesses, making them less reliant on foreign investment. This can include providing financial incentives such as grants, low-interest loans, and tax breaks to encourage local entrepreneurship. Additionally, the country must invest in infrastructure that benefits small- and medium-sized enterprises (SMEs), such as improving access to reliable electricity, Internet services, and transportation networks, which can enhance business operations and productivity. Offering training and development programs to help local business owners improve their management skills and business practices is also crucial. By fostering a supportive environment for local businesses, the government can establish a more resilient domestic economy that can thrive independent of foreign capital. Furthermore, establishing partnerships between local businesses and educational institutions can drive innovation and ensure that the workforce has the skills needed to meet the demands of the local market. Promoting local content policies can ensure that a significant portion of the value chain remains within the country, thereby boosting job generation and retaining economic benefits domestically. Ultimately, these measures can empower local businesses to grow sustainably, contribute more significantly to the economy, and reduce the dependency on foreign investments.

Ethiopia must negotiate with Chinese investors to secure better terms that ensure mutual benefits and safeguard Ethiopia's interests. This involves engaging in transparent and equitable negotiations that prioritize Ethiopia's development objectives while also addressing the concerns and priorities of Chinese investors. One approach could be to negotiate for more favorable financing terms, such as lower interest rates or extended repayment periods, to reduce the financial burden on Ethiopia and ensure the sustainability of infrastructure projects. Additionally, Ethiopia can seek to include clauses in investment agreements that promote technology transfer, skills development, and job generation for Ethiopian nationals. By leveraging its position as a recipient of Chinese investments, Ethiopia can negotiate for increased local content requirements and encourage the use of local labor, materials, and services in infrastructure projects. Moreover, establishing mechanisms for monitoring and evaluating the implementation of investment agreements can help ensure compliance with agreed-upon terms and mitigate potential risks or disputes. Overall, by engaging in proactive and strategic negotiations with Chinese investors, Ethiopia can maximize the benefits of foreign investments while safeguarding its sovereignty, promoting sustainable development, and fostering mutually beneficial partnerships.

It is also essential that Ethiopia uses existing Chinese investments as a foundation to attract additional investors by showcasing successful projects and highlighting Ethiopia's investment potential. Highlighting the successful collaboration with Chinese investors can serve as a testament to Ethiopia's business environment and capability to implement large-scale infrastructure projects effectively. Ethiopia can organize investment fora and trade shows to demonstrate the positive impacts of Chinese investments on the country's economy, infrastructure, and overall development. Additionally, publishing case studies and success stories of Chinese-funded projects in international business journals and media can enhance Ethiopia's visibility as an attractive investment destination.

Also, by leveraging its success stories, Ethiopia can target investors from diverse regions and sectors and promote technology, healthcare, education, and renewable energy opportunities. Ethiopia can build investor confidence and encourage new investments from emerging and established markets by demonstrating a proven track record of efficiently managing foreign investments and achieving tangible outcomes. Furthermore, Ethiopia can establish a one-stop-shop investment facilitation center to assist potential investors with information, permits, and support, and streamline the investment process and reduce bureaucratic hurdles. This approach will help to attract new investors and ensure the sustainable growth of various sectors, and thereby foster a robust and diversified economy.

Indeed, it is essential for all African countries to hire an outside expert to analyze their infrastructure projects like the ones in Nigeria, Kenya, and Ethiopia to determine if the aid and FDI projects benefit their countries. It is also essential that all African countries utilize their regional organizations and determine what is working and not working in their neighboring or regional countries. It is crucial to draw on the lessons learned to learn from the past and prevent making the same mistakes.

Also, it is also essential that each African country consistently reviews the terms of its contracts with China or any other country with which it is working to determine if the terms of an agreement still favor the country. This includes incorporating clauses emphasizing technology transfer and capacity building, ensuring that local workers are trained and employed in Chinese-funded projects, and promoting joint ventures that allow for greater local ownership and participation.

In addition, African countries must reiterate the importance of establishing clear environmental and social safeguards in infrastructure projects. These measures are crucial in mitigating negative impacts on local communities and ecosystems. Regularly reviewing and renegotiating contracts is a key strategy to adapt to changing economic conditions and ensure that the agreements continue to meet the evolving needs, just as it was recommended for Nigeria, Kenya, and Ethiopia. By taking these steps, African countries can better leverage Chinese investments to foster sustainable development, enhance economic resilience, and ensure that infrastructure projects contribute positively to their long-term growth and stability.

Furthermore, analysis indicates that more transparency and accountability are needed in the management of these projects. Implementing rigorous monitoring and evaluation frameworks can help track the progress and impact of infrastructure initiatives, thereby ensuring that they deliver the intended benefits. This includes setting up independent bodies to oversee project implementation and provide regular public reports on their status and outcomes.

Moreover, it is essential to be adamant about the benefits of fostering public-private partnerships (PPPs). These partnerships diversify the sources of investment and bring invaluable expertise from the private sector. By mitigating the risks associated with relying heavily on a single foreign investor, African countries can enhance the resilience of the infrastructure sector. They can also promote competition and innovation, leading to more efficient and effective project execution. Finally, given everything that has been discussed in the preceding chapters and this one, it behooves me to end this book with my goal for future research and the significance of this book.

8.1 Future Research

This is the first publication of a series of publications that will be issued to compare various African countries with one another to determine aid and FDI effectiveness. This book provides a comprehensive and nuanced understanding of how countries leverage foreign aid and investment for development. The series will enable policymakers, investors, and development agencies to determine what works and what does not in different contexts so that countries can adopt proven strategies and avoid pitfalls. This research will also help countries formulate targeted policies that maximize the benefits of aid and FDIs. Countries can in addition learn from one another's successes and challenges. For instance, a policy or project that worked well in one country can be adapted and implemented in another, thereby promoting regional development through shared knowledge and experiences. Regular publication of research findings will enhance transparency and accountability in utilizing aid and FDIs. Stakeholders, including regular citizens, can track progress and hold their governments accountable for the effective use of resources.

Also, the series will emphasize the importance of sustainable practices in aid and FDI projects. Highlighting projects that successfully balance economic growth with social and environmental sustainability can set standards for future initiatives. The research can foster greater cooperation among African nations by identifying regional trends and everyday challenges. Joint efforts and regional partnerships can be more effectively pursued to address shared issues and leverage collective strengths. Continuous research will provide up-to-date data and insights that will allow policymakers to adapt their strategies to evolving circumstances. This dynamic approach will ensure that policies remain relevant and effective in promoting long-term development goals.

8.2 Significance of the Book

The significance of this book hinges on the fact that it represents a pioneering effort to examine the impact of Chinese infrastructure development aid on the economic growths of Nigeria, Kenya, and Ethiopia through a comparative analysis of per capita GDP. Additionally, a regression analysis was conducted to investigate the correlation between Chinese infrastructure aid and the per capita GDPs in these countries. The theoretical framework employed is Dependency Theory, which provides a lens to analyze the extent to which these nations rely on Chinese aid and its implications for their economic autonomy.

This book also contributes significantly to the body of knowledge on Dependency Theory by evaluating its relevance to Chinese infrastructure aid in an Africa context. It underscores the principle that foreign aid should be mutually beneficial and aimed at fostering self-reliance. By utilizing Dependency Theory, the book assesses whether Chinese infrastructure aid helps these countries achieve self-sufficiency or perpetuates dependence.

The overall findings indicate that while Chinese infrastructure development aid has led to substantial economic improvements in Nigeria, Kenya, and Ethiopia, it also highlights ongoing concerns about the long-term economic independence of these nations. Like the recommendations regarding Chinese infrastructure development aid, Nigeria could focus on strengthening its domestic investment environment. This could involve incentivizing local businesses to invest in critical sectors, improving infrastructure, and reducing bureaucratic hurdles for local entrepreneurs. In addition, Nigeria could explore diversifying its economic partnerships beyond China. Strengthening ties with other countries or regions could provide alternative avenues for investment and trade, thereby reducing dependence on a single partner.

8.3 Chapter Summary

This chapter outlines the scope and future direction of a groundbreaking research series aimed at comparing infrastructure development aid and FDI effectiveness across African nations. As the first book in a planned series, this work presents a detailed comparative analysis of Chinese infrastructure development aid in Nigeria, Kenya, and Ethiopia, focusing particularly on its relationship to per capita GDP and economic development through the lens of Dependency Theory. This research not only enriches academic discourse on foreign aid and economic development but also provides actionable insights for policymakers, investors, and development agencies. This chapter emphasizes mutual learning among countries, promoting regional growth through shared successes and cautionary tales. Future publications in the series will provide continuous, data-driven updates to help nations adapt to changing circumstances, ensuring the relevance and effectiveness of their strategies.

Furthermore, this chapter underscores the relevance of this book by emphasizing the importance of sustainability, transparency, and accountability in aid utilization. By setting benchmarks for social, environmental, and economic balance, it encourages responsible development practices. The broader significance of this book lies in its contribution to evaluating whether Chinese infrastructure aid fosters economic autonomy or reinforces dependency, thereby providing the selected countries with guidance on diversifying partnerships and enhancing local investment climates. This research ultimately aims to promote long-term, self-sustaining growth and development across the continent.

References

Horn, S., Reinhart, C., & Trebesch, C. (2021). China's overseas lending. *Journal of International Economics, 133*, 103539. https://doi.org/10.1016/j.jinteco.2021.103539

International Monetary Fund. (2021). *Debt limits policy*. Retrieved June 5, 2024, from https://www.imf.org/en/Topics/sovereign-debt/debt-limits-policy

Ndwaru, J. (2022, July 7). Infrastructure development accelerates Kenya's economic revolution. The Exchange. Retrieved June 7, 2024, from https://theexchange.africa/industry-and-trade/infrastructure-development-accelerates-kenyas-economic-revolution/

Welz, A. "how Kenya's push for development is threatening its prized wild lands." Yale Environment 360, April 24, 2019. Accessed July 6, 2024. https://e360.yale.edu/features/how-kenyas-push-for-development-is-threatening-its-prized-wild-lands

Postscript

9

Chinese investments and infrastructure agreements across Africa rose by 34% in 2024 compared to 2023, according to Ecofin Agency (Ecofin Agency, 2024). This sharp increase is significant for understanding Chinese infrastructure development aid to countries like Nigeria, Kenya, and Ethiopia in support of its Belt and Road Initiative (BRI). The BRI reflects Beijing's strategic commitment to deepening its economic presence in Africa amid shifting global trade dynamics. As China seeks to reduce its dependence on Western markets, particularly considering its ongoing trade tensions with the United States, enhancing infrastructure in key African economies, positions these countries as critical elements in China's broader global supply chain strategy. For Nigeria, Kenya, and Ethiopia, this surge in infrastructure investment offers both opportunities for economic growth and risks of dependency, including rising debt burdens, reduced policy autonomy, and over-reliance on China. These risks highlight the need for transparent, inclusive, and mutually beneficial agreements that prioritize long-term sustainability and national interests.

This surge in investment is not only a product of China's long-term strategic goals but also a direct response to shifting global trade conditions. Heightened tensions in the US-China trade war have further accelerated Beijing's interest in Africa as a strategic economic partner. In 2024, the United States imposed tariffs of up to 145% on Chinese goods, prompting China to search for new export markets and investment destinations (Reuters, 2025). In response, Premier Li Qiang called on Chinese exporters to diversify their market reach and pledged to boost domestic consumption amid these global disruptions. As a result, African nations especially those with untapped infrastructure and resource potential are increasingly viewed as key alternatives to Western-dominated trade corridors (Reuters, 2025).

This strategic shift toward Africa is largely driven by the economic pressures resulting from escalating US-China tariffs. To understand China's growing interest in African markets, it's important to examine how these tariffs affect both

J. Guest, *China's Infrastructure Aid and Investment*, African Studies and Research Forum Series, https://doi.org/10.1007/978-3-032-11964-3_9

economies particularly in technology and manufacturing. For the United States, higher tariffs may result in increased consumer prices and disrupted supply chains. For China, they threaten export demand, strain its manufacturing sectors, and put pressure on the broader economy. As a result, many Chinese companies are forced to absorb financial losses or seek alternative markets making African countries increasingly attractive for trade and investment.

This matters significantly when considering Chinese infrastructure development aid to Nigeria, Kenya, and Ethiopia. The rise in tariffs could contribute to a slowdown in China's economy, limiting the financial resources it can allocate to overseas infrastructure projects. Many of Africa s large-scale initiatives such as railways, roads, and energy facilities depend on continued Chinese investment. A weakened Chinese economy could lead to delays, reduced funding, or the imposition of stricter loan conditions under the Belt and Road Initiative. This, in turn, would hinder economic growth and disrupt long-term development plans in recipient countries. Additionally, as China scales back its industrial activity, demand for raw materials from African nations may decline, impacting export revenues for countries that rely heavily on commodities like oil, copper, and minerals.

When viewed through the lens of dependency theory, especially as applied by African scholar Samir Amin, this relationship reflects structural patterns of unequal exchange. Amin argued that African economies remain trapped in a global system where they primarily serve as suppliers of raw materials to industrialized nations, while importing finished goods at higher costs. Chinese investment, while offering critical infrastructure, may replicate these colonial trade patterns unless African nations secure equitable, transparent agreements that support domestic industrialization and reduce structural dependence (Amin, 1976).

9.1 The Escalating US-China Trade War

The recent tariff dispute between the United States and China began in 2018 during President Trump's first term, sparked by a long-standing trade imbalance. At the time, the U.S, was importing significantly more from China than it exported, intensifying tensions that evolved into a full-scale tariff war on that continues to shape global trade today. Notably, the U.S, has maintained a trade deficit with China since 1985, when the gap stood at -$6 billion. By 2024, it had ballooned to approximately -$295 billion, and as of March 2025, the deficit had already reached -$70 billion (U.S. Census Bureau, 2025). Figure 9.1 illustrates the evolution of the US-China trade deficit from 2019 to 2025. These figures highlight the sustained pressure on the US economy and offer insight into China's strategic search for new markets including infrastructure engagement across Africa.

Examining the trade data between the United States and China from 1985 to 2025 reveals that there was no single year in which the United States had a positive trade balance with China or a balance between exports and imports. The table above shows the negative trade balance from 2018 to the present. This point is

Fig. 9.1 US Trade in Goods with China 2018–2024 (Thousands of Dollars). Self-generated by author from data at US Census.gov.

crucial because it highlights a long-standing structural trade imbalance that contributed to the escalation of tariffs and trade tensions beginning in 2018 under president trump's first term in office. The consistent deficit underscores the reason US policymakers have viewed the trade relationship with China as economically disadvantageous, justifying aggressive measures such as tariffs to reduce the gap, protect domestic industries, and push for more reciprocal trade practices.

As a result of this persistent trade imbalance between the United States and China, in 2018, the United States raised tariffs on Chinese goods from 10% to 25% on $34 billion of select Chinese imports. In late 2019, the United States raised tariffs from 10% to 25% on $200 billion of Chinese imports.

In January 2020, the United States and China signed a deal in which China agreed to purchase an additional $200 billion in US goods over 2 years period this agreement led to a halt in the tariff discussions between the two countries (Associated Press, 2023).

From 2020 to 2023, under the Biden administration, many of the tariffs that were put in place under the Trump administration remained in effect. Despite the existing high tariffs, the Biden administration introduced new duties May 2024 on items such as Chinese Electric Vehicles, solar technology, metals, and medical supplies (Associated Press, 2023).

In 2024–2025, under the second Trump administration, there were renewed discussions on tariffs between the United States and China. In February 2025, the United States raised tariffs to 10% on the remaining Chinese goods. In response, China imposed duties on US exports. The United States then increased the tariffs to 20% on all Chinese goods. China then increased tariffs on US exports of farm products to 15%. The back-and-forth retaliation between the United States and

China resulted in tariffs of 60%- 145% on Chinese goods and the same was placed on US goods (Mistreanu, Simina AP News, 2024–2025).

9.2 Implications of the Trade War for China's Global Strategy

Why is the trade war between the United States and China important to infrastructure development in Nigeria, Kenya, and Ethiopia? Africa offers an alternative source for exporting Chinese products and sustaining export-led growth and global influence. China is seeking alternative sources to export its products and reduce its dependence on the US market. Chinese investments in infrastructure in Nigeria, Kenya, and Ethiopia serve a dual purpose for China: opening new markets for its products and services, while also fostering long-term political and economic alliances. Nations such as Nigeria, Kenya, and Ethiopia have become crucial regional partners due to their strategic geographical positions, economic potential, and need for infrastructure development.

Not only is Africa a source for China to export its goods, but it is also an important avenue to build alliances in organizations such as the World Trade Organization (WTO) and the United Nations. China leverages its growing influence in Africa to solidify its voting power on global issues, from trade regulations to development finance. This strategy also garners support for initiatives that challenge existing US-led economic standards, particularly in areas like WTO reform and dispute resolution, which ongoing tariff disputes have impacted (Hopewell, 2017).

In addition to alternative sources for Chinese products and support in organizations such as the UN and WTO, as stated by the Global Business Outlook, China provides commerce, investment, and development assistance to African nations. In exchange, China gets political support in relationships between financial flows and African states, UN voting patterns on matters important to China, the speaker stated (Global Business Outlook, 2025).

9.3 China's Infrastructure Development Aid in Africa

As China deepens its economic engagement across Africa, one of the most consequential aspects is its growing role in infrastructure development. Through significant investments in roads, ports, and railways, China is not only building critical infrastructure but also gaining influence over strategic assets in countries such as Nigeria, Kenya, and Ethiopia. Chinese investments in infrastructure are crucial in creating alternative routes to bypass US global supply chains. This point is critical for the African countries to understand the leverage they gain by seeing the importance of their relationship with China. Understanding the impact of Chinese infrastructure aid on Nigeria, Kenya, and Ethiopia helps to determine whether this aid promotes economic development in these countries.

China's significant infrastructure investments in African nations like Nigeria, Kenya and Ethiopia including ports railways and energy projects, offer economic influence and geopolitical leverage. These initiatives align with China's goal of establishing trade corridors independent of Western systems, particularly amid ongoing US-China trade tensions.

While African countries may experience short-term benefits such as improved transportation, job creation, and increased market access, these gains come with potential long-term risk. These include escalating debt burdens, the possibility of losing control over national assets, and the marginalization of local industries due to the increase of Chinese goods and hopeful markets.

Therefore, it is critical to assess whether these projects genuinely foster equitable economic development in Africa will primarily serve China strategic and commercial interests. African nations must carefully navigate this relationship to ensure infrastructure development supports their national goals, promotes inclusive growth, and reinforces their long-term economic sovereignty.

It is important to note that there is also a trade imbalance between China and Africa. China primarily exports finished goods to Africa such as textiles, apparel, machinery, and electronics while Africa mainly exports raw materials to China, including crude oil, copper, cobalt, and iron ore. This imbalance has resulted in a persistent trade surplus in China's favor (Ecofin Agency, 2024). The persistent trade imbalance, when viewed alongside China's infrastructure development aid to Nigeria, Kenya, and Ethiopia, highlights underlying issues of potential economic dependency and structural asymmetry within these relationships. From a debt standpoint, a large amount of debt from the infrastructure loans combined with Nigeria, Kenya, and Ethiopia's ability to generate revenue from the Chinese funded infrastructure projects may lead to their inability to pay off the debt from the Chinese infrastructure projects. These countries may have to give up their rights to their assets such as ports, railways or mining rights to China's control. In Kenya for instance, there is speculation of the possibility of China taking control over the Mombasa port in the event Kenya is unable to pay its debt to China (Chatham House, 2023).

The trade surplus that exists between China and Africa resembles a colonial-style trade structure where China exports its finished goods to Africa, and Africa exports raw materials to China. Chinese infrastructure aid is frequently tied to Chinese companies, labor, and equipment, which could further exacerbate the imbalance by entrenching Africa's role as a raw material provider instead of fostering its industrial development. Chinese infrastructure assistance, often requiring the use of Chinese firms, workers, and materials, could worsen this disparity. This approach risks solidifying Africa's position as a mere supplier of raw materials, rather than promoting its own industrial growth. In addition, there is the potential for the local businesses in the individual countries that may be driven out of business due to the import of Chinese goods.

According to data from the World Integrated Trade Solutions (World Bank, 2018), Nigeria's exports to China from 2018 to 2022 resulted in a trade deficit for each year. While the United States is responding to the imbalance with China, it is also important that Nigeria is award that as China looks for alternatives to export its goods from the United States, it that they should be aware of their own trade imbalances with China. According to the data from World Integrated Trade Solutions (World Bank, 2018), during this five-year period, Nigeria's exports to China ranged from a high of approximately $1.85 million in 2021 to a low of $834,000 in 2022. While imports from China consistently exceeded $8million, peaking at nearly $16 million in 2020. The resulting trade deficits grew from about $7.3 million in 2018 to nearly $12.9million in 2022, illustrating an increasingly lopsided economic relationship between the two countries (World Bank, 2018).

In considering whether a dependency relationship exists, economies such as China through unequal trade relationships, in which Nigeria exports raw or low-value goods while importing higher-value manufactured products. The consistent trade deficits not only reflect Nigeria's limited industrial capacity and over-reliance on imports but also reinforces economic structures that prevent domestic value additions and industrial development. If unaddressed, these trade imbalances can trap Nigeria into a cycle of debt, inhibit its manufacturing growth, and reduce its bargaining power in international trade. This could potentially undermine long-term economic sovereignty and economic development (Fig. 9.2).

According to data from the World Integrated Trade Solutions (World Bank, 2018), in considering whether a dependency relationship exists, economies such as China often engage in unequal trade dynamics with African countries, including Nigeria, Kenya, and Ethiopia. Like Nigeria, Kenya has consistently experienced trade deficits with China from 2018 to 2022, exporting significantly less than it imports each year. In terms of Kenya, its exports to China from 2018 to 2022 resulted in a trade deficit for each year. While the United States is responding to the imbalance with China, it is also important that like Nigeria, Kenya look for alternative markets to export its goods.

According to the data from the World Integrated Trade Solutions (World Bank, 2018), during this five-year period, Kenya's exports to China ranged from a high

Fig. 9.2 Nigeria Trade with China 2018–2022 (In Thousands of Dollars). Self-generated by Author from dataset by World Bank World Integrated Trade Solutions

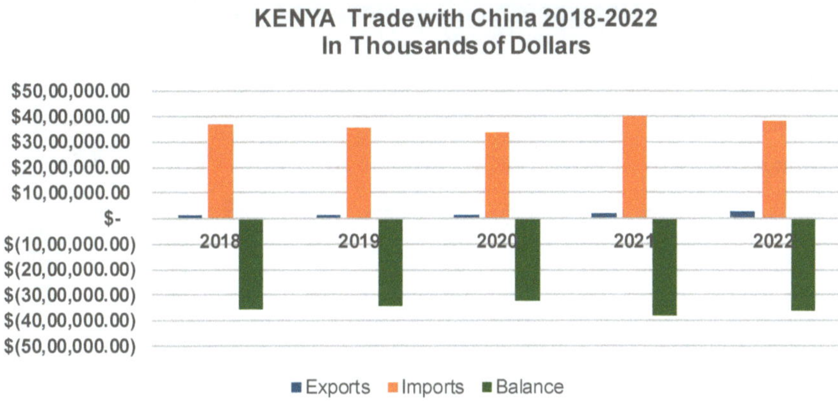

Fig. 9.3 Kenya Trade with China 2018–2022 (Thousands of Dollars). Self-generated by Author from dataset by World Bank World Integrated Trade Solutions (World Bank, 2018)

of approximately $233,714.55 in 2022 to a low of $109,896.48, but imported over $3.6 million, resulting in a $3.55million deficit. By 2022, although exports slightly increased to $233,714, imports remained high at $3.84 million, maintaining a deficit of $3.6 million. See Fig. 9.3:

According to the data from World Integrated Trade Solutions (World Bank, 2018), during the five-year period of 2018–2022, Ethiopia trade relationship with China highlights an even larger trade imbalance. Between 2018 and 2022, Ethiopia's exports to China were low, fluctuating from $138,514.05 in 2018 to $129,957.50 in 2022. In contrast, Chinese imports to Ethiopia consistently exceeded $4million annually during the same period, nearing $5million in 2022. This resulted in a substantial annual trade deficit ranging from $3.95 million to $4.83 million (World Bank, 2018).

Figure 9.4 strongly indicate that, much like Kenya, Ethiopia largely functions as an import-dependent nation in its trade with China. It primarily exports low-value goods while importing significantly higher-value manufactured products. This dynamic reinforces the central tenet of dependency theory: that developing countries frequently become in unequal trade patterns mirroring colonial economic structures. This makes them increasing reliant on powerful nations for essential goods, capital, and technology (Rodney, 1972). Without a decisive move toward robust domestic production and value addition, such patterns risk entrenching long-term underdevelopment.

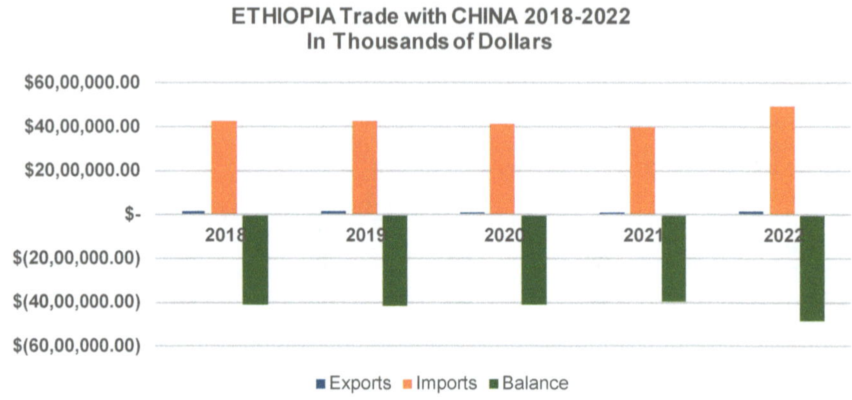

Fig. 9.4 Ethiopia Trade with China 2018–2022 (Thousands of Dollars). Self-generated by Author from dataset by World Bank World Integrated Trade Solutions

9.4 China's Infrastructure Development Aid in Africa (Nigeria, Kenya, and Ethiopia)

While the ongoing tariff war between the United States and China poses challenges for global trade, it also presents a strategic opportunity for African countries, particularly Nigeria, Kenya, and Ethiopia to assert greater agency in their economic partnerships with China. As Beijing seeks to diversify its export markets and reduce its dependence on the United States, these African nations can better position themselves not just as passive recipients of aid, but as influential negotiators in infrastructure and trade agreements. This shift can be used to secure more favorable loan terms and development agreements that promote domestic economic empowerment rather than perpetuate asymmetrical dependencies. Such demands could include requirements for technology transfer, local employment, use of African raw materials in infrastructure projects, and capacity-building initiatives. These provisions are essential to prevent the long-standing pattern described in dependency theory, where developing nations remain trapped in subordinate roles, exporting raw materials while importing manufactured goods leading to persistent trade deficits, limited industrialization, and loss of policy autonomy (Ake, 1981; Rodney, 1972).

The trade data between China and African countries such as Nigeria, Kenya, and Ethiopia support this theoretical framework. For example, Nigeria recorded trade deficits with China every year from 2018–2022, with a peak deficit of over $14 million in 2020 (World Bank, 2018). Similarly, Ethiopia's deficits remained consistently above $3.9 million annually, despite fluctuating export levels. These patterns underscore the structural imbalances that dependency theory critiques-imbalances that China's infrastructure aid could either entrench or help resolve, depending on the negotiation terms and development strategies adopted by African leaders. Moreover, this is a moment for African countries to evaluate how Chinese-funded infrastructure impacts their long-term sovereignty. African nations can also use their strategic value to demand favorable political concessions, such as increased voting power in global institutions or diplomatic support at the United Nations and World Trade Organization. Without a proactive, coordinated approach, the risk remains that Chinese aid will reinforce dependency rather that prevent it.

9.5 Opportunities for African Leverage

Since the trade war may disrupt some global supply chains, African countries can also use this time as an opportunity to export agricultural products or raw materials where the supply chains have been disrupted. Last, Nigeria, Kenya, and Ethiopia can position themselves as regional logistic hubs where they can better connect with regional economies to encourage intra-African trade. By enhancing ports, roads, and bridges, this helps to reduce trade barriers and reduce transportation costs. The countries may then become more attractive to local industries and external investors. This strategic positioning if done properly, would not only boost exports and regional integration but also create jobs, stimulate industrialization, and increase bargaining power in global and economic forums. To avoid failing into neocolonial patterns of extraction and debt dependency, it is crucial that infrastructure initiatives are paired with transparent loan agreements, local development requirements and policies that ensure long-term national ownership and sustainability.

9.6 Risks and Consequences for African Countries

If African countries fail to capitalize on this strategic moment to renegotiate agreements with China, they risk locking themselves into unfavorable loan terms and diminishing their future bargaining power especially while China is actively seeking alternative export markets due to its strained relationship with the United States.

Africa's growing economies and strategic trade position makes it vulnerable to the effects of the US-China trade war, which impacts its economic growth, commodity prices, foreign investment, and geopolitical relationships (Africa–China Review, 2025). In looking back under President Trump's first administration, the trade wars between the United States and China from 2018 to 2019, Chia redirected its agricultural needs to Africa, and while it did present the opportunity for some African countries to increase its exports, it led to countries such as Ethiopia and Kenya to have a surge in demand for certain commodities; which placed significant pressure of their logistical and regulatory infrastructures, exposing their limited ability to adapt effectively to global disruptions (Africa–China Review, 2025). The tariff wars between the United States and China have led to a reshuffling of global supply chains which allows for many African countries to become major players in the global market. However, there are some concerns in that many African country's ability to meet global demand is limited. Weak transportation systems, frequent power outages, and too much paperwork make it hard for Africa to take full advantage of becoming a key production hub. It is important for African countries to continue to invest in education, modern technology, and better leadership, or they may be left out as the global economy shifts (Africa–China Review, 2025).

This limited readiness is particularly concerning given the broader economic ripple effects of the U.S-China trade war. As China's economy slows due to increased US tariffs, its reduced industrial output has led to a decrease in demand for raw materials, many of which are sourced from sub-Saharan Africa (Economics Observatory, 2025). This shift threatens the export earning of resource-dependent African countries and add another layer of economic pressure to an already fragile situation because of higher US tariffs, China's economy is slowing down, which means it's producing less and buying fewer raw materials from places like sub-Saharan Africa. This drop in demand could hurt African countries that rely on exporting raw materials such as oil and minerals. As a result, their economies are expected to grow more slowly by approximately 0.4% less in 2025 and 0.6% less in 2026, bringing the overall growth rate down to 3.8% for 2025 and 2026 (Economics Observatory, 2025).

Marvellous Ngundu added the point "Where giants clash, smaller economies are often trampled-African must act now or risk becoming a dumping ground for displaced industrial overcapacity" (Ngundu, 2025). Africa faces two major challenges: it doesn't have enough factories and industries, and its trade and industrial policies are not well organized. As a result, if leaders don't act quickly, African countries could risk being stuck in a system where they become dependent on imports for most goods and lost eh ability to build and grow their own industries (Ngundu, 2025).

This is an important point to understand as it relates to the dependency terms highlighted in this book. One of the key theoretical frameworks of this book is the dependency theory: that underdeveloped nations, like many in Africa, can become economically dependent on more industrialized countries. Instead of developing self-sustaining economies, they risk becoming markets for surplus goods from powerful nations, particularly in the wake of global shifts like the US-China trade war. If Africa fails to strengthen its manufacturing base and coordinate industrial policy, it may reinforce its peripheral position in the global economy, serving mainly as a consumer of external goods rather than a producer. This could lead to structural inequalities and limiting long-term development. This could lead to a loss in jobs and the loss of local economies and local businesses, coupled with the potential loss of its manufacturing capabilities, high debt from the loans obtained from China for infrastructure projects, and a growing dependence on foreign powers for both goods and financial support. Over time, this dependence can erode national economic sovereignty, making it difficult for African countries to set independent development agendas. It may also limit their ability to invest in home-grown industries, deepen trade imbalances, and expose them to geopolitical risks tied to the interests of more powerful nations like China.

9.7 Policy Recommendations and Conclusion

As Marvellous Ngundu (2025) emphasizes, African countries must proactively develop industrial strategies that support self-reliance and long-term economic resilience. This involves targeted investments in local manufacturing sectors, particularly in food processing, textiles, renewable energy, and electronics. Governments should promote import-substitution industries by providing financial support to small and medium enterprises (SMEs), adopting public procurement policies that prioritize local goods, and enforce strategic import controls.

African nations should also maximize the potential of the African Continental Free Trade Area (AfCFTA). Strengthening intra-African trade can reduce dependency on external partners like China and promote regional value chains. To make this integration effective, countries must invest in cross-border infrastructure, such as roads, railways, and logistics networks, while at the same time harmonizing trade regulations and building regional industrial hubs (Ngundu, 2025).

Another key recommendation is to curb the inflow of substandard or under priced imports, particularly from China. These imports often undercut local products, harm domestic industries, reduce taxable revenue, and increase unemployment. Upgrading customs enforcement systems, strengthening product quality standards, and enforcing fair pricing mechanisms are essential to creating a level playing field for local producers (Ngundu, 2025).

Equally important is the renegotiation of infrastructure and trade agreements with China. African governments must avoid entering one-sided contracts that disproportionately benefit Chinese firms while providing limited value to local economies. Future agreements should include enforceable clauses on technology transfer, local labor and material sourcing, skill development and training, protection for infant industries, and equity sharing in major infrastructure projects. These contractual elements are critical to avoiding a repeat of historical patterns reminiscent of colonial-era resource extraction and economic marginalization.

From the perspective of dependency theory, these recommendations are vital. As theorized by scholars like Walter Rodney (1972) and Andre Gunder Frank, underdeveloped nations often remain in a subordinate position within the global capitalist system due to exploitative trade and investment relationships. Without strong policy interventions, African nations risk reinforcing their peripheral status, serving as exporters of raw materials and importers of manufactured goods. This structural imbalance perpetuates dependency, stifles domestic industrial growth, and undermines national sovereignty.

Finally, Nigeria, Kenya, and Ethiopia have a unique opportunity during this geopolitical realignment. By leveraging the cracks in global trade created by the US-China trade war, these countries can reposition themselves as regional leaders, not passive recipients of aid or foreign capital. If African leaders seize this moment with bold and strategic action, they can begin to reshape the continent's place in the global economy, moving from dependency toward interdependence, and from marginalization to leadership.

9.8 Chapter Summary

This chapter examines the historical and ongoing trade tensions between the United States and China, with a particular emphasis on how these global economic dynamics impact Chinese infrastructure investment and trade relations with African nations, specifically Nigeria, Kenya, and Ethiopia. The analysis begins with an overview of US-China trade data from 1985 to 2025, which highlights a consistent trade deficit in favor of China, which led to successive tariff escalations under both the Trump and Biden administrations. These trade tensions have driven China to diversify its export markets and deepen economic engagement with Africa. China's infrastructure development aid to African nations serves a dual strategic purpose: its ability to secure alternative markets for its exports and expand its geopolitical influence. While projects in Nigeria, Kenya, and Ethiopia have improved logistics, created jobs, and expanded access to markets, they have also raised concerns over mounting debt, lost control over national assets, and economic dependency. This chapter applies dependency theory to analyze whether such partnerships empower African nations or reinforce asymmetrical trade and development patterns reminiscent of colonial relationships.

Data from 2018 to 2022 showed growing trade deficits for all three countries, with significant reliance on Chinese imports. This data raises concerns about industrial stagnation, declining local businesses, and long-term economic vulnerability. Despite these challenges, this chapter identifies key opportunities for African nations to capitalize on. The shifting global supply chain presents an opportunity for African countries to reposition themselves as regional trade hubs and negotiate more favorable infrastructure terms. However, this requires strong policy coordination, investment in manufacturing, infrastructure upgrades, and increased participation in frameworks such as the African Continental Free Trade Area (AfCFTA). This chapter concludes with concrete policy recommendations for renegotiating a contract that includes provisions for local employment and technology transfer, investment in regional logistics, promotion of import-substitution industries, and strengthening trade enforcement mechanisms. Without these reforms, African nations risk deepening their dependence on China, which could lead to a loss of economic sovereignty and leave them behind in the evolving global economy.

References

Africa–China Review. (2025, May). How U.S.-China Trade Wars Affect Africa. *Africa–China Review*. https://africachinareview.com/how-u-s-china-trade-wars-affect-africa/.

Ake, C. (1981). *A political economy of Africa*. Longman.

Amin, S. (1976). *Unequal development: An essay on the social formations of peripheral capitalism*. Monthly Review Press.

Associated Press. (2023, September 18). Timeline of US-China Trade War as Tariffs Expand. *AP News*. https://apnews.com/article/china-us-tariffs-timeline-trump-xi-1eeed2865dc7b14e23d7eb8069ba41ea.

Chatham House. (2023). *China–Africa Relations*. January 2023. https://www.chathamhouse.org/2023/01/china-africa-relations.

Ecofin Agency. (2024). "China-Africa Trade up 4.8% to $295bn in 2024." *Ecofin Agency*. Retrieved May 26, 2025. https://www.ecofinagency.com/public-management/2001-46339-china-africa-trade-up-4-8-to-295bn-in-2024.

Economics Observatory. (2025, May 1). *How should Africa respond to America's new foreign economic policy?* Retrieved June 5, 2025. https://www.economicsobservatory.com/how-should-africa-respond-to-americas-new-foreign-economic-policy.

Global Business Outlook. (2025). The rise of China's influence in Africa. *Global Business Outlook Magazine*. Retrieved June 10, 2025, from https://globalbusinessoutlook.com/magazine/economy-magazine/the-rise-of-chinas-influence-in-africa/

Hopewell, K. (2017). The BRICS—Merely a fable? Emerging power alliances in global trade governance. *International Affairs, 93*(6), 1377–1396. https://doi.org/10.1093/ia/iix192

Mistreanu, Simina. AP News. (2024, May 14). "Timeline of US-China Tariffs." *AP News*. Updated April 5, 2025. Retrieved May 30, 2025. https://apnews.com/article/china-us-tariffs-timeline-trump-xi-1eeed2865dc7b14e23d7eb8069ba41ea.

Ngundu, M. (2025, April 24). *The US-China trade war and Africa's manufacturing crossroads*. Institute for Security Studies. Retrieved June 10, 2025. https://futures.issafrica.org/blog/2025/The-US-China-trade-war-and-Africas-manufacturing crossroads.

Reuters. 2025. *China's Premier Urges Trade Companies to Diversify Markets amid Drastic Changes*. Reuters, April 15, 2025. Retrieved June 1, 2025. https://www.reuters.com/markets/asia/chinas-premier-urges-trade-companies-diversify-markets-amid-drastic-changes-2025-04-15/

Rodney, W. (1972). *How Europe underdeveloped Africa*. Bogle-L'Ouverture Publications.

U.S. Census Bureau. (2025). *Trade in goods with China*. U.S. Department of Commerce. Retrieved May 5, 2025. https://www.census.gov/foreign-trade/balance/c5700.html.

World Bank. (2018). Ethiopia (excludes Eritrea) Product Exports to China 2018. World Integrated Trade Solution. Accessed June 12, 2025. Retrieved from https://wits.worldbank.org/CountryProfile/en/Country/ETH/Year/2018/TradeFlow/EXPIMP/Partner/CHN/Product/all-groups.

Index

J. Guest, *China's Infrastructure Aid and Investment*, African Studies and Research Forum Series, https://doi.org/10.1007/978-3-032-11964-3

MIX
Papier aus verantwortungsvollen Quellen
Paper from responsible sources
FSC® C105338

If you have any concerns about our products,
you can contact us on
ProductSafety@springernature.com

In case Publisher is established outside the EU,
the EU authorized representative is:
Springer Nature Customer Service Center GmbH
Europaplatz 3, 69115 Heidelberg, Germany

Printed by Libri Plureos GmbH
in Hamburg, Germany